The ABCs of the
Internet

The ABCs of the
Internet

Christian Crumlish

SYBEX®

San Francisco - Paris - Düsseldorf - Soest

Associate Publisher: Carrie Lavine
Acquisitions Manager: Kristine Plachy
Developmental Editor: Dan Brodnitz
Editor: Lee Ann Pickrell
Technical Editor: Sandra Teng
Book Design Director: Catalin Dulfu
Book Designer: Design Site, Tracy Dean
Desktop Publisher: GetSet! PrePress
Production Coordinators: Alexa Riggs, Robin Kibby
Indexer: Ted Laux
Cover Designer: Design Site
Cover Photographer: Dennis O'Clair, photograph furnished by Tony Stone Images

Screen reproductions produced with Collage Complete.

Collage Complete is a trademark of Inner Media Inc.

SYBEX is a registered trademark of SYBEX Inc.

TRADEMARKS: SYBEX has attempted throughout this book to distinguish proprietary trademarks from descriptive terms by following the capitalization style used by the manufacturer.

Netscape Communications, the Netscape Communications logo, Netscape, and Netscape Navigator are trademarks of Netscape Communications Corporation.

Library of Congress Card Number: 96-67838
ISBN: 0-7821-1887-9

Manufactured in the United States of America

10 9 8 7 6 5

To the Merry Punsters
(NTAP)

Acknowledgments

Of the many wizards I've met or asked advice of through the Net or in the real world, I'd like to particularly thank Richard Frankel. I'd also like to thank Mitch Goldman for checking some e-mail program details for me and James "Kibo" Parry for allowing me to reproduce a Usenet article. Most of all, I'd like to thank Nick "Griffin" Meriwether, whose cheerful assistance made the preparation of the manuscript possible.

At Sybex, I'd like to thank the following people: Richard Mills for suggesting that I adapt my book *A Guided Tour of the Internet* to the *ABCs* format and bring the information in it up-to-date; Dan Brodnitz for helping me think through what's needed for a beginner's Internet book these days; Lee Ann Pickrell for patiently editing the content; Sandra Teng for checking the technical accuracy of the book; Alexa Riggs and Robin Kibby for coordinating the production of the book; and David Kamola of Get Set! PrePress for desktop publishing.

Of the many people who worked on the previous *Guided Tour* version of this book, I'd like to thank Guy "Text Butcher" Hart-Davis for editing the original manuscript (and putting up with my various idiosyncrasies). Many readers have sent me e-mail to praise or complain about various aspects of that book and all the feedback is appreciated. I'd especially like to thank the following readers who sent me corrections: Brenda J. Panawash-Bielinski, Peter Glenn White, Glen, Bari Nirenberg, Baruch Kantor, Daniel Headrick, Daniel Rozenshein, Jeremiah Heller, Ilan Bukai, John B. Delack, Michael L. Canute, Santiago Cardoso, Susan Enabnit, and Wojciech Turski.

Thanks as always to Briggs, who has stood by me through my ridiculous way of working on too many projects at once.

Contents at a Glance

Table of Contents

Chapter 5: Finding Stuff on the Net 97

Chapter 6: Plugging In to Multimedia 120

Chapter 12: Making a Simple Home Page 261

Appendix A: Getting Connected and Getting Help 275

Introduction

Will the Internet hype never end? It seems like there's a newspaper article or magazine cover story every day. You probably saw hundreds of other Internet books on the shelf where you picked this up. Most of those books and magazine articles are full of breathless prose about an "information superhighway," or vague first impressions that betray not only a lack of understanding but also a deadline looming large.

Still, more and more people are connecting to the Net every day, and some businesses are beginning to rely on it for communication, for information, and even for transportation of certain types of products, such as software or writing. Maybe you've already got access to the Internet through your work or school, or maybe you're considering getting a modem and trying it out for yourself.

NOTE I assume you own a computer or have access to one, but it's not your favorite toy. You don't think like a computer wizard, and you don't want to know too much technical drivel, just enough to get going.

This book is different from most of the other books out there. It's not a puff piece, full of generalities and futuristic hype. Neither is it a technical manual. I assume that you generally don't care *why* things work the way they do. Instead, this book tells exactly *how* to get things done on the Internet.

WARNING The Internet changes rapidly, and it's more than likely that some of the screen shots I've shown in this book will have changed slightly or even drastically by the time you visit the displayed sites. Don't let that throw you!

How This Book Works

For most people, the basic appeal of the Internet is e-mail and the World Wide Web. I devote a lot of this book to those two topics because I realize that that's all some people are going to want to do. Eventually, though, you'll be tempted to look into some of the other resources available via the Net, and I cover some of the most interesting ones, such as Usenet and FTP.

> **NOTE** The Internet has two uses. One is person-to-person communication. The other is finding information. I cover both, starting with the person-to-person stuff because it's easier to get into, and it's what you hear about most.

The Internet is a great resource, and you're bound to learn more about it once you're connected. For now, I'm just going to tell you enough to get you over the threshold. That's all you really need.

The book contains twelve chapters and two appendices. The next sections discuss what these chapters cover.

Getting Oriented and Sending Mail

Chapter 1 gives you a basic overview of the Internet, e-mail, and the World Wide Web. I introduce most of the basic terminology you'll need to deal with to start learning about these subjects. I also explain the different ways you might connect to the Internet and how the book will handle those alternatives.

Chapter 2 introduces the most basic e-mail concepts, essentially how to send, read, and respond to mail. If you've already used e-mail, you should be able to skim this chapter. Chapter 3 explains some of the other useful and more elaborate uses of e-mail (such as attaching files). Both Chapters 2 and 3 cover a variety of e-mail programs, so either the program you use will be covered there or a very similar program will be.

The Web—Where the Action Is

Chapter 4 introduces you to the World Wide Web and the various programs (called Web browsers) that you might use to connect to it. Chapter 5 shows you how to search the Internet with your Web browser, so that finding things on the Net can be a little easier than just hunting around blindly. Chapter 6 explains how you can juice up your Web browser and connect to and play all kinds of multimedia content from the Internet.

The Internet as Community

In some ways the Net is like the phone system. It's another tool for contacting people, but it works only if the other people you want to reach are also on the system.

Chapter 7 tells you all about mailing lists—how to get on them, how to contribute to them, and how to find them. These lists will be your first taste of *virtual communities* of people united by common interests, no matter where they are geographically.

Chapter 8 explains the Usenet news network, a huge assortment of newsgroups devoted to interests and topics of every imaginable stripe, and tells you the practical details of running a newsreader program and reading and contributing to newsgroups yourself. No matter what newsreader you end up using—or even if you use your Web browser to read news—this chapter will have you covered.

Chapter 9 discusses live chatting using the IRC system and the various programs you can use to access IRC.

The Internet's Nooks and Crannies

Not everything on the Net is easily available via the World Wide Web, so Chapter 10 explains how to use some of the older Internet protocols, such as FTP and Telnet to find and connect to resources on the Net. Chapter 11 covers Gopher, a convenient way of browsing the Internet's archives, especially those at universities (although much of its usefulness has been overshadowed by the World Wide Web).

Your Name Here

The last chapter of the book shows you how to easily create a simple home page and how to find a place to publish it on the Web.

Appendices

Appendix A explains how to get an Internet connection, starting from scratch if necessary, as well as how to connect and what to do when things don't work the way they should. Appendix B is an essential glossary of the Internet jargon you hear bandied about nowadays (and other things you'll hear about on the Net and want explained).

Conventions I Use in This Book

When I want you to type something, I'll put it in boldface, and I'll use italics for new terms and jargon. When I want to give you useful Internet addresses or references, I'll put the information `in this font` or even

`on a line by itself.`

Sometimes, the specific text you need to type will vary from case to case. If so, I'll include some dummy text in *italics*. Don't type the italicized or underlined words! Instead, substitute the relevant file name, directory name, newsgroup name, etc. When the time comes, you'll know what to do. Usenet newsgroups also appear `in this font`. Program messages that appear on your screen are shown in quotation marks.

> **TIP**
> **Macintosh users should be aware that for programs that exist on both the Mac and Windows platform, I usually give the Windows shortcuts (such as Ctrl+P). Most of the time, the equivalent Macintosh shortcuts use the Command key instead of the Ctrl key.**

You'll notice (if you haven't already) that Web addresses (also called URLs) are often quite long, and it's important that you type them in exactly, if you're trying to visit a mentioned site with your Web browser. Because many of them are too long to fit snugly on one line of this book, I've allowed URLs to break after any forward slash (/) or dot (.), without a hyphen ever being inserted. If you see a URL that breaks over a line and continues on the next line (such as `http://ezone.org/ez/e5/articles/xian/backdrop.html`), just type it all on one line, without skipping a space for the line break!

Occasionally in this book I'll mention Unix programs. Because Unix is case sensitive, the names of many of these programs are traditionally written all lowercase (such as pine, irc, gopher, tin, vi, and so on). I will refer to these programs by capitalizing their initial letter (Pine, Irc, Gopher, Vi) to make the sentences easier to read and understand, but remember that you have to type the program's name in all lowercase to run it.

Sorting through the Many Programs

Because there are so many different ways to connect to the Net (at your office, through an online service, with an ISP) and so many different types of programs you can run to achieve many of the same goals, most of the chapters in this book are divided into two parts. In the first part, I usually explain the concepts you need to understand and, in generic terms, how to work the kind of program you'll need to send mail, browse the Web, post an article to a newsgroup, etc. In the second half, I'll cover the most popular and most common programs available for the feature in question and fill you in on the specific commands and idiosyncrasies of each.

You'll then have to read up on only one particular program (at least until you change to another one, at which time you can come back to the chapter and pick up the details for your new program).

> **TIP**
>
> Software changes rapidly on the Net and new versions of products come out all the time. Chapter 5 explains how you can make sure you always have the latest version of a program.

Stay in Touch

If you correct an error, I'll fix whatever's wrong in the next edition of the book, and even thank you in the acknowledgments.

If you find anything incorrect or misleading, if you'd like to point me toward something you think I've overlooked, or if you'd just like to give me some feedback (or even flame me), please write me at the following addresses:

Christian Crumlish

c/o Sybex Inc.

2021 Challenger Drive

Alameda, CA 94501

Or send me e-mail at **xian@pobox.com** and put the word ABC in the subject line of your message.

Chapter 1

JUST ENOUGH TO GET STARTED

FEATURING

- **Understanding the Internet**
- **Accessing the Internet at work and at home**
- **Discovering what you can do on the Internet**
- **Using Internet addresses**

I know, you're raring to go. You want to start sending and receiving e-mail, browsing the Web, and exploring the global library of fun stuff out on the Internet. Well, I don't want to hold you back. Feel free to skip to Chapter 2 and start right in on e-mail (or even jump to Chapter 4 to start messing around with the World Wide Web). However, if you've got some questions about what the Internet actually is, how you get access to it, and what you do once you're there, I'll try to answer those questions here.

I'll also try to explain most of the jargon you hear when people start babbling about the *Net*, so you can figure out for yourself what you want to learn about and what you'd like to ignore. (In addition Appendix B is a glossary of Internet terms used in this book.) Notice that I just used the word *Net* and not *Internet*. For the most part, the words are synonymous, although some people will use the word Net to refer to just about any aspect of the global inter-networking of computers.

NOTE	If you want a more thorough compendium of Internet jargon, terminology, and culture at your fingertips, try my *Internet Dictionary,* also from Sybex.

What Is the Internet?

In this chapter, there are no dumb questions. Everybody talks about the Internet these days but most people don't really know what it is. One reason for this is that the Internet looks different depending on how you come across it and what you do with it. Another reason is that everyone talks about it as if it's actually a network, like a local network in someone's office or even a large global network like CompuServe. Fact is, it's something different. A beast unto itself. The Internet is really a *way for computers to communicate*.

As long as a computer or smaller network can "speak" the Internet lingo (or *protocols*, to be extra formal about it) to other machines, then it's "on the Internet." If the Internet were a language, it wouldn't be French or Farsi or Tagalog or even English. It would be Esperanto.

Having said that, I might backtrack and allow that there's nothing wrong with thinking of the Internet as if it is a single network unto itself. It certainly behaves like one in a lot of important ways. But this can be misleading. No one "owns" the Internet. No one even really runs it. And no one can turn it off.

E-mail and a Whole Lot More

The Internet is also a collection of different ways to communicate or store information in a retrievable form. Take e-mail, for example. If you work in an office with a local-area network, then chances are you have an e-mail account and can communicate with people in your office by sending them messages. (See Chapters 2 and 3 for an in-depth discussion of all the ins and outs of e-mail.) This is not the Internet. Likewise, if you have an account at America Online and you send a message to someone else at

AOL, you're still not using the Internet. But, if your office network has a *gateway* to the Internet, and you send e-mail to someone who does not work at your office, then you're sending mail over the Internet.

> **NOTE** A *gateway* is a computer or the program running on it that transfers files (or e-mail messages, or commands) from one network to another.

Likewise, if you send a message from your AOL account to someone at CompuServe, or elsewhere, then, again, you are sending messages over the Internet (see Figure 1.1).

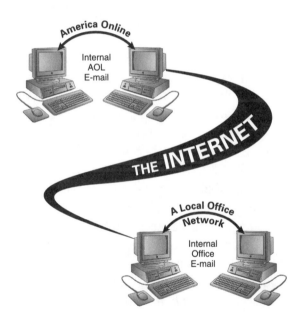

FIGURE 1.1: The Internet carries e-mail from one network to another.

But, from your point of view, the Internet is not just a collection of networks all talking to each other. A single computer can also participate in the Internet by connecting to a network or service provider that's connected to the Internet. And while the local office network I described and the big commercial online services are not themselves the Internet, they can and often do provide access through their gateways to the Internet. (I cover online services later in this chapter, in the section called *Accessing the Net at Home*.)

This can be confusing to first-time Internet users (universally referred to as *newbies*). Say you have an AOL account and you join one of the *discussion groups (bulletin boards)* there. It may not be obvious to you right away whether you're talking in an internal venue, one only accessible to AOL members, or in a public Internet newsgroup. One of the benefits of an online service is the seamlessness that makes everything within your grasp appear to be part of the same little program running on your computer.

> **NOTE**
>
> A *bulletin board* is a public discussion area where people can post messages—without sending them to anyone's e-mail address—that can be viewed by anyone who enters the area. Other people can then reply to posted messages and ongoing discussions can ensue. On CompuServe, a bulletin board is called a *forum*. On the Internet, the equivalent areas are called *newsgroups*.

The Web Is Not the Net, or Is It?

Nowadays, most of the hype about the Internet is focused on the World Wide Web. It's existed for under ten years now but it's been the fastest growing and most popular part of the Net for many of those years (except, perhaps, for the voluminous flow of e-mail around the globe). But what is the *Web* (also called *WWW* or *w3*) and is it the same thing as the Internet? Well, to answer the second question first: yes and no. Technically, the Web is just part of the Internet—or, more properly, a way of getting around part of the Internet. But it's a big part, because a lot of the Internet that's not strictly speaking part of the Web can still be reached through it.

So the Web, on one level, is an *interface.* A window onto the Net. A way of getting to where you're going. Its appeal derives from three different benefits:

1. It disguises the gobbledygook that passes for Internet addresses and commands. (See *A Few Words about Internet Addresses* at the end of this chapter.)
2. It wraps up most of the different features of the Internet into a single interface.
3. It allows you to see pictures, and even hear sounds or watch movies (if your computer can hack it), along with your helpings of text.

> **TIP**
>
> To play sounds, your computer needs a sound card, speakers, and some kind of software (such as MS Sound Recorder or Sound Machine for the Macintosh, but there are many others); to play movies, your computer needs software (such as Media Player for Windows or QuickTime for the Macintosh or Windows) and a lot of memory (or else the movies will play real herky-jerky).

It helps to know a little bit about the history of the Net to understand why these three features of the Web have spurred on the Internet boom. First of all, before the Web, to do anything beyond simple e-mail (and even that could be difficult, depending on your type of access) used to require knowing weird Unix commands and understanding the Internet's system for numbering and naming all the computers connected to it. If you've ever wrestled with DOS and lost, then you can appreciate the effort required to surmount this type of barrier.

Imagine it's 1991 and you've gotten yourself an Internet account, solved the problems of logging in with a communications program to a Unix computer somewhere out there, and mastered the Unix programs needed to send and receive mail, read newsgroups, download files, and so on. You'd still be looking at lots of screenfuls of plain text, reams and reams of words. No pictures. Well, if you were dying for pictures you could download enormous text files that had begun their lives as pictures and then were encoded as plain text so they could be squeezed through the text-only pipelines that constituted the Net. Next you'd have to decode the files, download them onto your PC or Mac, and then run some special program to look at them. Not quite as easy as flipping through a magazine.

The Web uses a method called *hypertext* to disguise the actual commands and addresses you use to navigate the Net. Instead of these commands and addresses, what you see in your *Web browser* (the program you use to travel the Web) is plain English key words highlighted in some way. Simply select or click on the key words, and your browser program talks the Internet talk, negotiates the transaction with the computer at the other end, and brings the picture, text, program, or activity you desire onto your computer screen. This is how all computer functions should work (and probably how they will work one day).

> **NOTE**
>
> You may have already encountered a form of hypertext on your desktop computer. If you have a Macintosh, think of hypercard stacks—the cards in those stacks are hyperlinked to one another. If you have Windows running on a PC, think about the Windows Help system, where clicking on highlighted words connects you to definitions or tangentially related help topics.

Early, Unix-based Web browsers such as Www (developed at CERN, the European particle physics laboratory where the Web was invented) and Lynx (developed at the University of Kansas) were not especially attractive to look at, but they did offer the "one-step" technique for jumping to a specific location on the Net or downloading a file or piece of software. Figure 1.2 shows Lynx, running on a Unix machine in a terminal window and connected to a PC by a modem.

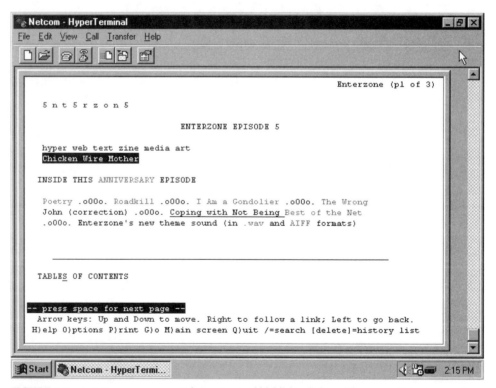

FIGURE 1.2: In Lynx, you can press Tab to get to and highlight a link, and then press Enter to execute the link and follow it to a file or another part of the Internet.

The next advance on the Web was the development of graphical Web browsers that could run on a desktop PC or Macintosh, permitting the user to employ the familiar point-and-click techniques available for other programs on the computer and incorporating text formatting and graphics into the browser screen. The first program of this type was NCSA Mosaic, which was developed at the National Center for Supercomputer Applications and distributed for free (see Figure 1.3).

FIGURE 1.3: Mosaic made it possible to point to a link and click on it, making the Internet much more accessible to non-technical users. It also pioneered the use of in-line graphics (meaning illustrations mixed in with text).

Furthermore, the various Web browsers can more or less substitute for a plethora of little specialty programs (such as Gopher clients, newsreaders, FTP programs, and so on) that you had to assemble and set up yourself "in the old days." The browsers all have their own little idiosyncrasies, but they're still remarkably uniform and consistent compared to the zoo of different programs and rules you had to follow just a few years ago. These days, the most popular browser is Netscape Navigator (see Figure 1.4).

> **NOTE**   "Just a few years ago" *is* the old days on the Internet. Changes happen so rapidly in the online world that time on the Internet is like "dog years," something like seven years go by for each one in the real world.

FIGURE 1.4:   Netscape Navigator is hands-down the most popular World Wide Web browser program. It works very much the way Mosaic does but with a number of additional features and improvements.

The Web has made it possible for browsers to display pictures right there in the midst of text, without you having to know how to decode files. A picture's worth a thousand watchamacallits, and pictures look better in newspaper articles and on TV than scads of typewritten text. So this ability was the final ingredient that made the Web seem so accessible and interesting to people who'd never in a million years care to learn what a Unix "regular expression" is.

So, I haven't really answered the question that heads up this section: Is the Web the Internet? Technically it's not exactly the same thing, but for all intents and purposes, it is. And Web browsers are the must-have programs that have made the Internet what it is today.

Getting on the Internet

So what exactly does it mean to be "on the Internet"? Generally, if someone asks you, "Are you on the Net?" it means something like, "Do you have an Internet e-mail address?" That is, do you have e-mail and can your e-mail account be reached over the Internet? With the popularity of the Web what it is, another common interpretation of what it means to be on the Net is, "Do you have the ability to browse the World Wide Web?" Often these two features—Internet e-mail, and Web access—go hand in hand, but not always. We're also getting to a time when being on the Internet will also entail having your own *home page,* your own "place" on the Web where information about you is stored and where you can be found.

Accessing the Net at Work

More and more companies these days (as well as schools and other organizations) are installing internal networks and relying on e-mail as one of the ways to share information. E-mail messages are starting to replace interoffice memos, at least for some types of announcements, questions, and scheduling purposes. The logical next step for most of these organizations is to connect their internal network to the Internet through a gateway. When this happens, you may suddenly be on the Net. This doesn't mean that anything will necessarily change on your desktop. You'll probably still use the same e-mail program and still send and receive mail within your office in the same way you always have.

What will change at this point is that you'll be able to send mail to people on the Internet outside of your office, as long as you type the right kind of Internet address. (Generally, this means adding @ and then a series of words separated by periods to the *username* portion of an address, but I'll explain more about addresses at the end of this chapter.) Likewise, people out there in the great beyond will be able to send mail to you as well.

Depending on the type of Internet connection your company has, e-mail may be all you get. Then again, it might also be possible for you to run a Web browser on your computer and visit Internet *sites* while sitting at your desk. Of course your company will only want you to do this if it's relevant to your job, but it works the same way whether you're researching a product your company uses or reading cartoons at the Dilbert site.

Accessing the Net at Home

If you're interested in exploring the Internet as a form of entertainment or for personal communication, then a work account is not really the way to do that. (An *account* minimally consists of a username and an e-mail in box; it may also provide storage space on a computer or access to a Web server.) You'll need your own personal account to really explore the Internet on your own time, without looking over your shoulder to make sure nobody's watching.

> **TIP**
>
> If your office is quite sophisticated, you may actually be able to dial into a company network from home via a modem to check your e-mail messages or even browse the Web, but again, this might not be an appropriate use of your boss's resources.

Your best bet is to sign up for an account from a commercial online service or a direct-access Internet service provider. (Appendix A explains how to find and get your own Internet account.) What's the difference between those two choices? Well, an *online service* (such as CompuServe, America Online, Prodigy, Microsoft Network, and so on) is first and foremost a private, proprietary network, offering its own content and access to other network members. An *Internet service provider* (also called an *ISP*) offers *just* access to the Internet and no local content (or only very limited local information and discussion groups). Figure 1.5 will help illustrate this distinction.

Online services have only recently begun offering full (or somewhat limited) Internet access. Because they are trying to do two things at once (sell you their own content and connect you to the Internet), they are usually an expensive way of exploring the Net. On the other hand, they tend to offer a single, simplified interface. I often recommend to people who just want to get their feet wet before plunging wholeheartedly into the Net, to sign up for a free trial account at one of the online services. If they like what the Internet has to offer or if they start using the Net so much they run up an expensive bill (after that first free month), then I recommend that they switch to a direct-access Internet service provider.

ISPs can be much cheaper than online services, especially if you can find one that offers a *flat rate*—a monthly charge that doesn't vary no matter how much time you spend connected to the Net. They also don't try to compete with the Internet by offering their own content and sponsors. Instead, they function as a gateway, getting you onto the Internet and letting you go wherever you want.

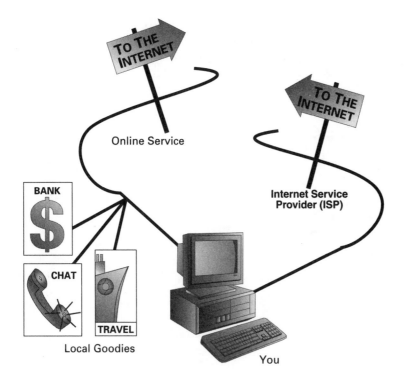

FIGURE 1.5: Online services connect you to the Internet but encourage you to explore their own offerings, whereas ISPs just connect you to the Internet and let you fend for yourself.

What Kinds of ISP Accounts Are There?

An ISP account generally includes, along with the e-mail address, an account with some storage space on a computer somewhere on the Net, usually in a directory (a folder) with the same name as your username. An account is also a billing entity, and your account will be billed monthly, sometimes with a surcharge based on the amount of time you spent connected that month (depending on the provider) or the amount of space you used on their hard drive.

But how do you use an account? Well, you need a computer with a modem, and you need software that knows how to use that modem to call up (dial up) your provider and allow you to log in to your account. Appendix A has more on the nitty-gritty of connecting to an account. If you want more than simply a connection to a Unix command-line and a plain text account (and I suspect that you do), then nowadays you need something called a *PPP* or *SLIP account.* (The other kind is usually called a *shell account* or sometimes a *Unix shell account*.) Again, I'll explain more about these distinctions in Appendix A, if you're really interested. A PPP (or SLIP) account lets your computer behave like it's connected directly to another computer on the Internet—when it's really connected over a phone line whenever you dial in—and it enables you to run software, such as graphical Web browsers like Mosaic and Netscape Navigator, that functions in your computers' native environment (for example, Windows or the Macintosh operating system) instead of forcing you to deal with plain-text programs like the text-only browsers Lynx and Unix (see Figure 1.6).

PPP-Type
Internet Connection

Unix-Shell Type
Internet Connection

FIGURE 1.6:
If you can get a PPP (or SLIP) account, then your connection to the Internet will be much more seamlessly integrated into your computer's normal environment.

Once you're set up, you won't have to think much about whether you have a PPP or SLIP account or any other kind of account, but I just wanted to introduce the terminology so you'll know what I'm talking about when I mention it again.

WARNING By the way, the speed of your modem—and that of the modem at the other end of the dial-up line, that is, your provider's modem—determines the speed of your Internet connection, and even the fastest modems these days are still slower than a direct network connection to the Net, such as you might enjoy at your office.

The Internet Doesn't Care What Kind of Computer You Use

One of the nice things about the Internet is that it makes some of the seemingly important distinctions between types of computers a lot less important. Sure, if you use a Macintosh, you have to run Macintosh software, and if you use Windows 95, you have to run Windows software, but the information out on the Internet, the public discussion areas, and the World Wide Web look and act more or less the same, no matter what kind of computer you use.

In fact, the Web is quickly becoming a sort of universal computer platform now that certain types of programs and services are being designed to run on the Web, rather than to run on one specific type of computer. In this book, most of the screen shots (such as in Figure 1.2) show Windows 95 screens, because that's the kind of computer I do most of my work on, but many of the programs featured also exist for the Macintosh, and when they do, I'll be sure to fill you in on the Macintosh equivalents and where to find them. Figure 1.7 shows a Netscape Navigator window on a Macintosh. Notice how similar it looks to the Windows 95 version shown in Figure 1.4.

Part of the elegance of the Internet is that much of the heavy duty processing power and storage of large programs and dense information takes place "out there," not on your computer. Your computer—whether it's a PC, a Mac, or a Unix workstation—becomes just a convenient beanstalk to climb up to the land of the Internet giants. You'll sometimes refer to this common structure of Internet facilities as *client-server* (sorry for the jargon). In this scenario, you are the client (or your computer or the program running on it is) and the information source or World Wide Web site or mail-handling program is the server. *Servers* are centralized repositories of information or specialized handlers of certain kinds of traffic. All your client has to do is connect to the right server and a wealth of goodies are within your reach, without you having to overload your machine. This is a major reason why it doesn't matter what kind of computer you prefer.

What You Can Do on the Net

I've touched on the most popular facilities on the Internet—e-mail and the World Wide Web—but I'll run down some of the other useful features covered in this book.

FIGURE 1.7: Netscape Navigator for the Mac works almost exactly the same way as the PC (and for that matter, Unix) version of the program, except for the normal Macintosh user-interface features, such as the menu bar being at the top of the screen instead of below the title bar.

All of these things are interrelated, and you may notice me mentioning something *before* I cover it in detail. I don't want to leave you scratching your head when I'm forced to sputter terms of the trade, such as FTP, Telnet, and Gopher.

Once you start exploring the Web you might start to get tired of its disorganization (imagine a library where every card-carrying member worked part-time as a librarian for one of the shelves, and each micro-librarian used their own system for organizing their section) or with not knowing for sure where *anything* is on the Internet. Fortunately, there are a lot of useful *search engines* available on the Net, and I'll show you where to find them and how to use them. Not as thorough as a card catalog, perhaps, but easier to use.

NOTE   A *search engine* is a program or Web page that enables you to search an Internet site (or the entire Internet) for a specific key word or words (see Chapter 5).

The Web itself is becoming more of a whiz-bang medium with some of the bells and whistles we've come to expect in television advertisements and big budget movies. To take full advantage of some of the more dynamic Web offerings, though, you have to learn how to plug special tools into your browser. I'll show you where to find the tools and how to plug them in.

Those newsgroups I alluded to before, the Internet's public message boards, are organized (to use the term loosely) into a system called *Usenet*. I'll tell you how Usenet works, how to get and install a *newsreader,* and how to start participating in this public forum without getting called a jerk. If you plan to join in on the public discourse of the Net, you have to learn a thing or two about something called *netiquette*—the traditional rules of civilized behavior online. (Usenet and netiquette are explained in Chapter 8.)

If you prefer the idea of communicating with people "live" rather than posting messages and waiting for people to reply later, then you'll want to know about the various *chat* facilities available on the Internet, particularly *IRC* (*Internet Relay Chat*).

If you're willing to get your hands a little dirty and want to start tunneling your way around the Internet, connecting to computers all over the globe and moving files hither and yon, you might be able to do all that from your Web browser, or you may want to pick up the basics of *FTP* (*File Transfer Protocol*) and *Telnet*, a system that allows you to log into remote computers over the Net).

Finally, if you want to join the ranks of people with their own home pages on the Web, so you can create a "presence" on the Net or publicize your favorite Internet sites, I'll show you how to do that as well.

A Few Words about Internet Addresses

One of the confusing things to Internet newbies is that the word *address* is used to mean at least three different things on the Internet. The most basic meaning—but the one used least often—is the name of a computer, also called a *host* or *site,* on the Internet in the form `something.something.something` (to really use the lingo properly you have to pronounce the periods "dot"—you'll get used to it and it saves a lot of time over the long haul). For example, I publish a magazine (or 'zine) on the Internet called *Enterzone;* it's stored on a machine at Vassar that's part of the American Arts and Letters Network. The address of that machine is

`ezone.org`

Reading from right to left, you first have the *domain,* `org`, which stands for (non-commercial) organization. Next you sometimes have a *subdomain.* Finally you have the *hostname,* `ezone`, which is the name (or a name) of the specific computer the magazine is stored on.

Another type of address is an e-mail address. An e-mail address consists of a *username* (also called a *login,* a *log-on name,* a *userID,* an *account name,* and so on), followed by an "at sign" (@) and then an Internet address of the type just described. So, for example, say you want to send mail to me in my capacity as editor of *Enterzone.* You could address that e-mail message to a special username created for that job (it will stay the same even if someone else takes over in the future):

`editor@ezone.org`

The third type of address is the kind you see everywhere these days, on billboards, on TV commercials, in the newspaper, and so on—a Web address, also called a *URL* (*Uniform Resource Locator*). I'll explain more about how to read (or ignore) URLs in Chapter 4. For now, it's enough just to know what one looks like. The Web address of that magazine I told you about is

`http://ezone.org/ez`

Fortunately, you often can avoid typing in Web addresses yourself and can zip around the Web just by clicking pre-established *links.* Links are highlighted words or images that when clicked on or selected take you directly to a new document, another part of the current document, or some other type of file entirely.

Well, I think I've kept you waiting long enough. Are you ready for e-mail?

Chapter 2

SENDING AND RECEIVING E-MAIL

FEATURING

- **Sending e-mail**
- **Reading e-mail**
- **Replying to e-mail**
- **Deleting e-mail**
- **Working with America Online, cc:Mail, CompuServe, Eudora, MS Exchange, NetCruiser, Netscape Mail, Pegasus Mail, Pine, and QuickMail**

This is the real stuff. The reason why you're on the Net. E-mail! Instant (more or less) communication with people all over the globe. Sure, we'll get to the World Wide Web soon (see Chapter 4), but first things first. Once you can send and receive e-mail, you're wired.

This chapter will cover the most basic e-mail concepts—mainly, how to send and receive e-mail. If you have an internal network at your office and you're already familiar with how to send and receive mail, you can probably skip this chapter (though you might want to read the parts about how to write an Internet e-mail address to send mail beyond your network). If you don't yet have an e-mail account or Internet access, look in Appendix A for how to get connected to the Internet, and how to get started once you are connected.

NOTE When you get used to sending e-mail, you'll find that it's as useful a form of communication as the telephone, and it doesn't require the other person to drop whatever they're doing to answer your call. You can include a huge amount of specific information, and the person you sent mail to can reply in full in their own good time. And unlike the telephone, with e-mail you can write your message and edit it first before you send it.

E-mail is the lifeblood of the Internet. Daily, millions of written messages course through the wires, enabling people all over the planet to communicate in seconds. One reason for the widespread use of the Internet as *the* international computer network is that it's a flexible enough system to allow just about any type of computer or network to participate. The upside of this is that whether you have a Mac, PC, or more exotic type of computer; whether you connect by modem or from a smaller network; and no matter what e-mail program you have you can still send and receive mail over the Internet.

The downside is that there are so many different e-mail programs available that I can't hope to cover each one in detail, so I'll start off by explaining the most common activities associated with e-mail, the kinds of things you'll want to know how to do no matter what program you have. I'll use generic terminology in this part of the chapter, such as In box and Out box, even if some specific programs use different terms for the same ideas. Focus on the concepts and the standard features, not what they're called in one program or another. Then, I'll cover specific commands and tips for a heaping handful of the most common e-mail programs—chances are you'll be using one of them.

In the unlikely circumstance that you have none of the specific programs that I cover, the first part of the chapter will still provide you with a list of actions to look for in the help portion of your e-mail program or to discuss with your system (or network) administrator.

Your E-Mail Program May Depend on Your Type of Service

If you have a typical dial-up account, or if you connect to the Internet through a network at your work or school, then you'll run a stand-alone mail program in your normal operating environment. If you get your Internet access through a commercial network, such as America Online or CompuServe, then you'll use their built-in mail programs, and sending mail over the Internet will require only that you use the proper sort of Internet mailing address.

If you've got a Unix shell account, then you'll handle your mail either by running a Unix e-mail program (such as Pine) or by setting up an offline mail program, such as Eudora, that will run in your normal computer environment and connect with your shell account only to send and receive mail.

TIP	Throughout this book, I will provide alternative approaches to the various Internet services that provide only e-mail. Then, as long as you have e-mail access to the Internet, you'll be able to use some of the services that your provider does not offer directly.

Working with E-Mail

These are the things that you will do most often with e-mail:
- Run the mail program
- Send mail
- Read incoming mail
- Reply to mail
- Delete mail
- Exit the mail program

In Chapter 3, I'll show you some additional e-mail tricks you might find useful, such as how to forward mail and create an electronic address book.

Running a Mail Program

You start most e-mail programs the way you do any program, usually by double-clicking an icon or by choosing a program name from a menu (the Start menu in

Windows 95, the Apple menu on a Mac). If your Internet connection is not already up and running, your e-mail program may be able to start that process for you. (If not, see Appendix A for how to connect to the Net.)

Your e-mail program will start and either show you the contents of your In mailbox or will show you a list of all your mailboxes (in which case you'll want to open the In box).

In addition to an In mailbox where just-arrived messages appear, you'll automatically have an Out mailbox in which copies of your outgoing messages can be saved (some programs will do this automatically), and usually a deleted-messages or Trash mailbox where discarded messages are held until they're completely purged. Figure 2.1 shows a Microsoft Exchange Inbox.

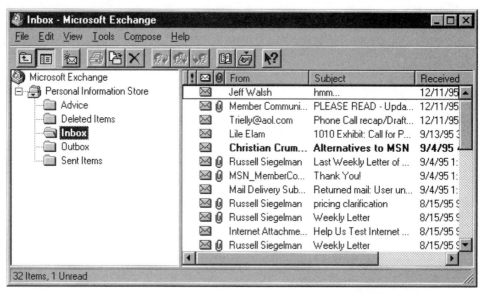

FIGURE 2.1: My Microsoft Exchange Inbox with messages listed in the order they were sent, from the most recent to the oldest

Mailboxes generally list just the sender's name and the subject line of the message (and probably its date as well). When you double-click on a message in any of your mailboxes, the message will open up in a window of its own.

Sending Mail

All mail programs have a New Message or Compose E-mail command, often located on a message menu, and they usually have a keyboard shortcut for the command as well, such as Ctrl+N for New Message. When you start a new message, your program will open a new window. Figure 2.2 shows a new message window in Exchange.

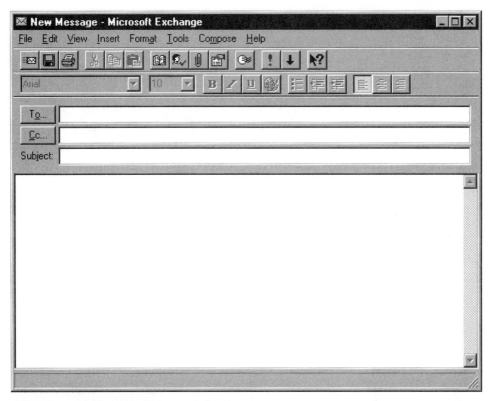

FIGURE 2.2: A blank New Message window

> **TIP**
>
> **Most e-mail programs enable you to save addresses and then select them from an address book or list of names rather than type them in directly. See Chapter 3 for more on this.**

Type the address of the person to whom you wish to send the mail. The person's address must be of the form **username@address.domain**, where *username* is the person's identifier (the name they log in with); *address* is the identifier of the person's network and or machine on the network (the address might consist of several words—the *host* and *subdomain*—separated by dots); and *domain* is the three-letter code indicating whether the address is a business (.com), a non-profit (.org), a university (.edu), a branch of the government (.gov), a part of the military (.mil), and so on. (Some e-mail programs require special text before or after the Internet e-mail address.)

By the way, all the rules mentioned in the previous category apply only to sending mail over the Internet. Generally, if you're sending mail to someone on your own network (or another member of your online service or subscriber of your service provider), you only have to specify the username, not any of the Internet information.

> **TIP**
>
> The easiest way to send mail to someone is to reply to mail that they've sent you. If you're not sure exactly how to form someone's e-mail address, ask them to send you some mail and then simply reply to it. That's what I always do.

One of my addresses is `xian@netcom.com` (you pronounce the "@ sign" as "at," and the "." as "dot"). I log in as "xian," my service provider is Netcom, and Netcom is a commercial business.

Sending Mail to People on Other Networks

Many people have Internet addresses even though they are not, strictly speaking, on the Internet. Most other networks have gateways that send mail to and from the Internet. If you want to send mail to someone on another network, you'll need to know their identifier on that network and how their network address appears in Internet form. Here are examples of the most common Internet addresses:

Network	Username	Internet Address
America Online	Beebles	Beebles@aol.com
AT&T Mail	Beebles	beebles@attmail.com
CompuServe	75555,5555	75555.5555@compuserve.com
Delphi	Beebles	beebles@delphi.com
Fidonet BBSs	1:2/3	f3.n2.z1@fidonet.org
GEnie	Beebles	beebles@genie.com
MCI Mail	555-7777	555-7777@mcimail.com
Microsoft Network	Beebles	beebles@msn.com
Prodigy	Beebles	beebles@prodigy.com

As you can see, the only tricky ones are CompuServe, for which you have to change the comma in the CompuServe address to a dot in the Internet address; and Fidonet, for which you have to reverse the order of the three numbers and then put them after *f*, *n*, and *z*, respectively. (If you are only given two numbers, in the form a/b, then assume that they are the *n* and *f* numbers and that the *z* number is 1 [one].)

After entering the address, press Tab and then type a subject on the next line (keep it short). This will be the first thing the recipient of your mail sees.

> **TIP**
>
> In almost all e-mail programs, you can press Tab to jump from box to box or from area to area when filling in an address and subject. Generally, you can also just click directly in the area you want to jump to in most programs.

To send a copy of the e-mail message to another recipient, press Tab again and type that person's address on the Cc: line. Press Tab a few more times until the insertion point jumps into the message area.

> **NOTE**
>
> Would you rather write up your message ahead of time and then just paste it in when it comes time to send it? See Chapter 3 for how to include a text file you've already prepared.

Most mail programs can word-wrap your message, so you only have to press Enter when you want to start a new paragraph. I recommend leaving a blank line between paragraphs, to make them easier to read. Figure 2.3 shows a short e-mail message.

When you are done, send the message or add it to a *queue,* a list of outgoing messages to be sent all at once.

Reading Mail

Whenever I connect to the Net, the first thing I do is check my e-mail. It's like checking your mailbox when you get home, except the contents are usually more interesting. Some mail programs combine the process of sending queued messages with checking for new mail. Most also check for new mail when you first start them.

Unread (usually new) mail typically appears with some indicator that it's new, such as the Subject line appearing in bold, or a bullet or checkmark appearing next to new messages. This is supposed to help you avoid accidentally missing messages.

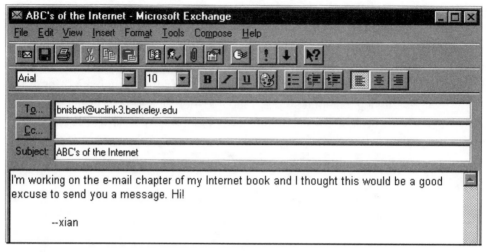

FIGURE 2.3: A short e-mail message to a friend

To view the contents of a mail message, highlight it in the window and press Enter (or double-click on it). The message will appear in its own window, much like an outgoing message. Figure 2.4 shows an incoming message in Exchange.

If the message continues beyond the bottom of the window, use the scroll bar to see the next screenful.

After reading the message, you can close or reply to the message.

> **TIP** I keep my mail around until I've replied to it. I could save it to a mailbox (as I'll explain presently) but then I might forget about it. When my In box gets too cluttered, I bite the bullet and reply to mail I've been putting off, and then delete most of it.

Replying to Mail

Somewhere near the New Message command (probably on the same menu or button bar), you'll find the Reply command. To reply to mail, highlight the message in the In box, or open it and then select the Reply command.

> **TIP** If you start a reply by mistake, just close the message window and don't save the reply if prompted.

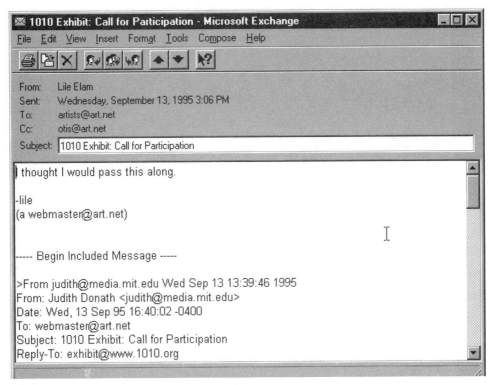

FIGURE 2.4: Here's an e-mail message I received.

Your program will also start a new message automatically addressed to the sender of the message you're replying to. Some mail programs will also automatically include the contents of the original message (or will give you the choice of including the contents or not). Often, especially with e-mail programs that were designed primarily for use on the Internet, the included message will appear with each line preceded by a ">" character to indicate that it is quoted text, although different mail programs have different ways of showing quoted messages. Some, for example, just indent the quoted material (see Figure 2.5).

Sometimes, you'll want to reply to everyone who was sent a copy of the original message. Most e-mail programs also offer a variation on the normal reply command that includes all original recipients in your reply.

Type a subject and press Tab. (People often fail to change the subject line of messages, even when the conversation has evolved its way onto a new topic.) Add other recipients if necessary or tab your way into the message area to type your reply, and then choose the Send (or Queue) command. But before we go on, there are a few rules of netiquette to follow.

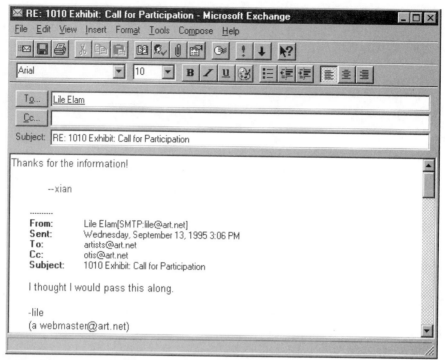

FIGURE 2.5: A reply with the original message included

Keep Your Messages to the Point

Try to minimize the amount of quoted text that you keep in your return message. Leave enough so it's clear what you're replying to (people don't always remember exactly what they wrote to you.)

Don't Fly off the Handle

In this book I'm trying to not give you too much advice about how to behave on the Net, for several reasons. First, I assume you are an adult and can decide for yourself how to behave. Secondly, the Net has a strongly interactive culture, and you will receive plenty of advice and cues from others if you overstep the bounds of good behavior.

Nevertheless, I will point out that e-mail is a notoriously volatile medium. Because it is so easy to write out a reply and send it in the heat of the moment, and because text lacks many of the nuances of face-to-face communication—the expression and body cues that add emphasis, the tones of voice that indicate joking instead of insult, and so on—it has become a matter of course for many people to dash off ill-considered replies to perceived insults and therefore fan the flames of invective.

NOTE Issues of netiquette (as it's called) arise even more frequently when you are communicating with large numbers of people on mailing lists or Usenet. See Chapters 7 and 8 for more details.

This Internet habit, called *flaming*, is widespread and you will no doubt encounter it on one end or the other. All I can suggest is that you try to restrain yourself when you feel the urge to fly off the handle. (And I have discovered that apologies work wonders when people have misunderstood a friendly gibe or have mistaken sarcasm for idiocy.)

Deleting Mail

If you have read a piece of mail and you're positive that you have no need to save it, you should delete it so it doesn't clutter up your In box (and waste precious hard-disk storage space). To delete a message, you typically highlight it and press Delete (or click on the Delete or Trash button, if there is one). In most programs, this moves the message to the Deleted-mail or Trash mailbox until you empty the trash (or quit the program).

WARNING In some programs, you don't get a chance to undelete a message, so be sure you know how your program works before deleting messages willy-nilly.

If you change your mind, try opening the Trash mailbox (or Deleted-Mail mailbox) and then look for a command that allows you to transfer mail from one box to another. It may even be called Transfer (as it is in Eudora). When you find it, transfer the mail back to your In box.

I cover saving messages in Chapter 3.

Exiting a Mail Program

When you are finished sending, reading, and replying to mail, you can quit your program or leave it running to check your mail at regular intervals. You can quit most mail programs by selecting File ➤ Exit or File ➤ Quit.

Using Specific E-Mail Programs

Well, now you know the basic e-mail moves no matter what program you have. In the rest of this chapter, I'll detail the specific commands for most of the popular e-mail programs (listed here in alphabetical order). Look ahead to see if I cover yours and just read that section unless you're interested in checking out another program. Then you're done with this chapter. Chapter 3 covers some of e-mail's more interesting possibilities, and Chapter 7 tells you all about mailing lists. Jump to Chapter 4 if you're impatient to get onto the World Wide Web.

America Online

America Online (also known as AOL) is the most popular online service today. It has an easy-to-use mail interface both for sending mail to other members of the service as well as for sending Internet mail. Figure 2.6 shows what the America Online mail program for Windows looks like.

> **TIP**
>
> America Online lets you compose messages offline; then you can log in and send them in something called a Flash Session, so you're not paying for connect charges while racking your brains over what to write. You can also arrange file transfers this way.

Send

With America Online, choose Mail ➤ Compose Mail or click on the Compose Mail button to send mail. Type the recipient's address (if they're on AOL, you can just use their *screen name*—which is what AOL calls a username). Press Tab twice to jump to the Subject box and enter a subject line. Press Tab again to begin typing your message. When you're done, click on the Send or Send Later button.

Send
Later

To read mail, select Mail ➤ Read New Mail, and then double-click the title of the message in the New Mail dialog box. Read the message and close the window when you're done. Once you've read a message, AOL moves it to the Old Mail dialog box. To read an old message, select Mail ➤ Check Mail You've Read. AOL also keeps copies of outgoing messages. To read them, select Mail ➤ Check Mail You've Sent. Close all open dialog boxes when you're done.

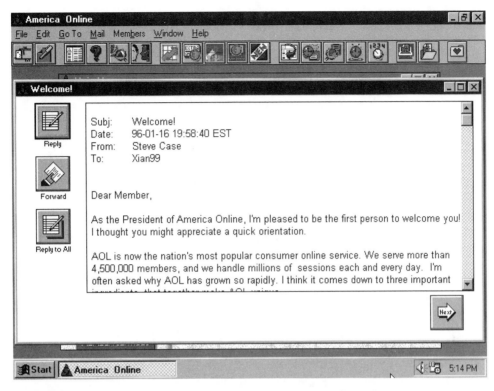

FIGURE 2.6: America Online's e-mail program is very easy to get the hang of.

TIP If you have received new mail since the last time you logged on, the Welcome dialog box will tell you, "You have new mail." Click on the picture above the message to open the New Mail dialog box.

To reply to a message, click on the Reply button (or click on Reply to All to send your reply to all of the recipients of the original message). This opens up a new mail window just like the kind you get when you send a new message.

To delete a message, select it and then click the Delete button at the bottom of the dialog box.

WARNING You can't undelete AOL e-mail messages.

cc:Mail

Lotus's cc:Mail is a popular network-oriented mail program (see Figure 2.7). To send mail with cc:Mail, click on the Prepare SmartIcon. A new window will appear. After typing the recipient's address, press Tab to jump to the Subject text box to enter a subject.

Press Tab until you reach the text area. Type your message, and then click on the Send SmartIcon.

To read a message in your In box, just double-click on it. To reply to a message, click on the Reply SmartIcon. To delete a message, click on the Delete SmartIcon.

To exit cc:Mail, select File ➤ Exit or click on the Exit SmartIcon.

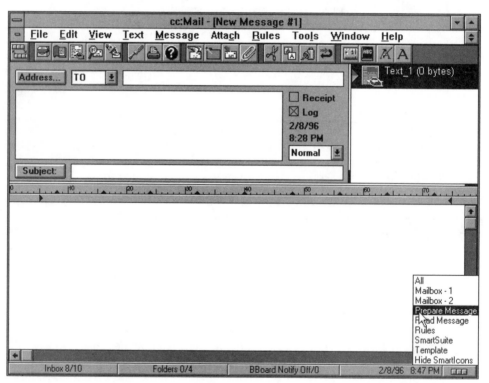

FIGURE 2.7: cc:Mail has easy-to-understand toolbar buttons for all the most common e-mail commands.

CompuServe

After America Online, CompuServe is the next most popular online service. If you're using one of the other services, the commands will likely be very similar to either AOL or CompuServe.

With CompuServe, choose Mail ➤ Create/Send Mail to send mail. In the Recipient List dialog box, either choose your recipient's name in the address book window and click on Copy>> or type their name, press Tab, type their e-mail address, press Tab again, select Internet at Address Type:, and then click on the Add button. Click on the OK button when you're done. For Internet addresses, CompuServe will append INTERNET: to the front of the e-mail address.

Write your message in the Create Mail dialog box (see Figure 2.8). Then click on the Send Now button or on the Out-Basket button.

> **TIP**
>
> **CompuServe lets you compose any number of messages offline and put them in your out-basket. You can then use the Mail ➤ Send/Receive All Mail command to send and receive all your mail as quickly as possible so you can get back offline. You can also arrange file transfers this way.**

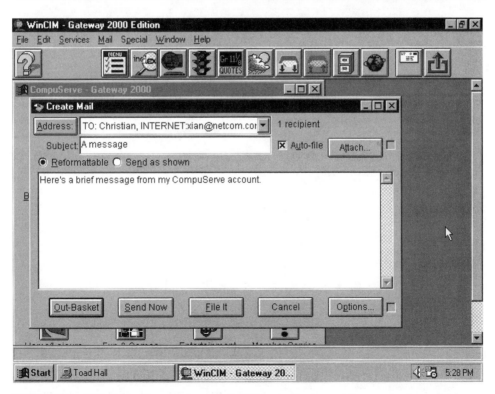

FIGURE 2.8: With CompuServe, click on the Send Now button to send the message immediately or on the Out-Basket button to store the message until you next connect.

To retrieve mail on CompuServe, choose Mail ➤ Get New Mail. Double-click on a message to read it. To reply to a message, click on the Reply button at the bottom of the message window. To delete a message, click on the Delete button at the bottom of the window and then click on Yes.

If you want more information about CompuServe's mail feature, choose Go ➤ Mailcenter.

> **WARNING**   CompuServe e-mail messages cannot be undeleted.

Eudora

Eudora is one of the most popular and dependable Internet e-mail programs. It can work on a network connection, with a PPP or SLIP dial-up account, or as an offline mail reader with a Unix shell account.

> **TIP**   A free evaluation copy of Eudora (called Eudora Lite) can be downloaded from http://www.qualcomm.com. See Chapters 5 and 10 for how to download files off the Net.

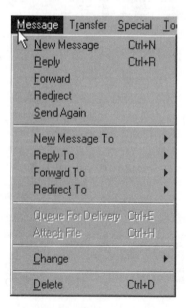

Most of the useful Eudora commands are available on the Message menu (shown here).

To send mail, select Message ➤ New Message (or press Ctrl+N in Windows, Command+N on the Mac). Type the address of the person to whom you wish to send the mail and press Tab a few times until the insertion point jumps to the area below the gray line. Figure 2.9 shows a short e-mail message.

When you are done, click on the Send button in the upper-right corner of the message window. The button might read Queue instead of Send. That means that it will be added to a list (a queue) of messages to be sent all at once either when the program checks for new mail or when you quit the program.

To check your mail with Eudora, select File ➤ Check Mail or press Ctrl+M (or Command+M). Eudora will connect to something called a *POP server* (POP stands for *Post Office Protocol*, but you can forget that) to pick up all your mail.

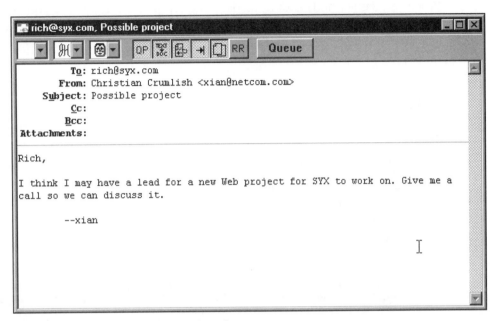

FIGURE 2.9: A new message window in Eudora

Unread mail will appear with a large dot (or bullet) in the left column of the In box. To view the contents of a mail message, highlight it in the window and press Enter (or double-click on it).

After reading the message, you can close its window or select Message ➢ Reply (or Ctrl+R) to reply to the message. If you start a reply by mistake, just close the message window and don't save it when prompted.

> **TIP**
> If you want to reply to everyone who was also sent a copy of the message, press Ctrl+Shift+R instead of Ctrl+R (or hold down Shift while selecting Message ➢ Reply).

To delete a message, place the highlight on it and press Delete (or click on the Trash icon at the top of the mailbox window). This moves the message to the Trash mailbox. It won't actually be deleted until you empty the trash (Special ➢ Empty Trash).

If you change your mind, select Mailbox ➤ Trash to open the Trash box, highlight the message, and then select Transfer ➤ In to move the message back into the In box.

When you are finished sending, reading, and replying to mail, you can quit Eudora or leave it running so you can check your mail. To quit Eudora, select File ➤ Exit (or File ➤ Quit in the Macintosh version of Eudora), or select Ctrl+Q (or Command+Q for the Mac).

Microsoft Exchange

Microsoft Exchange (formerly Microsoft Mail) comes built in with Windows 95. If you join the Microsoft Network (MSN), Exchange will be your mail program, but it can also handle network mail. You can start it by double-clicking on the Inbox icon on the desktop.

Exchange starts you off in a window showing two panes. The pane on the left shows your mailboxes (folders), and the pane on your right shows you your In mailbox (but if you choose another folder in the left pane, Exchange will show its contents in the right), as shown in Figure 2.10.

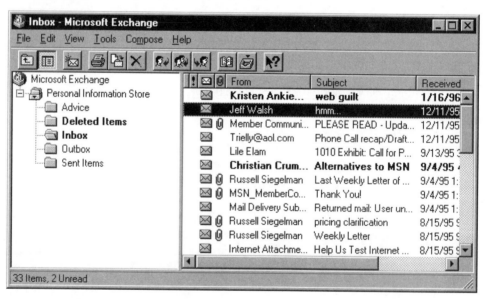

FIGURE 2.10: The main Exchange window shows you the messages in your Inbox or in whichever mailbox you've selected.

To send a new message with Exchange, select Compose ➢ New Message (Ctrl+N). This will open up a new message window (as shown back in Figure 2.2). Type an address and press Tab to get down to the message area.

Type your message and then click on the Send button.

To read a message in your Inbox, just double-click its subject line. The message will appear in its own window. To reply to the message, select Compose ➢ Reply to Sender (Ctrl+R). Exchange will supply the recipient's address. Proceed as if you were sending a new message.

To delete a message, just highlight it and press Delete. It will be moved to the Deleted Items folder until you specifically open that folder and delete its contents (even then Exchange will warn you that you are permanently deleting the message).

> **TIP**
>
> **To undelete a message, open the Deleted Items folder and select the message you want to restore. Then select File ➢ Move, choose the Inbox folder to move it to from the dialog box that appears, and click on OK.**

To exit Exchange, select File ➢ Exit.

NetCruiser

NetCruiser is an all-in-one Internet program from Netcom, for both Windows and the Macintosh. NetCruiser has its own mail program, but it also allows you to run outside programs, such as Eudora or Pegasus.

To send mail with NetCruiser, click on the Send Mail button on the button bar.

This brings up the Address Mail To window. Type the recipient's address, click on the Use button, and then click on OK. After entering a subject line, press Tab to enter the message area and type your message (NetCruiser will take care of word-wrapping). When you're done, click on the Send Current Message button (it looks the same as the Send Mail button on the main button bar, but it's on the Send Mail window's button bar instead).

To read incoming mail, click on the Read Mail button on the button bar

This brings up the Select a Folder window. Choose Inbox and click on OK. In the Read Mail window, messages are listed by author and subject line in the top pane and message contents are displayed in the bottom pane. To read a message, double-click it in the top pane (see Figure 2.11).

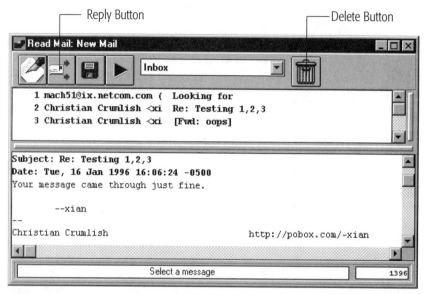

Reply Button — Delete Button

FIGURE 2.11: Incoming messages can be read in the bottom half of NetCruiser's Read Mail: New Mail window.

To reply to a message, click on the Reply button. To delete a message, click on the Delete button (the Trashcan icon). To exit the mail module of NetCruiser, just close the window. To exit NetCruiser, select File ➢ Exit.

Netscape Mail

Netscape Navigator 2 is mainly a Web browser, but it also sports a full-featured mail program that earlier versions of Netscape did not have.

NOTE You'll learn more about Netscape's Web capabilities in Chapter 4.

To send mail with Netscape mail, first select File ➢ New Mail Message (or press Ctrl+M). Type an address in the Mail To box. Press Tab twice and type a Subject. Then press Tab again to enter the message area and type your message (see Figure 2.12). When you're done, click on the Send button (or press Ctrl+Enter).

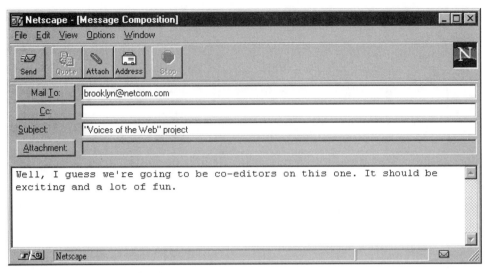

FIGURE 2.12: Sending mail with Netscape

If you receive mail while working in Netscape (the little envelope in the lower-right corner of the Netscape window will alert you), select Window ➢ Netscape Mail to open the Mail window (see Figure 2.13). The first time you do this, Netscape will require that you enter your password.

TIP   Any Web addresses mentioned in e-mail messages to you will function as clickable links. That means when you finish reading, all you have to do is click on a highlighted word to go to that Web page and start surfing. For more information on the Web, see Chapter 4.

Just highlight a message in the top-right pane to see its contents in the bottom pane. To reply to a message, select Message ➢ Reply (or press Ctrl+R). To delete a message, just highlight it and press Delete. Netscape will move the message to a Trash folder. To undelete a message, just select the Trash folder in the top-left pane, and then drag the message you want to restore back into the Inbox folder (also in the left pane).

You can close the Mail window but keep Netscape running—in Windows 95, just click on the close button in the upper-right corner—or you can quit Netscape entirely by selecting File ➢ Exit.

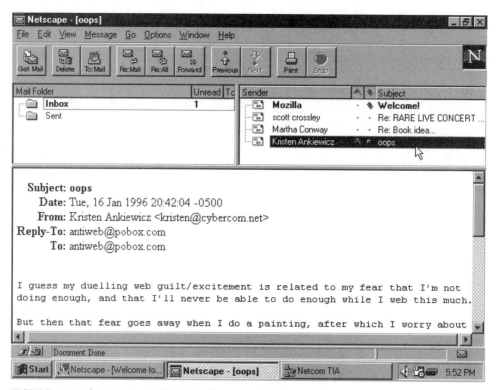

FIGURE 2.13: The Netscape Mail window has panes showing your mail folders, the contents of the selected folder to the right, and the selected message below.

Pegasus Mail

Pegasus is a popular, free mail program that can run on networks and over dial-up Internet connections.

> **TIP**
>
> You can download Pegasus from its Web site (`http://www.cuslm.ca/pegasus/`). See Chapters 5 and 10 for how to download files off the Net.

To send a new message with Pegasus, select File ➤ New Message (or press Ctrl+N). Type the recipient's name, press Tab, and type a subject. Then press Tab two more times to get down to the message area and type your message (see Figure 2.14).

When you're done, click on the Send button to either send your message immediately or put your message in a queue, depending on how your version of Pegasus is set up. To send all queued messages, select File ➤ Send All Queued Mail.

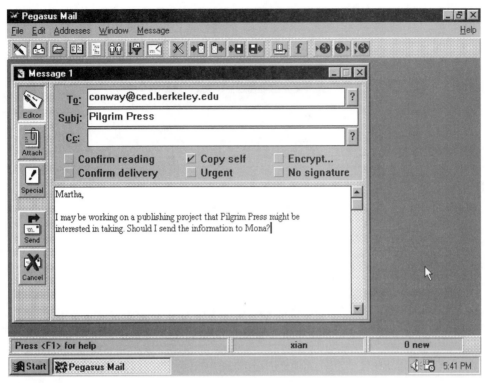

FIGURE 2.14: A new message window in Pegasus

To read new mail, select File ➤ Read New Mail (or press Ctrl+W). This opens the New mail folder. (Once you've read a message, it will automatically be moved to the Main mail folder after you close the New Mail folder or exit Pegasus.)

To check for new messages, select File ➤ Check Host for New Mail. Double-click on a message to read it. Figure 2.15 shows an incoming message.

To reply to the message, click on the Reply button. To delete it, click on the Delete button.

To exit Pegasus, select File ➤ Exit.

Pine

If you're determined to get your hands dirty and log in directly to a Unix account to read mail with a Unix mail reader, then here's a quick rundown of the most useful commands in the most popular Unix mail program, Pine.

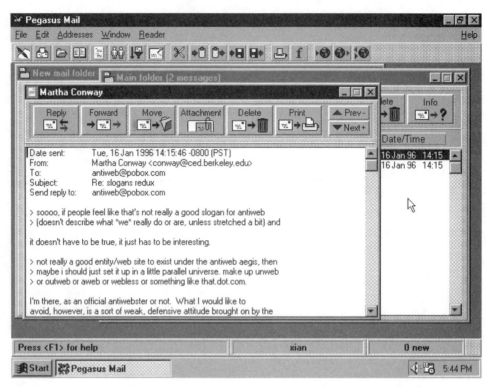

FIGURE 2.15:   An incoming message in Pegasus has useful shortcut buttons at the top of its window.

TIP   Another popular Unix e-mail program is Elm. For information
about Elm, send mail to `mail-server@cs.ruu.nl` with
no subject and the lines `send NEWS.ANSWERS/elm/FAQ`
and `end` each on their own lines.

To run Pine, type **pine** (yes, all lowercase—it matters) at the Unix command prompt
and press Enter. Pine starts you off at a main menu. To enter your In box, type **i**.

To send mail, type **c**—and don't press Enter. Pine will start a new message (see
Figure 2.16). Type the recipient's address, press Tab, and type a subject. Press Tab
again until you're in the message area. Then type your message. Pine will handle
word-wrapping, so you only have to press Enter when you're starting a new paragraph. When you're done, press Ctrl+X to send the message.

To read a message, highlight it in your In box (you can use the up and down arrow

FIGURE 2.16: Pine is a *full-screen* editor, so it works something like a *normal* Windows or Mac program, even though it's text only and runs in Unix.

keys to move through the list of messages) and press Enter. To return to the message list from a message, type **i**. To reply to a message, type **r**. To delete a message, type **d**. To undelete a message, type **u** (deleted messages don't disappear until you quit the program). To quit the program, type **q**.

The following list summarizes what you need to type to perform some of the specific functions mentioned in this section:

Function	Type
To run Pine	Type **pine**
To send mail	Type **c**
To return to your message list	Type **i**
To reply to a message	Type **r**
To delete a message	Type **d**
To undelete a message	Type **u**
To quit Pine	Type **q**

Chapter 3

MAKING THE MOST OF E-MAIL

- **Forwarding mail and sending it to multiple recipients**
- **Composing mail messages in your word processing program**
- **Sending attachments with your messages**
- **Saving e-mail messages and addresses**
- **Spell-checking an e-mail message**
- **Attaching a signature to mail messages**
- **Finding Internet e-mail addresses**

After you know the basics of e-mail—sending, reading, and replying to messages—there are a few more things you'll want to know about that will come in very handy as you start communicating over the Internet.

Mail-Sending Tricks

So you know how to send messages and how to reply to them, but there are a few more tricks in the basic e-mail grab bag—namely, forwarding a message on to a new recipient, sending mail to more than one person at a time, and saving old messages somewhere besides in your In box.

Forwarding Mail

If someone sends you mail and you'd like to send a copy of it to someone else, with most mail programs, you can select a Forward command. (Never send mail to a third party without the express permission of the original sender.)

The Forward command is often near (such as on the same menu as) the Reply command, and it works in almost the same way. The difference is that your mail program won't insert the original sender's e-mail address into the To: line. Instead it will be blank, as in a new message. But the original message will be automatically included in the new message, often with some characters (like the standard ">" Internet e-mail quoting character) or other formatting to distinguish it from what you yourself write.

To forward a message, type the recipient's name on the To: line and then Tab your way down to the message area. Edit the message and/or add your own note, perhaps an explanation of why you are forwarding the message, to the beginning. Then send the message as usual.

Sending Mail to Multiple Recipients

Sometimes you'll want to send a message to more than one recipient. You can usually do this in one of several ways. Most programs allow you to list multiple recipients in the To: line, usually separated by commas (some programs require that you use a different character, such as a semicolon, to separate addresses). Most also have a Cc: line which, so far, I've suggested you just Tab right past to get to the message area. As with traditional paper office memos, the Cc: line, in an e-mail message is for people who you want to receive a copy of the message, but who are not the primary recipient.

Some programs also offer a Bcc: line, which lets you list one or more people to receive *blind* copies of that message. This means that the primary (and Cc:) recipients will not see the names of people receiving blind copies.

**WARNING** You can typically include as many names on the Cc: line as you want, but some mail servers will choke on a message if its headers are too long.

Filing E-Mail Messages

Even after you have deleted all the messages you've replied to or no longer need to leave lying around in your In box, your undeleted messages can start to pile up. When your In box gets too full, it's time to create new mailboxes to store those other messages in. Different programs offer different commands for creating mailboxes and transferring messages into them, but the principles are more or less the same as those used for real-life filing. Don't create a new mailbox when an existing mailbox will suffice, but do file away as many messages as you can (even if you have to create a new mailbox to do so), to keep your In box a manageable size.

NOTE Your e-mail should conform to your general scheme of organization. I arrange mine alphabetically, chronologically, and/or by project, depending on the person involved. Think about the best system for you before you find your In box filled with 200 messages to sort.

Using Your Word Processor to Write E-Mail Messages

If you're more comfortable writing in a word processing program than you are writing in your e-mail program, you can write your message there, copy it using the Copy command, and then switch to your e-mail program and paste it into a new message window.

TIP If you're writing your message in a word processing program and planning to eventually insert it into an e-mail program that doesn't do word-wrapping, use a large font size when you write your message to ensure that your lines aren't too long.

One problem with putting word-processed text into e-mail messages is that some word processors substitute special characters for apostrophes and quotation marks. These special characters come out as garbage characters that make your mail harder to read. Also, there are sometimes problems with line breaks, either with lines being too long or with extraneous ^M characters appearing at the end of each line.

After composing your message, first save it as a text file. Figure 3.1 shows a text file I created in Word for Windows 95. Then close the file and open it again. To ensure

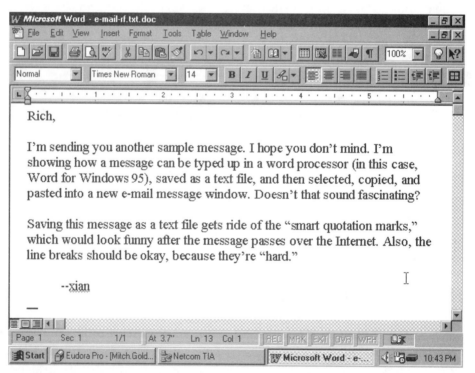

FIGURE 3.1: I created this file in Word for Windows 95. Now I'm going to save it as a text file.

that none of the special (nontext) characters are still in the file. Select the entire document and copy it (usually you press Ctrl+C or Command+C to do this). Then switch to your mail program. Start the message, go to the message area, and then paste the text you copied (usually you press Ctrl+V or Command+V).

The text will appear in the mail program as if you had typed it there.

Sending Files via E-Mail

One of the most important functions of e-mail is its ability to let you send files called *attachments* along with your messages. An attachment is any data file, in any form, which your program will send along with your e-mail message. Each program is different in the way it handles file attachments, and some of the online services still don't let you send or receive files over the Internet. Also, since different programs have different ways of *encoding* attached files (translating the files into a form that can be shipped over the Internet), you may have to compare details with your sender or recipient to make sure that both of your programs can "speak" the same code. For example, a big part of the revision of this book involved transferring files between a Macintosh running one version of Eudora and my PC, which was running another version, and it took several file transfers before things worked seamlessly.

Internet mail generally consists of only straight text files, although there are some protocols for sending other forms of information. For example, some mail programs use *MIME* (*Multipurpose Internet Mail Extensions*) to send other kinds of data, including color pictures, sound files, and video clips. If you are sent e-mail with a MIME attachment, you may not be able to see the pictures, hear the music, or view the movies, but the text in the attachment should come through just fine. You'll be asked if you want to view it or save it.

Quite aside from e-mail issues, you might be trying to send a file that your recipient doesn't have the right application for reading, so that's another thing you may have to work out in advance. For example, if you use Word for the Macintosh and your recipient uses WordPerfect for DOS, let's say, then you may have to save your file in a format that your recipient's program can understand; this may involve both of you poking around your program's Open and Save As commands to see what options are available.

When you receive a file attachment, your e-mail program will usually decode it and tell you where it's been placed (unless it doesn't recognize the coding format, in which case you'll get a bunch of garbage at the end of the message and no file attachment— if this happens, you need to negotiate with the sender as I just discussed).

NOTE See Chapter 10 to learn about some of the other ways to send and receive files.

Saving E-Mail Addresses

If there are people with whom you correspond regularly through e-mail or people whose e-mail addresses are hard to remember or difficult to type correctly, most e-mail programs enable you to create *aliases* (sometimes called *nicknames*) for these people. Aliases are shorter words that you type instead of the actual address. Other programs offer you an address book with which you can save e-mail addresses and other information about your correspondents.

When you type an alias or choose a name from an address book, your e-mail program inserts the correct address into the To: line of your message (some programs can also insert an address into the Cc: line).

You can also set up an alias for a list of addresses so you can send mail to a group of people all at once. I've got an alias for a group of people to whom I send silly stuff I find on the Net (no one's complained yet) and another one for contributors to my online magazine.

TIP When you make up a nickname or alias for an e-mail address, keep it short—the whole point is to save you some typing—and try to make it memorable (although you can always look it up if you forget).

Checking Your Spelling in E-Mail Messages

Most e-mail programs now offer spell-checking (so the traditional excuses for sloppily edited e-mail messages are vanishing fast!), but the specific techniques vary from program to program (as you might expect). It's a good idea to check the spelling in a message before sending it, especially if the message is long, formal, or for some business purpose.

| **NOTE** | For more on using e-mail with specific programs, flip to the end of this chapter. |

If you write your messages ahead of time using a word processing program, then you can use your word processor's spell checker to check the message. You may find this easier than working with two different spell checkers.

Attaching a Signature to an E-Mail Message

On the Internet, it's traditional to include a short *signature* at the end of each message. A signature is a few lines of text, usually including your name, sometimes your postal (*snail mail*) address, and perhaps your e-mail address. Many people also include quotations, jokes, gags, and so on. Signatures (also called *sig blocks, signature files, .signatures,* or *.sigs*) are a little like bumper stickers in this respect.

Some e-mail programs do not support signature files, particularly those designed for local networks and those of some online services where signatures are less common, but many do and more are adding the feature all the time. Here's my current signature (I change it from time to time):

```
 --
 Christian Crumlish              http://www.pobox.com/~xian
 Internet Systems Experts (SYX)     http://www.syx.com
 Enterzone (latest episode)         http://ezone.org/ez
 American Arts and Letters Network  http://www.aaln.org
```

It includes my name; the address of my home page on the Web; the name of my company and its home pages address; and the name of my online magazine, along with its address.

I'll show you how to create your own signature when I discuss the specific programs that support them.

Finding Internet E-Mail Addresses

Because the Internet is such a large, nebulous entity, there's no single guaranteed way to find someone's e-mail address, even if you're fairly sure they have one. Still, if you're looking for an address, here are a few things you can try.

Say "Send Me E-Mail"

If you're not sure how to send mail to someone but you know they're on the Net, ask them to send you some mail. Once their mail comes through okay, you should have a working return address. Either copy it and save it somewhere, make an alias for it, or just keep their mail around and reply to it when you want to send them mail (try to remember to change the subject line if appropriate, not that I ever do).

> **TIP**
>
> Really, the best way to collect e-mail addresses is from people directly. Many people now have their e-mail addresses on their business cards, so you can get people's addresses this way too.

Send Mail to Postmaster@

If you know someone's domain, such as the company where they work, or you know they're on one of the online services, you can try sending mail to `postmaster@` `address` and asking politely for the e-mail address. Internet standards require that every network assign a real person to the postmaster@ address, someone who can handle questions and complaints. So, for example, to find someone at Pipeline, you could send mail to `postmaster@pipeline.com` and ask for the person by name.

Ask the Knowbot

The Knowbot is a semireliable source of missing persons information. When you ask it for information, it conducts a few searches of its own and then mails the search results back to you.

You contact the Knowbot via e-mail, by sending a message to **kis@nri·reston·va·us**. It doesn't matter what you put in the subject line of the message; however in the body of the message, type **query _firstname_ _lastname_** (you can also submit a query for an e-mail address or part of one, if you know it). You can include as many query lines as you like.

> **TIP**
>
> **To learn more about Knowbot, about how it works, and what else you can do with it, put the word "man" on a line by itself in your message. You'll be sent a Knowbot manual.**

If you normally have a signature attached to your mail messages, put the word **end** on a line by itself after your last Knowbot command. This will prevent the robot from trying to interpret your signature lines as additional commands.

Figure 3.2 shows my message to the Knowbot. I'm asking Knowbot to find my own address, using my username and my real name; I'm also asking for a Knowbot manual.

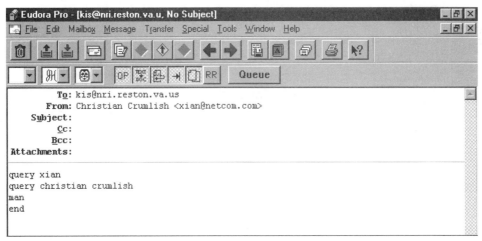

FIGURE 3.2: A message for the Knowbot: two queries and a request for a manual.

More E-Mail with Specific Programs

The e-mail techniques and features I've just outlined should bring you up to speed as a full participant in the e-mail world of the Internet. In the rest of this chapter, I'll revisit the most popular e-mail programs to tell you which of the features are available to you and exactly how to use them. Again, look ahead to see if I cover your program to read that section (they're in alphabetical order).

AOL

Forward

It's easy to forward America Online mail to another address; just click on the Forward button in the message window.

To send mail to multiple addresses, just type the addresses in the To: box, separating them with a comma, or press Tab and type some of the addresses in the Cc: box.

To create a folder for filing messages, select Mail ➢ Personal Filing Cabinet. In the dialog box that appears, click on the Mail folder and then click on the Add Folder button. Type a folder name and then click on OK. To file a message in that folder, select its subject in a mail window and drag it to the folder you just created.

Attach

Until recently, you couldn't attach files to AOL messages sent over the Internet, but now you can. While in the Compose Mail window, click on the Attach button.

Select a file in the Attach File dialog box that appears (this looks just like the typical Open dialog box you see in any normal program) and then click on OK. The message will be attached using the MIME format. Make sure your recipient's e-mail program can understand that format. You can also receive files sent to you from Internet e-mail addresses—as long as the sender's program can send MIME attachments.

TIP   If someone is planning to send you more than one file, ask them to send each one in a separate message. When this book went to press, AOL could handle only a single-file attachment (although you can get around this limitation by creating a single compressed file, such as a *zipped* file, containing many files).

When you receive a message with an attached file, two buttons will appear at the bottom of the message window: Download File and Download Later. Choose Download File to download the file immediately (the message will also give you a rough estimate of how long the download should take). Click on Download Later to leave the file lying around until you're ready to download it.

AOL provides you with an address book for managing your e-mail addresses. To add an address to it, select Mail ➢ Edit Address Book. In the Address Book window that appears, click on the Create button, type a name in the Group Name box, press Tab, and then type the address in the Screen Names box.

To use your address book when sending a new message, click on the Address Book button in the Compose Mail dialog box. Choose a name and then click on the To: button. Click on OK to insert the corresponding address into the To: box.

AOL's mail program does not include a spell checker or a way to attach signatures to outgoing messages.

If you want more information about AOL e-mail, select Mail ➢ Post Office for up-to-date information.

cc:Mail

When you want to forward mail, click on the Forward button in the message window and then type the recipient's address as you normally would. To send mail to multiple addresses, type the first address and press Enter. Then type the next address and press Enter again. Repeat this process as often as necessary.

To create a new folder, click on the New button. Select Folder and click on OK. Then type the name of the new folder and press Enter. To transfer a message to a folder, simply click on the message and drag it into the folder.

As in other programs, click on the Attach button to attach a file to an e-mail message. Choose the file you want in the dialog box that appears. To attach more than one file, click on the Add button and then select the next file. When you're done, choose OK.

To add an e-mail address to your address book, click on the AddrBk button. Type **internet** in the address field and press Enter. Type the e-mail address and then click on the Add to List button. To send a message to a recipient listed in your address book, click on the AddrBk button. Choose the address you want from the Internet drop-down list and then press Enter.

In order to check the spelling of a message select Tools ➢ Spell Check. cc:Mail will start scanning the message for words it doesn't recognize. If you've ever used the spell checker in Word or any other standard word processor, then you should be familiar with this drill:

- To skip a word, click on Ignore.
- To accept a suggestion, click on Change.
- To make your own correction, enter it in the Change To box and click on Change.
- To add the word in question to the spell checker's dictionary, click on Add.

> **NOTE** cc:Mail does not enable you to attach a signature to your mail messages.

CompuServe

To forward mail to another recipient, click on the Forward button at the bottom of the message window, then proceed as you would with a normal message. To send mail to more than one recipient, simply repeat the normal procedure in the Recipient List dialog box for each recipient (except don't click on OK until you've selected all the recipients you want).

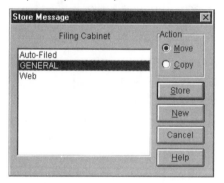

Click on the File-It button at the bottom of the message window to file an e-mail message away. This brings up the Store Message dialog box.

To create a folder, click on the New button, type a name for the folder, and click on OK. To transfer a message to a folder, select the folder and then click on the Store button.

You cannot currently send or receive file attachments from Internet e-mail addresses, although you can send and receive files to and from other CompuServe addresses.

To send just a file:

1. Select Mail ➢ Send File.
2. Choose a recipient address from the Recipient List dialog box as described in Chapter 2.
3. In the Send File Message window, click on the File button and choose a file from the Open dialog box that appears (see Figure 3.3).
4. Type a short message (one line only) to describe the attached file and click on Out-Basket or Send Now.

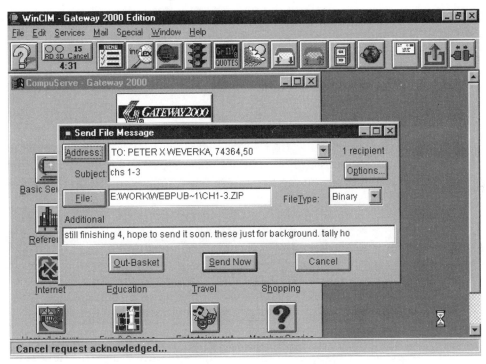

FIGURE 3.3: The Send File Message window

To send a file attached to a full e-mail message:

1. Start the message as usual (Mail ≻ Create/Send Mail).
2. Click on the Attach button when you get to the Create Mail dialog box.
3. Select a file from the Open dialog box that appears.
4. Type your message and then click on the Out-Basket or Send Now button.

To add an address from an existing message to your address book, click on the Address button just to the left of the To: information near the top of the message window. In the Add to Address Book dialog box that appears, select the address and click on the Copy ≫ button.

At any other time, you can add an address to your address book by selecting Mail ≻ Address Book. Then click on the Add (or Add Group) button and fill out the Add to Address Book dialog box, clicking on OK when you're done.

To select an address from your address book when sending a message, simply click on the address in the left side of the Recipient List dialog box and then click on Copy ≫.

> **NOTE**   CompuServe does not currently have a spell checker or a way of attaching signature blocks to mail messages.

Eudora

In order to forward a message, select Message ➢ Forward. Then proceed as you would with a new message. To send the message to additional recipients, include their e-mail addresses on the Cc: or Bcc: lines, separated by commas if there are more than one on any single line.

> **TIP**   If you want to add some explanatory text before the forwarded message, but you don't want the forwarded message to have the ">"'s before each line, select Message ➢ Redirect instead of Message ➢ Forward.

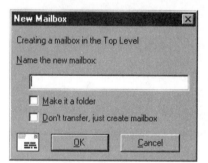

To transfer a message to a new mailbox in Eudora, select the message and pull down the Transfer menu. Either choose an existing mailbox from the menu or select New. In the New Mailbox dialog box that appears, type a name for the mailbox and then click on OK.

When you want to attach a file, first start a new message. Then, either drag the file from a folder window into the Eudora message window (this only works in recent Windows versions of Eudora) or select Message ➢ Attach File or press Ctrl+H or Command+H. Choose a file from the Attach File dialog box (it's just like a normal Open dialog box) and then click on OK.

Depending on your version of Eudora, you might have the choice of several different formats for the attached file, including MIME, *UUencode,* and *BinHex,* all different ways of translating files into a format that lets them ship across the Internet. Discuss the options with your intended recipient to find a format in common.

To create a nickname in Eudora, highlight a message from the person whose e-mail address you want to save and then select Special ➢ Make Nickname (or press Ctrl+K). Type a short name in the New Nickname dialog box that appears and click on the Put It on the Recipient List check box if you want to be able to select the nickname from a pop-up menu (this is useful if you expect to send mail to this address regularly). Then click on OK.

Now, whenever you want to use the nickname, just type it instead of the full Internet address. (If you added the nickname to the recipient list, then you can send or forward mail to the address by selecting Message ➢ New Message To ➢ *the nickname* or Message ➢ Forward To ➢ *the nickname*.) Eudora will do the rest. If you forget a nickname, select Tools ➢ Nicknames (in earlier versions of Eudora, it's Window ➢ Nicknames—so poke around a little if you can't find the command), select the nickname you want and click on the To: button.

The free version of Eudora doesn't have a spell checker, but the commercial version does. To check the spelling in a message, select Edit ➢ Check Spelling. Eudora will scan the message for words it doesn't recognize. If you've ever used the spell checker in Word or any other standard word processor, then you should be familiar with this drill:

- To skip a word, click on Ignore.
- To accept a suggestion, click on Change to accept a suggestion.
- To make your own correction, make it in the Change To: box and then click on Change.
- To add the word in question to the spell checker's dictionary, click on Add.

To create a signature in Eudora, select Tools ➢ Signature (Window ➢ Signature in some earlier versions of Eudora), type in your signature, and then close the window and agree to save it when prompted. Eudora will automatically append this signature to all your outgoing mail unless you choose None in the Signature drop-down list box at the top of the new message window.

TIP

The commercial version of Eudora also allows you to create an Alternate Signature. This means you can, for example, have one signature for business e-mail and one for personal e-mail.

MS Exchange

If you want to forward a message in MS Exchange, select Compose ➤ Forward (or press Ctrl+F) and then proceed as you would with a new message. To send mail to multiple recipients, type their addresses in the To box—separated by semicolons, *not* commas—or type additional addresses in the Cc box.

To make a new folder for messages, first press Backspace to jump up to the Personal Folders window. Then select File ➤ New Folder. In the New Folder dialog box that appears, type a name for the folder and click on OK. To move a message to a folder, simply click on it and drag it to the folder you want.

Attaching a file to a message is a little different in MS Exchange; to attach a file, either open the window the file is in, click on it and drag it into the new message window, or select Insert ➤ File and choose the file you want from the Insert File dialog box that appears and click on OK. Figure 3.4 shows an attached file in an MS Exchange message.

To add a name to your address book, select Tools ➤ Address Book (or press Ctrl+Shift+B) and then select File ➤ New Entry. In the New Entry dialog box that

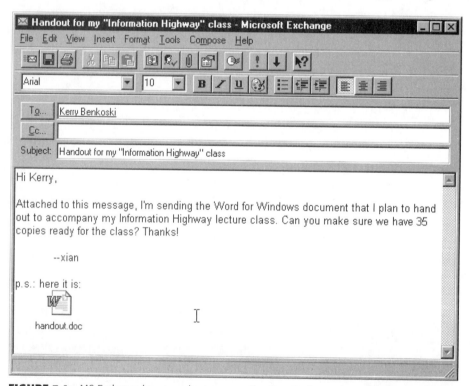

FIGURE 3.4: MS Exchange inserts an icon representing the attachment into your message at the insertion point. Your recipient double-clicks on the icon to open the attached file.

appears, choose Internet Mail Address and click on OK. Type the name, press Tab, and type the e-mail address. When you're done, click on OK. To send a message to someone in your address book, start a new message as usual, but instead of typing a recipient's address, click on the To button to the left of the To box. Select a name from the Address book list, click on the "To–>" button, and then choose OK.

Select Tools ➤ Spelling (or press F7) to check the spelling of a message. Exchange will start scanning the message for words it doesn't recognize. If you've ever used the spell checker in Word or any other standard word processor, then you should be familiar with this drill:

- To skip a word, click on Ignore.
- To accept a suggestion, click on Change.
- To make your own correction, type the correct word in the Change To: box and click on Change.
- To add the word in question to the spell checker's dictionary, click on Add.

NOTE Exchange does not enable you to attach a signature to your mail messages.

NetCruiser

There are two ways to forward mail in NetCruiser: select Mail ➤ Forward or click on the Forward button on the Read Mail dialog box. Then proceed as you would for a new message.

To send mail to multiple recipients, just repeat the normal procedure by typing an address and clicking on the "Use–>" button as many times as necessary before clicking on OK.

NOTE NetCruiser currently does not enable you to create mailboxes or folders to file your messages in.

When you want to send an attached file with an e-mail message, click on the Attachment button in the Send Mail window. Select a file in the Open dialog box that appears and then click OK.

To add an address to your address book, select Mail ➤ Address Book (or Internet ➤ Address Book if you don't currently have a mail window open). Then click on the New

Entry button. Type a name, press Tab, and type the e-mail address. Click on OK, then on Done. To send a message to someone in your address book, select Internet ➤ Send Mail - Out. Select a name from the …Or Choose Address from Address Book box, click on the "Use–>" button, and then choose OK.

> **NOTE** **NetCruiser currently does not have a built-in spell checker and does not allow you to attach signature blocks to messages.**

Netscape Mail

When you want to forward a message, select Message ➤ Forward (or press Ctrl+L or Command+L). Then proceed as you would with a new message. To send mail to multiple recipients, type the addresses in the Mail To: box, separated by commas, or enter additional addresses in the Cc: box.

To create a new folder, select File ➤ New Folder. Type a name for the folder in the dialog box that appears and then click on OK. To move a message to a folder, click on it in the upper-right pane and drag it to the folder you want in the upper-left pane.

In Netscape Mail, you can attach a file to an e-mail message by clicking on the Attachment button in the Message Composition window. In the Attachments dialog box that appears, click on the Attach File button. Choose a file in the Enter File to Attach dialog box (it's just like the normal Open dialog box), and then click on Open followed by OK.

Select Window ➤ Address Book to add an e-mail address to your Address Book. In the Address Book window that appears, select Item ➤ Add User. Type a nickname, press Tab, type the user's full name (if you wish), press Tab, type the e-mail address, and then click on OK. Select File ➤ Close to close the Address Book window.

To send a message to someone in your address book, type their nickname in the Mail To box in the Message Composition window. If you don't remember the nickname you made up, click on the Mail To button, choose your recipient, click on the To: button, and then on OK.

> **NOTE** **Netscape Mail doesn't have a spell checker.**

To attach a signature file to outgoing messages, first create the file with a text editor and save it. Then, in Netscape, select Options ➤ Mail and News Preferences. Select the Identity tab in the Preferences dialog box and type the file's full path and file name in the Signature File box (or click on the Browse button, find and select the file, and click on OK), as shown in Figure 3.5.

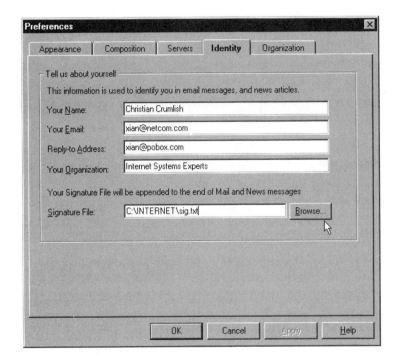

FIGURE 3.5:
Netscape can attach a signature file to messages if you create the file with any text editor.

When you're done, click OK. If your signature exceeds the recommended four lines (this rubric is a widely accepted netiquette standard, though many people violate it), Netscape will warn you, but all you have to do is click on OK again to accept it.

Pegasus Mail

Forwarding a message in Pegasus Mail is simple; just click on the Forward button at the top of the message window.

Then proceed as you would with any new message. To send mail to multiple recipients, type the addresses in the To: box, separated by commas, or enter additional addresses in the Cc: box.

To create a new mail folder, first select File ➤ Mail Folders to open the Folders dialog box. Click on the New button, type a name for the folder, and click on OK. To move a message from one folder to another, double-click on the folder currently containing the message; choose the message you want and drag it to the new folder.

Click on the Attach button on the left side of the message window to attach a file to an e-mail message.

Select a file in the bottom part of the window that appears and then click on the Add button (top right).

If PC users—especially on a local-area network—sometimes have trouble bringing up the path the folder is in, you may have to move the file around in File Manager.

Pegasus can handle a wide variety of file-encoding formats; you can choose one from the Encoding drop-down list or allow the mailer to choose one for you. Then click on the Editor button (on the left side of the window) when you're ready to return to typing the message. Or if you're done typing the message, you can just click on Send.

To create an address book, select Addresses ➤ Address Books and then click on New in the Select an Address Book dialog box that appears. Type a name for the address book and then click on OK. To open an address book, select Addresses ➤ Address Books and double-click on the address book's name. To add a name to the address book, click on the Add button. Pegasus suggests the name and e-mail address from the currently selected message, but you can type any name. Press Tab seven times to get to the E-mail address box and type a different e-mail address, if you like. Then click on OK.

When you want to send mail to someone in one of your address books, either type their name in the To: box or open the address book (as just described); scroll down to select the person you want, and click on the Paste button. Then click on Close.

You can access the spell-checking feature by selecting Edit ➤ Check Spelling. Pegasus will start scanning the message for words it doesn't recognize. If you've ever used the spell checker in Word or any other standard word processing program, then you should be familiar with this drill:

- To skip a word, click on Skip.
- To accept a suggestion, click on Change.
- To make your own correction, type in the correct word and click on Change.
- To add the word in question to the spell checker's dictionary, click on Add.

Pegasus will tell you when you've reached the end of the message and ask if you want to start over from the top. Choose No (unless you want to). Then click on Close.

To create a signature for your messages, select File ➤ Preferences ➤ Signatures ➤ For Internet Messages. Type your signature in the dialog box that appears and click on the Save button.

Pine

When you receive a message you want to forward on to another recipient, press **f**. Pine will clear the screen and put you in the Forward Message screen, which is exactly the same as the Compose Message screen except that the message area will include the original message, preceded by

```
----------Forwarded Message----------
```

Proceed as you would with a normal message.

To send mail to multiple recipients, type each e-mail address on the To: line, separated by commas, or type additional e-mail addresses on the Cc: line.

If you want to save a piece of mail for future reference, press **s** either in the index or while reading the mail. Pine will suggest **[saved-messages]** as a folder name, but you can replace it with anything you like.

> **TIP**
>
> You can always go back to your INBOX folder by pressing g (for Go to) and then Enter to accept the default.

To look at the contents of a folder, press **l** to see a folder list and Tab to get to the folder list you want to see, and then press Enter. When you are done, press **l** to get back to the folder list and choose the INBOX folder.

You can also send a file with Pine. In the Compose Mail screen, press Tab twice to get to the Attachment: line. Then press Ctrl+T. This will bring up a list of the files in your Unix directory. Using the arrow keys, select a file and press Enter. Pine will send the file as a MIME attachment.

> **TIP**
>
> Okay, but how do I get the file to my Unix directory? You need to use a modem transfer program, such as Zmodem or Kermit, as explained in Chapter 10.

In order to automatically add the sender of the current message to your address book from the Folder Index screen, press **t** and then type a nickname for the sender and press Enter. Press Enter twice to accept the full name and address of the sender.

To create an address book—a list of e-mail addresses you regularly send mail to—press **a** (from the Main Menu screen). This brings up the Address Book screen.

To add a new address to the address book:

1. Press **a**. Pine will prompt you with

    ```
    New full name (last, first) :
    ```

2. Type the last name, a comma, and then the first name of the person whose Internet address you want to add to your address book. After pressing Enter, Pine will prompt you with

    ```
    Enter new nickname (one word and easy to remember):
    ```

3. Type a short nickname and press Enter. Then Pine will ask you

    ```
    Enter new e-mail address :
    ```

4. Type the address and press Enter. The new address will be added to the address book.

5. Press **i** to return to the INBOX folder index, or press **m** to return to the Main Menu.

Now, whenever you want to use the nickname in the address book, just type it instead of the full Internet address. Pine will do the rest.

To check the spelling of a message, press Ctrl+T (while in the message area itself). Pine will highlight any suspicious words and prompt you to correct it and press Enter—but Pine won't suggest any possible spellings.

If you want to have Pine attach a signature to the end of your messages, create a text file named .signature. To do so, at the Unix prompt, type **pico .signature** and press Enter. Type whatever you want for your signature (but keep it under four lines as traditional netiquette dictates). Then press Ctrl+X, type **y**, and press Enter.

> **TIP**
>
> The required location of the signature file might vary from one system to the next, so if your signature file does not appear at the end of your messages, ask your system administrator where it should be stored.

Your signature will appear at the end of your mail messages. When you reply to a message and quote the text in your reply, Pine will put your signature at the beginning of your new message, before the quoted text. The idea is for you to write your message before the signature and then delete as much of the quoted text as possible.

Chapter 4

BROWSING THE WEB

One of the newest media available over the Internet is the World Wide Web. The Web (or sometimes WWW, w3, or W^3) is a huge collection of interconnected *hypertext* documents. (See *What Is Hypertext?* to learn more about hypertext.) Hypertext documents can contain links to other documents, to other kinds of files entirely, and to other sites on the Internet. With a Web browser, you can jump from one link to the next, following the trail of links in any direction that interests you. Not everything on the Internet is available via the Web, but more and more of it is linked together.

What Is Hypertext?

On the Web, hypertext is simply text with links. *Links* are elements of the hypertext documents that you can select. Click on a link and you'll be transported to the document it's linked to (or to a different part of the current document). As I mentioned in Chapter 1, if you use Windows, then you've got hypertext right in front of you, in the form of Windows help files. Whenever you select options from the Help menu of a Windows program, you are shown a hypertext help document with definitions and links available at the click of a mouse.

In addition to taking you to other documents, links can take you to Gopher servers, FTP sites, Telnet sites, Usenet newsgroups, and other Internet facilities. Links can also bring to you other programs and connect you to pictures, sounds, movies, and other binary files.

Once we start expanding the idea to include other media besides text, the rubric of hypertext is replaced by the word *hypermedia*. But the idea behind it is the same: links. An advantage of hypertext (or hypermedia) is that it allows you to navigate through all kinds of related documents (and other kinds of files), using one simple procedure—selecting a link.

A drawback is that, for now, you generally must follow links that other people have created, so the medium is not yet fully interactive. Of course, you can always make your own Web page—see Chapter 12. Also, there's a lot more text out there than hypertext. A Web browser can lead you to a plain text document as easily as to a hypertext document. You won't be able to jump anywhere else from a plain text document, so it's a sort of cul-de-sac, but you can always turn around.

The beauty of the Web is that the browser programs with which you "read" the Web are incredibly easy to use. This gives you access to all kinds of data, programs, news, pictures, and so on, without having to master the syntax of difficult protocols and arcane Unix commands.

Throughout the rest of this book, there will be references to the Web. It has become such a ubiquitous *front end* (a way to connect to the Net), that much of your use of the Net will take place through a Web browser.

Web Addresses (URLs)

If you've ever noticed an advertisement that says "check out our web site," you've seen the arcane way they describe how to find it, giving you the address, or *URL,* which almost always begins with the letters **http:.** (URL stands for *Uniform Resource Locator.*) A Web address starts with the name of a protocol (a method for connecting to information); most of the time it is *HTTP*. HTTP stands for *Hypertext Transfer Protocol* and means that the resource in question will be found on a Web server. This protocol is followed by **://** (the oft-heard "colon-slash-slash," or even more cumbersome, "colon–forward-slash–forward-slash"), and then an Internet address of the form **site.subdomain.domain**, as explained in *A Few Words about Internet Addresses* in Chapter 1. After that, you might find a colon and a port number (this is fairly rare), a path which is a list of folders or directory names leading to the resource in question, separated by more forward slashes. After the path, you might find a file name, which often ends with the extension **.html**. An *HTML* file (which means *Hypertext Markup Language file*) is the primary type of document on the Web.

Fortunately, most of the time, you won't have to type in Web addresses yourself, since you'll be following links that have the URL encoded into them.

Different Types of Web Browsers

Most online services are now offering access to the World Wide Web. Some do it by launching an external browser program (usually some variety of Mosaic) alongside the main access program. Others have their browser built-in, as with any other module available within the access program. Netcom's NetCruiser has a built-in Web module, but it also enables external Web browsers to run alongside NetCruiser, piggybacking on the Internet connection provided by the Netcom software. (Similarly, some online services, such as CompuServe and Microsoft Network enable you to do the same with external Web browsers).

Direct-access ISPs usually enable you to run whichever Web browser you like over the dial-up connection (and most people opt for Netscape Navigator), but Unix shell-only accounts require that you run a character-based Unix browser, such as Lynx or the original browser, Www. They won't be able to show you pictures and won't allow you to click your mouse to select links, but they can take you anywhere you want to go, and you can always download binary files that the character-based browsers aren't able to display.

HTTP, HTML, and URLs

Don't get thrown by the alphabet soup of acronyms you're confronted with when you start looking into the Web. URL, as I mentioned before, stands for Uniform Resource Locator. It's a form of address that all Web browsers can understand. URLs always take this form:

```
protocol://host:port/dir/filename.
```

So the URL `gopher://dixie.aiss.uiuc.edu: 6969/11/ urban.legends` tells a browser "use the gopher protocol to connect to the host machine called `dixie.aiss.uiuc.edu`, connect to port `6969` there, look in directory `/11`, and get the file called `urban. legends`."

The protocol generally used to connect to hypertext documents is called HTTP. HTTP stands for Hypertext Transfer Protocol because browsers use it to transfer you to hypertext documents. If that protocol is called for, the URL will begin with http: (other protocols are ftp:, telnet:, and so on—there's also a protocol called file:, which is equivalent to ftp:).

The other confusing acronym you might come across is HTML. HTML stands for Hypertext Markup Language, and it is the code used to mark up text documents to make them into hypertext documents. Hypertext documents on the Web generally end in the extension .html.

NOTE While graphical browsers such as Netscape Navigator are certainly a pleasure to use and a great way to surf the Net, reading the Web with Lynx or Www can be just as fascinating—after all, it's the information itself that is most interesting on the Net.

Using Web Browsers

Generally, when you start a browser, you begin at a *home page,* a starting place you designate (or your browser designates) for your Web-crawling sessions. (Hypertext documents on the Web are commonly referred to as *pages.*) This will either be the default home page for your browser or a custom home page that you have created. You can also start some browsers by pointing them directly at a Web address. Some e-mail programs, such as Eudora, now allow you to double-click a URL in an e-mail message to automatically start up your most recently installed browser and bring up the selected Web page.

NOTE

The Web is growing more popular all the time, and you may experience delays connecting to new addresses. Attempts to follow links may even result in *timing-out* (meaning that some computer along the line gives up and you get an error message) and failure. If this happens, just try again later, first right away and then, if necessary, during off-hours.

Figure 4.1 shows the Netscape home page that comes up automatically when you start Netscape Navigator (until or unless you change it to start at a different page). Now that you're connected, you can

- Follow the links that interest you. At any point you can retrace your steps so far or bring up a complete history of where you've been this session and then jump immediately back to one of those pages.
- Go to a specific Web address (URL) when you start your browser. Generally, to stop it from loading the default home page, you press the Stop button and enter an address directly.
- Insert bookmarks that enable you to jump back to an interesting page without having to retrace your steps or bring up a history of where you've been.
- Save (download) or mail interesting documents and files.
- View the hidden URL (Web address) that a given link points to.
- Customize your program's home page so that you always start at a page with links that interest you, rather than having to start at a generic home page.
- Access Help through a command or menu to get tips about using the program and information about the Web itself.
- Find out what's new on the Net.

Read on to discover how to do all these things … and more.

FIGURE 4.1: Unless customized, Netscape Navigator starts you off at the Netscape home page.

Reading a Page in a Web Browser

Web pages can consist of formatted text and headings, illustrations, background art and color effects, and hyperlinks, which can be highlighted text or art. In most graphical browsers, links are shown in blue (unless the creator of the page has decided otherwise) and are underlined (unless the creator has decided otherwise and has customized the program).

Often a page won't fit on the screen all at once. Graphical browsers use scroll bars, just as other programs do, to enable you to see material that doesn't fit on the screen. If you're hunting for a specific piece of information on a long document page, try searching for key words, usually with a menu command.

TIP
If you find browsing too slow, if pictures take too long to load, or if your browser has trouble displaying some of the art on some of the Web pages, consider turning off automatic picture loading. Most browsers have an option on one of their menus for doing so. You'll still be able to load any specific pictures you want to see or even see all the art on a page at once, but it will make your browsing go much more quickly and smoothly.

Following a Link

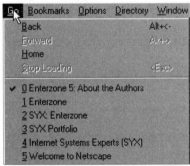

In graphical browsers, following a link entails positioning the mouse pointer over the link (the pointer will change to show you that you're over an active link—in Netscape it changes to a little hand) and then clicking once (get out of the habit of double-clicking).

All browsers have a Back command, often a shortcut button, for retracing your steps back to the previous page. Once you've gone back, you can also go forward, using the Forward command, to return along your original path to the furthest point you had gotten to. Also, you can usually bring up a *history list* (on a menu, in a graphical browser; on a separate page, in a text-only browser) of all the pages you've been to since you started the program that session.

WARNING
The history list will actually show you only the pages you've visited in a straight line from your starting point. Any time you back up and then follow a different link, you will lose the history path beyond the point you backed up to. For example, if I go to sites *A, B, C,* and *D,* then back up to *B* and then go to *E,* my history path will read *A, B, E.*

Knowing Where to Go

It's hard to get oriented in the Web, since there's no real starting point. Your default home page should provide some pretty useful places to start though. I recommend surfing around for a while to see where these points lead.

> **NOTE**   For pointers toward directories and methods of searching the Web, see Chapter 5.

In most browsers, if you have a specific Web address in mind (say one you saw in an advertisement or one that was e-mailed to you), you can type in a URL directly to visit a Web page without having to follow a trail of links that leads to it.

Also at any time, you can return to the default home page. Graphical browsers have a Home button, often decorated with an icon representing a house, for this purpose.

Making a Bookmark

As you travel around the Web, you can save interesting destinations by making bookmarks (also called Favorites or Favorite Places in some browsers, and Items on a Hotlist in others). Once you've made a bookmark, you've created your own personal shortcut to a favorite destination. You won't have to find your way back to the page in question next time you want to go there.

> **TIP**   Make bookmarks as often as you want. You can always weed out your bookmark list later, but it's very difficult to find a page you stumbled across while wandering around when you try to retrace your steps later.

Saving or Mailing a Document

If a Web page contains information you want to send to someone or have stored on your own computer, you can either use your browser's mail command to send the document to yourself or to someone else, or you can use the save command (File ➢ Save As in graphical browsers) to save a copy of the document on your hard disk, much the same way you'd save a file in a word processor.

NOTE   **For more on downloading documents, see Chapter 5.**

Peeking behind the Scenes

If you need to see the URL associated with a specific link, you can do so. For instance, in most browsers, when you place the pointer over a link, the associated link appears in the status bar at the bottom of the program. Some browsers enable you to copy a URL by right-clicking or clicking-and-holding the link to it. You can then paste it into another document for future reference or paste it into an e-mail message to tell someone else how to get to the page in question.

If you want to see how a Web page was constructed, you can generally view the source file underlying a page. In graphical browsers, you do this by selecting View ➢ Source (or something similar). Figure 4.2 shows the source underlying the Netscape home page.

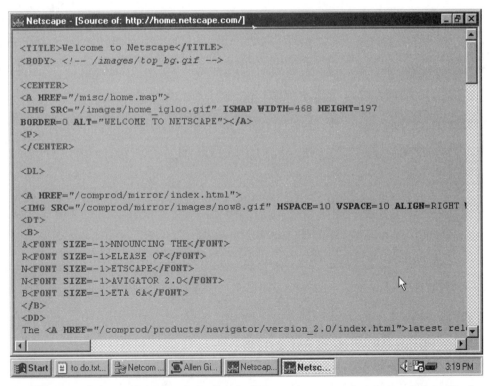

FIGURE 4.2: The HTML document that makes the Netscape home page look the way it does. (Don't let it spook you!)

Changing Your Home Page

The commands differ from browser to browser, but most Web browsers allow you to change your default home page to a different page (or even to a list of your bookmarks) so you can start exploring the Web from any vantage point.

Generally, the way you change you home page is to go into the Options or Preferences area of your browser and either specify an exact URL or tell the browser to use the current page as the new home page. Why would you change your page? Well, you might find a useful page out there on the Net that connects to most of your favorite sites. Or you might want to make one of the directory or search pages (as discussed in Chapter 5) into your new starting page.

Web Help and Info

There are a number of helpful resources for the Web, both hypertext and plain text documents. Try the WWW FAQ, an excellent document. Its URL is `http://www.boutell.com/faq/`. The W3 Consortium is the official source of information about the Web, and you can connect to their home page at `http://www.w3.org/`. (But be forewarned, much of their information is highly technical!) Many individual browsers also offer dedicated help files, accessible through a menu command. I'll cover some specific browsers and their help functions at the end of this chapter.

Get EFF's Internet Guide as Hypertext on the Web

The Electronic Frontier Foundation has published a hypertext version of its Internet Guide on the World Wide Web. You could hunt around for it by looking in one of the many indexes or other jumping-off pages on the Web, but why don't I just tell you the URL? Point your browser at `http://www.eff.org/papers/eegtti/eegttitop.html` to go to the main page for the Guide.

Keeping Up with What's New

If you want to keep up-to-date on the latest interesting home pages, visit the NCSA What's New Page (the unofficial newspaper of the Web) at `http://www.ncsa.uiuc.edu/SDG/Software/Mosaic/Docs/whats-new.html`. Most

Web browsers have a What's New command or button (and some also have a What's Cool option as well), leading to some similar compendium of the latest interesting sites.

Surfing the Web with Your Web Browser

The program you choose to wander around the Web with is largely a matter of taste, need, and budget. In fact, you may eventually end up with more than one browser on your hard drive. I'll discuss a few of the more common browsers now.

Browsing the Web with AOL

You can start the AOL browser by going to the Internet Connection area and choosing World Wide Web, by double-clicking on any AOL content that includes the word *Web* at the end of its title, or by going to the keyword *Web*.

Figure 4.3 shows the AOL home page that comes up automatically when you connect to the Web without specifying a particular site.

AOL's browser has no search command for the contents of a Web page. It has Back and Forward buttons, and you can see a list of sites you've visited in the drop-down list box directly below the buttons (that's also where you type an address if you want to go there directly).

Click on the Home button to return to the AOL home page.

You can save interesting Web destinations by adding them to your Favorite Places list, just as you do with any other AOL resource. Simply click on the Heart icon in the upper-right corner of the window. AOL will ask you to confirm that you want to add the current page to your favorites. Click on Yes. To go to a favorite place, click on the Favorite Places button, choose an item in the window that pops up, and click on Connect.

Save a document with File ➢ Save (or Save As); however, there's no way to mail a document directly from the AOL browser. Also, the AOL browser doesn't allow you to see the underlying HTML source file for a Web page.

FIGURE 4.3: AOL's browser starts you off at the AOL home page.

To change your home page with AOL's browser, click on the Prefs button. In the dialog box that appears, type a new URL in the box at the bottom and then click on OK (see Figure 4.4).

TIP You may have to go to the page and copy its address from the box at the top of the window before doing this. That will make it easier to insert the correct address in the box.

To get help with AOL's browser, click on the Help button, and to keep up with what's new, visit the Internet Connection every now and then to see which new Net resources have been listed there.

Browsing the Web with CompuServe Mosaic

CompuServe offers a licensed version of the original graphical Web browser, Mosaic. You can start it by selecting Services ➢ CompuServe Mosaic.

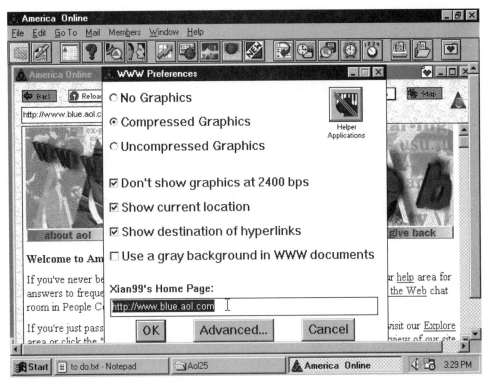

FIGURE 4.4: Changing your home page with AOL's browser

> **TIP**
>
> CompuServe also provides you with a full *PPP (Point-to-Point Protocol)* connection to the Internet, which means you can launch any external Web browser, such as Netscape, alongside your CompuServe connection.

Figure 4.5 shows the CompuServe home page that comes up automatically when you connect to the Web without specifying a particular site.

In CompuServe, you can search a long Web page, select Edit ➤ Find, type the text you're looking for, and press Enter. The Search command and its shortcut button on the toolbar lead to a Web page for searching the Internet. It has Backward and Forward buttons, and you can bring up a list of the sites you've visited by selecting Navigate ➤ History. To go somewhere directly, type the URL into the Web Page box at the top of the window.

FIGURE 4.5: CompuServe Mosaic starts you off at the CompuServe home page.

Click on the Home button to return to the CompuServe welcome page.

You can save interesting Web destinations by clicking on the Add button. The page you add will instantly become a menu item on the Personal Favorites menu. To go to a Favorite, just select it from that menu.

To save a Web document with CompuServe Mosaic, select View ➢ Load to Disk Mode to place a checkmark next to this command. Then all of the pages you visit will be saved on your hard disk (you'll be prompted to confirm each file name). If you just want to save a single page this way, be sure to uncheck the Load to Disk Mode command on the View menu when you're done. Unfortunately, you can't mail a document directly from CompuServe Mosaic.

In order to view the HTML source of a Web document, select File ➢ Web Page Source.

If you want to change your home page with CompuServe Mosaic, select View ➢ Options and click on the Pages tab in the dialog box that appears. Type a new URL in the Home Page box and then click on OK. (As you sometimes have to do with AOL, you may have to go to the page and copy its address from the box at the top of the window before typing in the address.)

To get help with CompuServe Mosaic, select Help ➢ Help Topics. To keep up with what's new, go to the Internet topic (GO INTERNET) and then click on the What's Cool button.

> **WARNING**   CompuServe Mosaic sometimes has trouble downloading artwork and "conks out" before finishing. When this happens, you should still be able to read the text contents of a page with no problem. If this happens a lot, consider running an external Web browser over your CompuServe connection.

Browsing the Web with Lynx

If your connection to the Internet is through a character-based Unix account, then the best Web browser for you is Lynx. Lynx is a full-screen program that is very easy to use. You might also have the Www browser available, which only allows you to type on the bottom line of the screen—you follow links by typing their number and pressing Enter—but you're better off using Lynx if possible.

There are some graphical Web browsers that can run over a Unix shell account connection, most notably SlipKnot, from MicroMind. You can download SlipKnot from `http://plaza.interport.net/slipknot/slipknot.html`. See Chapter 10 for more on downloading. See also Appendix A for other strategies for coping with a Unix shell account.

You start Lynx by typing **lynx** at the Unix prompt and pressing Enter. This will start you off at Lynx's default home page, for your system. On my system, Lynx starts off at the University of Kansas home page. Figure 4.6 shows the About Lynx page (`http://www.cc.ukans.edu/about-Lynx/about-Lynx.html`).

If you don't have Lynx installed on your system, Unix will tell you "lynx: Command not found." You can still run Lynx by "telnetting" to a public-access browser. Type `telnet ukanaix.cc.ukans.edu` and press Enter; log in as `www` (no password required). See Chapter 10 for more on Telnet.

If you have a specific Web address (URL) in mind, you can also start Lynx by pointing it at that URL. Type **lynx *url*** and press Enter, substituting the actual URL for *url*, of course.

> **TIP**
>
> **Different installations of Lynx may function differently. Lynx is sometimes set up to prevent users from entering URLs directly. If you run into problems trying to follow these instructions, ask your system administrator for help.**

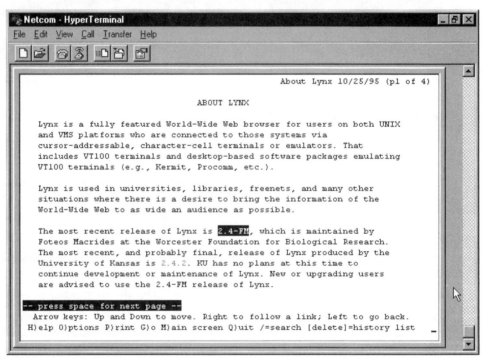

FIGURE 4.6: The About Lynx page at the University of Kansas Web site.

Most of a Web page will be regular text and headings. In Lynx, hypertext links are shown in boldface, and the current link is shown in *reverse video* (white-on-black text, instead of vice versa). The first link on the page is the current link when you first arrive at a page.

Often a page won't fit on the screen all at once. The commands necessary to move around a Web page in Lynx are detailed in the table below.

Action	Commands
To see the next screenful of a page	Press the spacebar or type + (or PageDown or **3** on your numeric keypad if NumLock is on)
To go back up a page	Type **b** or **–** or PageUp (or **9** on the numeric keypad with NumLock on)
To move down to the next link	Press Tab + ↓ (or **2** on the numeric keypad with NumLock on)
To move up to the previous link	Press ↑ (or **8** on the numeric keypad with NumLock on)
To fix a messed up screen, say, if reverse video is left all over the screen	Press Ctrl+W to redraw it
To search for specific text	Type **s** or **/**. Then type the text you want to search for and press Enter
To repeat a search	Type **n**
To select the current link (and jump to the address it refers to)	Press Enter (or → or **6** on the numeric keypad with NumLock on)
To return to the previous link	Press ← (or **4** on the numeric keypad with NumLock on)

> **TIP**
>
> **If the arrow keys don't work and you have a numeric keypad, try turning NumLock on and then using the number keys on the numeric keypad. Your communications program might be reserving the arrow keys (along with some Control keys and scrolling commands) for their standard uses in your operating environment. Check the terminal-emulation settings to see if you can change this.**

Though you can always retrace your steps in Lynx, by pressing **4** (NumLock) repeatedly, you can also jump back to any previous point in just two steps: First press Delete to see your history page, a list of all the links you've followed in this session, (try Backspace if Delete doesn't work) and then select the page you want to return to and press Enter.

At any point you can type **i** to go to the Internet Resources Meta-Index, which includes many more starting points for you to try. Figure 4.7 shows the first screen of the Meta-Index page.

At any point, you can type **g** to enter a URL directly. Lynx will prompt you with "URL to open:". Type (or paste in) the URL and press Enter.

> **TIP**
>
> If you've done this once already, the previous URL will already be there. Delete it by pressing Ctrl+U before typing in the new one.

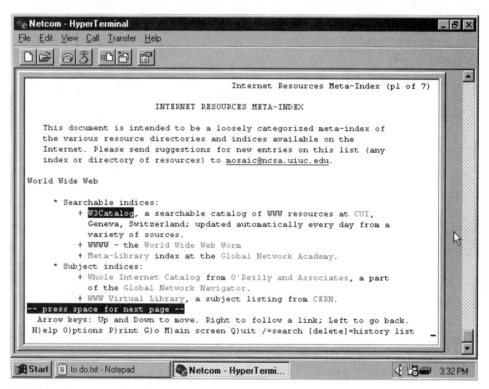

FIGURE 4.7: Not sure how to get started? Check out the Meta-Index.

Also at any time, you can return to the default home page by typing **m**.

You can save interesting Web destinations by adding bookmarks to your bookmark page. (Lynx will create one for you if you don't have one.) To add a bookmark link to the current page, type **a**.

You can then view your bookmark page at any time by typing **v**.

If you want to save a copy of a document you're reading on the Web, type **p**. This will bring up the Printing Options page. Press Enter to save the document to a file. Lynx will prompt you to "Please enter a file name:" and suggest one. Press Enter or type in a different name and press Enter.

> **NOTE** To send mail to the owner of the page you're on, type **c**. (The *owner* just means the person who created and who maintains the page.)

At some point you may want to mail the document to yourself (sometimes that's the easiest way to store a copy of a document); press Tab to go to the next link (Mail the File to Yourself) and then press Enter. Lynx will prompt you with "Please enter a valid internet mail address:". If you've told Lynx your address, it will appear there. If not, type your address. Then press Enter.

To see the URL associated with the current link, type **=**. Type **=** again to go back to the normal view. To see the actual HTML text of the current page, type **\. Type ** again to go back to the normal view.

Follow these steps to change some of the Lynx settings:

1. Type **O**. This brings up the Options Menu.
   - Type **e** to change the default editor for sending e-mail to mail to URLs.
   - Type **b** to change your bookmark file.
   - Type **p** to enter or change your e-mail address.
2. When you are done, type **>**. This saves your changes.
3. To return to where you left off without saving the changes, type **r**.

To make a different document your default home page, enter the line **setenv WWW_HOME *url*** (using the correct URL for the page you want) in your startup file (usually called .login, .profile, or .cshrc).

You can get help at any time in Lynx by typing **?**. Quit Lynx at any time by typing **q**. Then press Enter. To quit without being prompted, type **Q**.

Browsing the Web with Microsoft Internet Explorer

The Internet

Internet Explorer works seamlessly with the Microsoft Network, but it also stands alone as a Web browser that can work with any Internet connection. On the Windows 95 desktop, it's represented by the presumptuous "The Internet" icon.

A trial version of Internet Explorer for the Macintosh has just been announced and should be available by the time this book reaches your hands.

> **TIP**
>
> You can download Internet Explorer from Microsoft's Web site. To do so, start at http://www.microsoft.com. If you have trouble connecting to that site, try http://www.msn.com.

Figure 4.8 shows the Microsoft Network home page that comes up automatically when you connect to the Web without specifying a particular site. Internet Explorer, by the way, calls the page you start on your *start page*, not your *home page,* as most other browsers refer to it.

To search a long Web page, select Edit ➢ Find, type the text you're looking for, and press Enter. Internet Explorer has Back and Forward buttons, and you can return to any of the recent sites you've visited by pulling down the File menu and selecting the page from the list just near the bottom of the menu (just above the Exit command). To go somewhere directly, type the URL into the Address box (it will change to an Open box when you click in it).

> **NOTE**
>
> You can leave off the http:// part of any Web URL when typing it into the Address box, though you will have to type other protocols, such as ftp://, gopher://, and so on.

Click on the button at the right end of the Address box to drop down a list of all the addresses you've ever entered.

Click on the Home button to return to the Microsoft Network home page.

You can save interesting Web destinations by selecting Favorites ➢ Add to Favorites. The page you add will instantly become a menu item on the Favorites menu. To go to a Favorite, just select it from that menu.

To save a Web document with Internet Explorer, select File ➢ Save As. You can also save a shortcut to a file—to a tiny file containing the Web address—by selecting File ➢ Create Shortcut. To mail a shortcut to someone, select File ➢ Send Shortcut. Internet Explorer will open a Microsoft Exchange New Message window with the shortcut already attached.

Back ——— ——— Forward

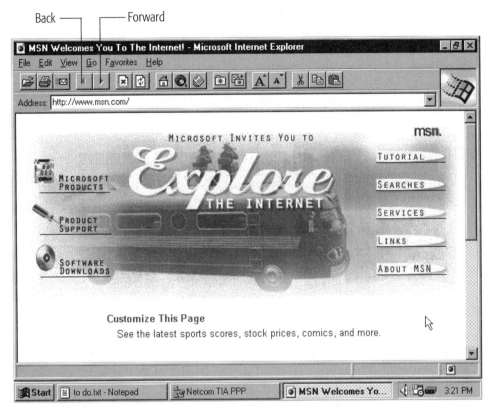

FIGURE 4.8: Internet Explorer starts you off at the Microsoft Network start page.

To view the HTML source of a Web document, select View ➤ Source.

Changing your start page is simple:

1. First go to the page you want to use.
2. Then select View ➤ Options and click on the Start and Search Pages tab in the dialog box that appears.
3. Click on the Use Current button.
4. When you're done, click on OK.

To get help with Internet Explorer, select Help ➤ Help Topics. To keep up with what's new, click on the Links button on the Microsoft Network start page. It features a pick of the day and other useful links.

Browsing the Web with Mosaic

Mosaic is the original graphical Web browser, and versions of it now exist for just about every graphical user interface. The original version is NCSA Mosaic (NCSA, the National Center for Supercomputing Applications, is where Mosaic was first created), but there are other licensed versions out there, including Spyglass Mosaic, AIR Mosaic, and the version CompuServe uses. All versions of Mosaic work more or less the same way.

NOTE You can get NCSA Mosaic from `ftp://ftp.ncsa.uiuc.edu/Web/Mosaic`. **See Chapter 10 for more on FTP.**

Figure 4.9 shows the NCSA Mosaic for Microsoft Windows home page that comes up automatically when you connect to the Web without specifying a particular site.

To search a long Web page, select Edit ➤ Find, type the text you're looking for, and press Enter. Mosaic has Back and Forward buttons, and you can return to any of the recent sites you've visited by selecting Navigate ➤ Session History. This will bring up a small dialog box listing the recent sites. Choose one and click on the Load button. To go somewhere directly, type the URL into the box on the Location bar, and click on the button at the right end of the Address box to drop down a list of all the addresses you've ever typed in.

Click on the Home button to return to the Mosaic home page for your version.

You can save interesting Web destinations by selecting Navigate ➤ Add Current to Hotlist. The page you add will instantly become a menu item on the Hotlists ➤ Starting Points menu. That menu includes many useful hotlist items preloaded. To go to a hotlist item, select Hotlists ➤ Starting Points ➤ *hotlist item*.

To save a Web document with Mosaic, select File ➤ Save As. To mail a Web document to someone, select File ➤ Send Email. Mosaic will open a Mail window. To include the text of the document in the message, click on the Include Text button and then click on Yes to "quote" the document using the ">" character or No to insert the text as is.

In order to view the HTML source of a Web document, select File ➤ Document Source.

If you want to change your home page, first go to the page you want to use or copy its URL. Then select Options ➤ Preferences and click on the Document tab in the dialog box that appears. Either click on the Use Current button in the Home Page area or type (or paste) the address you want. Then click on OK.

Back ———┐ ┌——— Forward

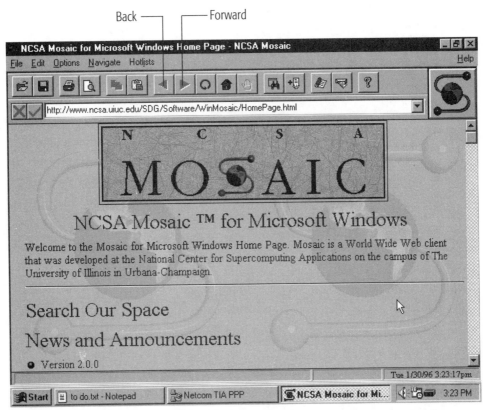

FIGURE 4.9: NCSA Mosaic has a different home page for each version (Windows, Macintosh, X Window, and so on). This is the home page for the Windows version.

To get help with Mosaic, select Help ➢ Contents or Help ➢ Online Resources. To keep up with what's new, select Hotlists ➢ Starting Points ➢ NCSA Mosaic's 'What's New' Page or any of the other preloaded starting-points links.

AutoSurf with Mosaic

Users familiar with Mosaic will be delighted to learn of its new AutoSurf feature. Now when you browse a Web site, Mosaic can pull down and cache all of the pages at a site, letting you browse them at your leisure—and in a lot less time.

Browsing the Web with NetCruiser

 NetCruiser includes a browser module for the Web (it comes up automatically when you start NetCruiser unless you say otherwise). To run it, click on the Web icon. This takes you to the Netcom HomePort, a pretty good jumping-off point (see Figure 4.10).

> **TIP**
>
> **The connection to the Internet that NetCruiser establishes for you can support external programs, such as stand-alone Web browsers. So if you get tired of the limitations of NetCruiser's Web module, consider running an outside browser, such as Netscape Navigator (although, as of this writing, you can only use the 16-bit version of Navigator with NetCruiser).**

The Web browser module has a Back and Forward button. To see the list of recent sites you've visited, select WWW ➢ History. Choose a site in the dialog box that appears, and then on click the Jump To button. You can go to a specific page by typing its URL in the Address box at the top of the WWW module window. When you click on the arrow on the right end of the Address box, a list drops down, showing you the history list of recent sites you've visited.

To search a page, click on the Search button (or select Edit Find). Type the text you're looking for and click on OK.

When you want to make a bookmark, click on the Book Mark button (or select WWW ➢ Book Mark). Click on the Add button in the Book Mark dialog box that pops up to add the current page to your bookmark list. Select a bookmark and click on Jump to go directly to that page. Click on Close when you're done in the window.

There are two ways to save a document: click on the Save button or select File ➢ Save. However, NetCruiser does not provide a way for you to mail documents to other people.

In order to see the underlying HTML source for a Web document, select View ➢ Source File.

First select Settings ➢ WWW Options to change your home page. Make sure the General button appears pushed in. Type or paste the URL you want into the box in the Home Page File area and then click on OK.

To get help with NetCruiser, select Help ➢ Contents.

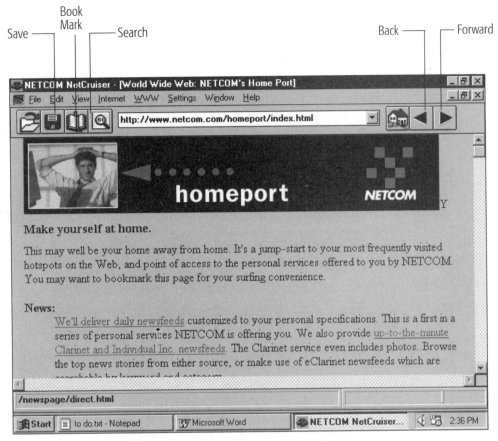

FIGURE 4.10: Netcom's HomePort offers a variety of destinations on the Web.

To keep up with Netcom news, click on the New button at the bottom of the Homeport page. You can also

- Click on the Search Engines & Directory Listings link on the Homeport page.
- Click on the What's New link on the Web Directory Listings page that appears.
- Choose one of the listed What's New pages.

WARNING NetCruiser's Web module sometimes has trouble downloading artwork and "conks out" before finishing. When this happens, you should still be able to read the text contents of a page, no problem. If this happens a lot, consider running an external Web browser over your NetCruiser connection.

Browsing the Web with Netscape Navigator

Netscape Navigator (commonly referred to as just Netscape) is by far the world's most popular Web browser. When you start it (by connecting to your Internet service provider and then double-clicking on the Navigator icon), it connects to the Netscape home page and starts you off there (see Figure 4.11).

FIGURE 4.11: The Netscape Home Page has Web-surfing destinations and up-to-date information about Netscape.

Use the Back and Forward buttons to move between pages, and the Go menu to see a list of all of the pages you've visited in the current session—your history list. To go to a specific Web page, type its address in the Location box, which will change into a Go To box as soon as you start typing. You can pull down a list from that box to see every page you've ever typed in directly.

To make a bookmark with Netscape, select Bookmarks ➢ Add. To go to a bookmark, pull down the Bookmarks menu and choose the item.

In order to save a Web document with Netscape, select File ➢ Save As. To mail a document to someone, select File ➢ Mail Document. Click on the Attachment button in the message window to control how the document is sent—as an HTML source file (the default) or as plain text.

When you want to view the underlying HTML source of a Web page, select View ➢ Document Source (previously View ➢ Source in earlier versions of Navigator).

To change your home page in Netscape, first copy the URL of the page you want to use. Then select Options ➢ General Preferences and click on the Appearance tab. Type or paste the Web address into the Start With box in the Startup area and then click on OK.

Any time you want to get help with Netscape, choose Help ➢ Handbook (or any of the other commands on the Help menu). To see what's new on the Net, choose one of the following options:

- Select Directory ➢ What's New!
- Select Directory ➢ What's Cool!
- Click on the What's New! directory button
- Click on the What's Cool! directory button

Chapter 5

FINDING STUFF ON THE NET

- **Looking in Web directories such as Yahoo**
- **Searching the Web from pages such as Lycos**
- **Visiting the Netscape directory pages**
- **Downloading files and updating your software**
- **Looking for e-mail addresses**
- **Searching Usenet and the rest of the Internet**

Once you've had the chance to explore the Web a bit, you may start wondering how you're ever going to find anything there. As easy as it is to follow tangents and get lost wandering from interesting site to interesting site, there's no clear path through the Web and no obvious way to find a destination if you don't know its address.

Fortunately, various clever individuals and companies have set up sites to help you find information on the Web. While there's no single, definitive location for searching, there are, in fact, quite a few ways to search the Web, (and more coming on line all the time), and the Net is changing so rapidly that any central listing of sites is bound to be out of date in some ways. Still the process of "mapping the Net" is going on all the time, and the work in progress is useful enough to usually help you find what you're looking for.

TIP — Because there's no single, definitive way to search the Web, it's sometimes best to try several different approaches.

Also in this chapter, I'll show you how to download (save) files from the Web to your own computer and how to hunt for information on the Net that might not be directly on the Web.

Searching the Web

There are a number of pages on the Web that offer one of two models for finding specific information. One model is that of a *directory,* where Web sites are organized by topic and subtopic, something like a yellow pages phone book. The other model is that of a searchable index, where you enter a key word to search for, and the search page gives you a list of suggested sites that seem to match what you're searching for. I'll show you an example of each approach.

Searching through a Directory

One of the best directories on the Web is the Yahoo site. To see it for yourself, type `http://www.yahoo.com` into the address box at the top of your Web browser. Figure 5.1 shows how Yahoo looks as I'm writing this chapter (remember, most Web sites update their design and layout from time to time, so the site may look slightly different to you today).

TIP — Make a bookmark for Yahoo, as discussed in Chapter 3, so you can come back here easily any time you want to start looking around.

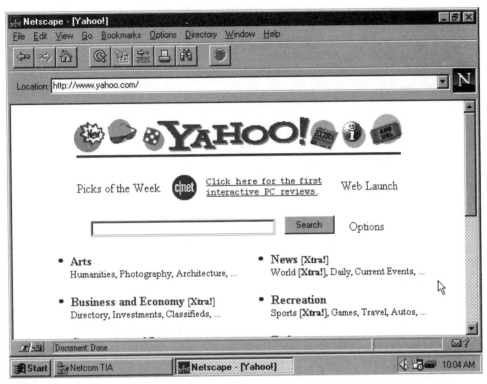

FIGURE 5.1: The popular Yahoo directory site

Searching by Topic

Yahoo is organized hierarchically, which means that you can start with a general topic area and then narrow it down to more specific topics as you go. Some of the major subtopics are listed under each topic as well, so you can skip one step, if you like.

NOTE   At Yahoo, category listings are in boldface, whereas *endpoint* listings (that don't lead to further subcategories) are in plain type.

- **Health**
  Medicine, Drugs, Diseases, Fitness, ...
  http://www.yahoo.com/Health/Medicine/

Let's say you're interested in the subject of medical ethics, such as the question of who among several candidates should get an available organ transplant. You could start by choosing the Medicine subcategory of the Health topic.

This will take you to Yahoo's Health:Medicine page (see Figure 5.2).

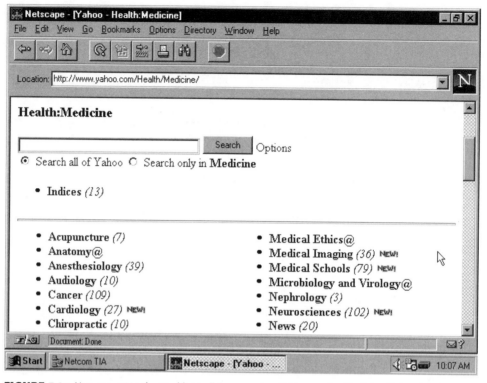

FIGURE 5.2: You can get to the Health:Medicine page by clicking on the Medicine link or by clicking on the Health link and then choosing Medicine on the Health page.

As you can see, one of the sub-subtopics of Health:Medicine is Medical Ethics. (The @ sign after the listing means that topic appears in several different places in Yahoo's listings—this means you can reach topics of interest by more than one route, without having to read the minds of the people who set up the site.) Click on Medical Ethics to go to the page listing pages on that subject. It turns out to be part of the Arts hierarchy—Arts:Humanities:Philosophy:Ethics:Medical Ethics (see Figure 5.3).

> **TIP** Remember to use the Back button if you want to return to a previous topic in Yahoo's hierarchies.

Needless to say, when you reach a listing for a page that sounds interesting, simply click on the hyperlink to that page to jump to it.

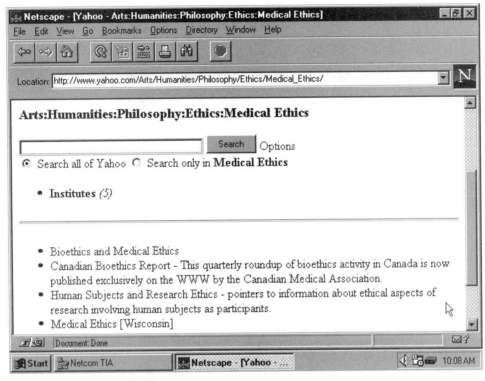

FIGURE 5.3: The Medical Ethics page at Yahoo

Searching by Key Word

Of course, it's not always easy to guess where a page or topic might be listed in an organized structure such as Yahoo's. Fortunately, the site also includes a search feature at the top of each page.

To perform a search, type a word (or a few words, to make the search more specific) in the box near the top of the page and then click on the Search button.

> **TIP**
>
> **If you perform your search from any of the pages besides the home page, you have the choice of searching the entire Yahoo directory (Search All of Yahoo) or just the items in the current category (Search Only in *Topic*).**

So, let's say you're interested in kayaking and want to see if there are any good resources for kayakers on the Net. Type the word **kayak** into the search box and click on the Search button. Yahoo quickly returns a list of sites relating in some way or another to your key word (in fact, the word will appear in boldface in a blurb for each page), as shown in Figure 5.4.

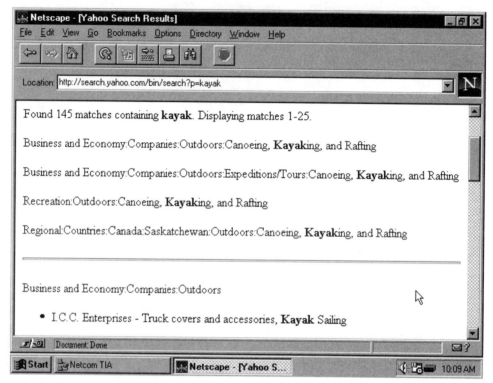

FIGURE 5.4: Some of the kayaking-related pages listed as the result of a Yahoo search

From there, all you have to do is start clicking on the interesting looking sites you want to visit.

Searching with a Search Engine

So now that you know how to search the contents of a directory site, it's easy to perform a search of the entire Net from a search site. Conceptually, the only difference is that a site like Yahoo is organized into hierarchies that have been edited, meaning that only "worthy" sites are listed. Most of the *search engines* attempt, instead, to include every single page on the Web—although that's obviously impossible. (A search engine is a Web site designed to perform searches of the Net.) Either way, of course, you're searching someone's list of sites, but the search engines generally return results from a broader pool.

Most search engines allow you to enter very specific, even complicated search queries, much like you would submit to a database program, but fortunately, for your everyday searches, you shouldn't need those advanced features. Instead, a single key word—or a couple, for a narrower search (such as *medical ethics*)—will usually do the job.

One of the more popular search engines is Lycos. Everyone has their favorites, but Lycos, which has been around for awhile, seems to crop up most often when I ask around. (Another popular one is Alta Vista at `http://www.altavista.digital.com`. See "Ziegen Speaks.") Lycos is at (what else?) `http://www.lycos.com` (see Figure 5.5).

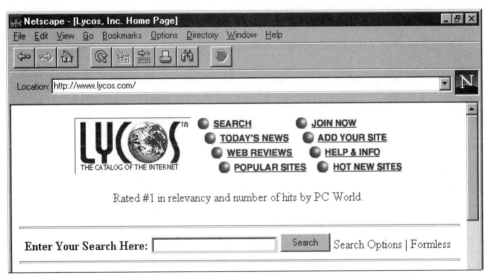

FIGURE 5.5: The Lycos search engine is powerful and easy to use.

TIP   Make a bookmark for the Lycos site as well.

Zeigen Speaks

Date: Mon, 5 Feb 1996 12:23:07 -0800
From: Zeigen <estephen@emf.net>
Subject: Re: best search engine(s) for
beginners?
X-URL: http://www.emf.net/ estephen

Let me put in one final plug for Alta Vista over
Lycos:
Lycos is *seriously* out of date in many places.
Their backlog of new indexing to be done is way
greater than their robot machine's capacity to
index. The frequency of their garbage collection
(that is, removing the old/removed/moved pages
from the index) is far less than Alta Vista's. I
don't mean to decry someone else's desert-island
favorite-searcher, but I think objectively Alta
Vista has a larger and more updated catalog.
Plus there's that Usenet searching side. It's
funny to watch the frequency of the indexers as
they come by my place. Scooter (from digital,
for Alta Vista) comes by every month if not more
often, and grabs EVERYTHING. The Lycos robot
hasn't come by in several months, and when it
does, it only gets a small fraction of the four
megabytes that constitute chez Zeigen.
It's not like I own stock in Digital or
anything. If they started charging to access
Alta Vista I would start insulting them like
crazy. Like for limiting basic searches to 200
hits.

--Zeigen

P.S. Heck - why not put them both up?

As with the search feature in Yahoo, just type a key word (or several words) into the box and click on the Search button. Lycos will return a list of sites, ranked in order of their likeliness to match your key words (this is especially useful when you've entered more than one word). Figure 5.6 shows the results of a Lycos search on the word *kayak*.

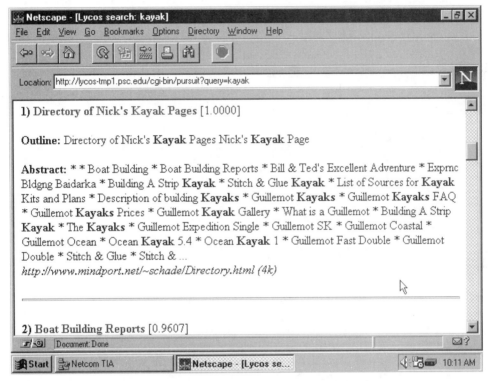

FIGURE 5.6: Web sites turned up by Lycos in a search using the word *kayak*.

Click on any of the hyperlinked listings to visit the listed site. (Lycos boldfaces the key word in the page abstracts only to show you where your search words turned up.)

Visiting a Central Search Page

Most of the Web browsers have a shortcut to one or more directory or search pages built into the program.

> **TIP** Even Lynx, the character-based Unix browser, has a shortcut. Type the letter *l* to go to a directory site.

Net Search | Net Directory
With Netscape Navigator, you can click on the Net Search or Net Directory buttons on the directory button bar to jump straight to Netscape's own central search pages, each of which have links to the sites already mentioned in this chapter along with many others. Although I tend to hide the buttons since they're easily accessible on the Directory menu—choose Options ➤ Show Directory Buttons to do so.

You can also simply select Directory ➤ Internet Directory or Directory ➤ Internet Search. Figure 5.7 shows Netscape's Internet Directory page.

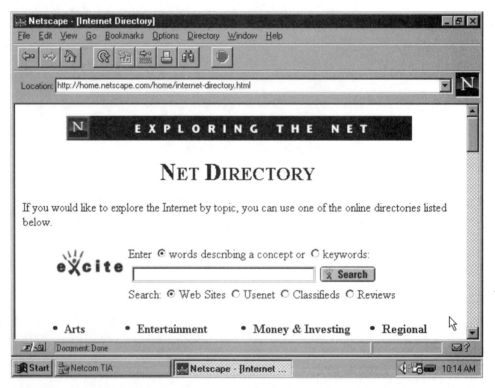

Figure 5.7: Netscape's Internet Directory page currently shows a direct search box for the Excite directory (like all Web pages, it's subject to change without notice) and then a list of other good directories below.

As with any of the directory or search pages, enter a key word in the Excite text box and click on the Search button or choose a category and start browsing.

Scrolling down the page past Excite's Choose a Category items, there's a list of other good directory sites (including Yahoo, naturally). There's no need to bookmark this page if you use Navigator, since you have a built-in shortcut. If you're using another browser, go to `http://home.netscape.com/home/internet-directory.html` and create a bookmark so it will be easy to return to any time you want.

If you want to perform a broader search, select Directory ➤ Internet Search. Figure 5.8 shows Netscape's Internet Search page.

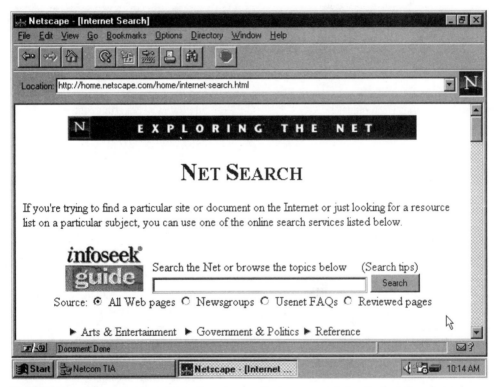

FIGURE 5.8: Netscape's Internet Search page currently shows a search box for the Infoseek search engine and then a list of other good search engines below.

As in the previous examples, enter a key word in the Infoseek Guide text box and click on the Search button or choose a category and start browsing.

At the bottom of the page, there's a list of other good search sites (including Lycos, of course). There's no need to bookmark this page if you use Navigator since you have a built-in shortcut. If you're using another browser, go to `http://home.netscape.com/home/internet-search.html` and create a bookmark so it will be easy to return any time you want.

Some Search Addresses

Here are the addresses of just about all the good search resources (most of them—and more—are listed at the bottom of the Netscape pages I just discussed):

Resource	Web Address
Search Directories	
A2Z	http://a2z.lycos.com
Amazing Environmental Organization WebDirectory!	http://www.webdirectory.com
Excite	http://www.excite.com
Magellan	http://www.mckinley.com
Point	http://www.pointcom.com
World Wide Arts Resources	http://www.concourse.com/wwar/default.html
Yahoo	http://www.yahoo.com
Search Engines	
Alta Vista	http://www.altavista.digital.com
Berkeley Public Library's Index to the Internet	http://www.ci.berkeley.ca.us:80/bpl/bkmk/index.html
Infoseek	http://www.infoseek.com
Inktomi	http://inktomi.berkeley.edu
Lycos	http://www.lycos.com
NlightN	http://www.nlightn.com
Open Text	http://www.opentext.com/omw/fomw.html
shareware.com	http://www.shareware.com
Web Crawler	http://www.webcrawler.com
WhoWhere?	http://www.whowhere.com

Downloading Files and Keeping Your Software Up-to-Date

Sometimes when you search the Net you're looking for information, but other times you're looking for files to download from the Internet to your computer. For example, there's a lot of software out there available either for free or as *shareware* (meaning you're expected to pay for it after evaluating it, if you decide to keep using it). Also, a lot of programs, especially Internet-related software programs, are updated from time to time, with newer versions that can be downloaded available on the Net.

Once you start using Internet software (such as Web browsers, newsreaders, mail programs, and so on), you have to get used to the idea that if you want to have the latest version of the program, you occasionally have to check the software manufacturer's Web site to download the latest update.

No matter what your reason for downloading a file, the procedure with most Web browsers is about the same. It generally involves finding your way to the appropriate site, working your way through some links, and ultimately clicking on a link that goes directly to the file in question.

When you do this, your browser will realize that you've requested something that can't be displayed in a browser window, and it will offer to download or even try to run the file for you.

> **TIP** The file you're downloading may be a compressed file. See Chapter 10 for how to unsquish files.

Figure 5.9 shows the dialog box that Netscape Navigator displays when you choose a link to a file for downloading.

Click on Save File and then select a folder to save the file to in the Save As dialog box that appears. Usually a Temp folder is best, since most of the time you'll be unpacking a compressed file or running an installation program to actually set up the software you're downloading.

Your browser will then download the file, showing you its progress, either in a special dialog box or in the bottom-right corner of the browser window.

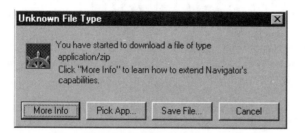

FIGURE 5.9:
Netscape gives you four choices when you download a file.

> **WARNING** Be careful when downloading files from the Internet. Only take files from reputable sources. If you download a file from some unofficial archive, it could easily house a virus or other software designed to damage your computer. If you're downloading from a well-established company site, though, you have nothing to worry about.

For more on transferring files, see Chapter 10. For more on "teaching" your browser how to use an external application to open a file (the Pick App option in Navigator), see the full discussion in Chapter 6.

Looking for People on the Internet

In Chapter 3, I mentioned a few ways to look for people's e-mail addresses. Now that you have the hang of using a Web browser to search, I will point you to a few more useful sites for looking for people.

Using Whois

The first place to try looking for someone is the Whois gateway at the *InterNIC* site. InterNIC is the Internet's Network Information Center—a resource worth knowing about. To perform a Whois search, first point your browser at `http://rs.internic.net/cgi-bin/whois` (see Figure 5.10).

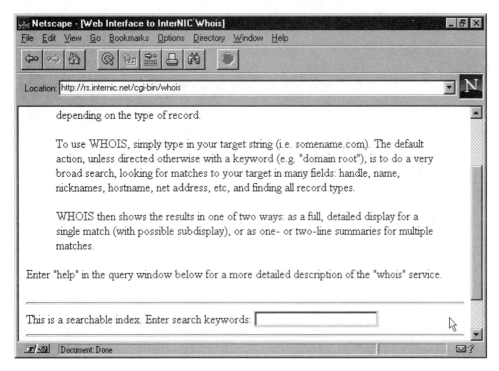

FIGURE 5.10: Type a name in the Enter Search Keywords box and press Enter to search for a person's e-mail address.

Then just type a name and press Enter. Whois will return a list of e-mail addresses and domain names that match the words you type.

NOTE Whois is primarily designed for looking for domain names (such as sybex.com, ibm.com, syx.com, ezone.org), not necessarily individuals' addresses; however, it will turn up many e-mail addresses as part of its data, so it's generally worth a try.

Using WhoWhere?

Another good site to use to look for e-mail addresses is called WhoWhere? To try it out, point your browser at `http://www.whowhere.com/` (see Figure 5.11).

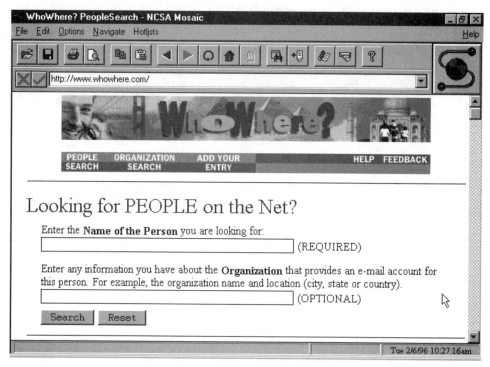

FIGURE 5.11: Type a name in the Enter the Name of the Person You Are Looking For box and then click on the Search button.

Type a name in the Enter the Name of the Person You Are Looking For box. If you know an organization that the person you're looking for might be listed with, type the organization's name in the second box (but that's optional). Then click on the Search button.

The Whois search finds nothing for **Christian Crumlish,** but WhoWhere? finds me with no trouble (see Figure 5.12).

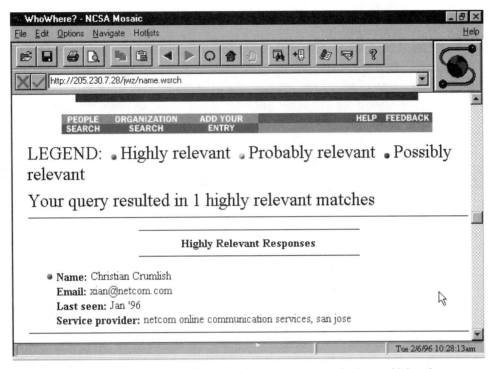

FIGURE 5.12: A WhoWhere? search: I just entered my name—no organization—and it found me.

Searching off the Web

Because the Web doesn't constitute the entire Internet, there are some Internet resources that don't show up when you're searching for Web sites. Fortunately, there are search engines and gateways out there that specialize in finding information in these other non-Web media.

WARNING Some of the non-Web resources can be even flakier than the Web when you're trying to make a connection, especially during the business day in the continental U.S.A. If you have trouble getting through, try, try again (and then give up and try a couple of hours later).

Searching Usenet

Usenet and related newsgroups are the public discussion *bulletin boards* of the Internet. Because articles posted to Usenet expire after several weeks or months (depending on the news server), there's no way to search everything that's ever been posted there, but it is possible to search all the posts made during a recent enough period.

Probably the best Usenet search engine is DejaNews at `http://www.dejanews.com/forms/dnq.html` (see Figure 5.13).

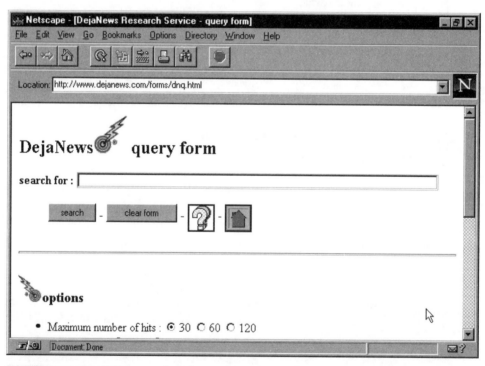

FIGURE 5.13: As with most search engines, you can choose all sorts of complicated options with DejaNews, but you can also just type a key word and then click on the Search button.

Type a word or words in the Search For box and click on the Search button. DejaNews will give you a list of articles containing your key words, with links to the text of the articles themselves and to the author of each article (see Figure 5.14). Clicking on the article's subject takes you to the article's contents. Clicking on the author takes you to a "profile" of the author that includes statistics about the author's Usenet posting habits.

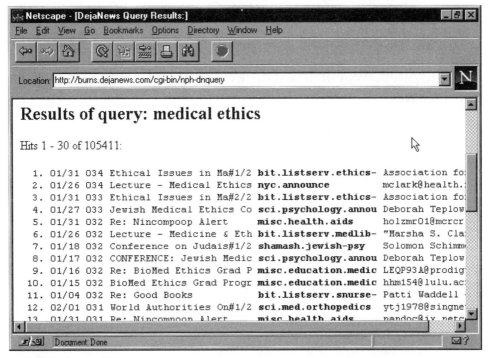

FIGURE 5.14: DejaNews has found many articles containing the key words *medical ethics*.

Searching Gopherspace

Before the Web existed, the easiest way to browse the Internet was by using Gopher. Gopher programs present you with a list of menu items. Choosing an item either accesses a document or another menu. Although you can use a special Gopher client program to view Gopher menus (see Chapter 11 for more on this), Web browsers are also capable of displaying Gopher information. However, Gopher sites are not indexed (at least not as thoroughly) with the major Web search engines, so if you're looking for something in *Gopherspace*—the set of all Gopher servers out there serving up Gopher menus and documents—then you're better off performing a Gopher search.

The easiest way to do such as search on the Web is to point your browser at `gopher://veronica·psi·net:2347/7-t1%20%20` (see Figure 5.15).

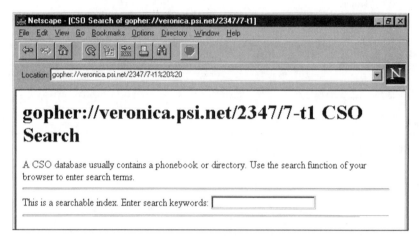

FIGURE 5.15: A Gopher search page. As with other search pages, type a key word or words in the Enter Search Keywords text box and press Enter.

After you enter keywords in the text box, the search page will give you an ad hoc Gopher menu with items that match your search words. Figure 5.16 shows the results of a search for **medical ethics.**

Searching University Libraries

Another popular Internet resource not easily reached via Web search engines are university libraries, many of which use a Telnet or Gopher interface (see Chapters 10 and 11) for their offerings. A program called Hytelnet has a fairly up-to-date list of university libraries, though, and you can reach it via the Web if you need that sort of information for your research.

To get to a Hytelnet Web page, point your browser at `http://library·usask·ca/hytelnet/` (see Figure 5.17).

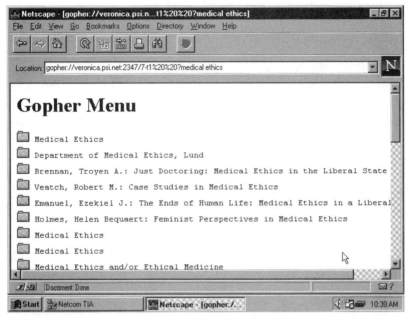

FIGURE 5.16: Click on an item to reach another Gopher menu or (and ultimately) a document.

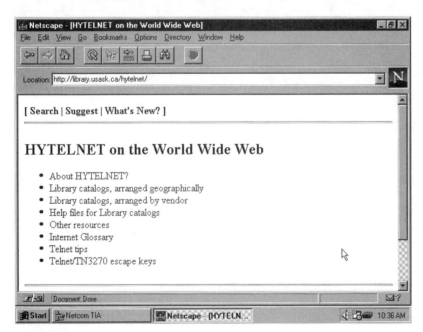

FIGURE 5.17: Perform a Hytelnet search from the HYTELNET on the World Wide Web page to look for library catalogs.

Looking for a Specific University Library

To look for a university library, click on Library Catalogs, Arranged Geographically. Then choose a geographical region and start zooming in on the library you're looking for. Figure 5.18 shows the information for the Cornell University library.

Click on the Telnet link to connect to the library, and then follow the login instructions given in the library listing. Your browser will attempt to start a Telnet program for you to make the connection. If you don't have a Telnet program, see Chapter 10 for where to get one. See Chapter 6 for how to tell your browser where your Telnet program can be found. Figure 5.19 shows the Telnet connection to the Cornell library catalog.

Performing a General Search of University Libraries

To perform a general search, click on the Search link at the top of the main Hytelnet page (see Figure 5.17). This will take you to a search page. Enter a key word (or words) and press the Search button. Figure 5.20 shows the results of a Hytelnet search on the words **medical ethics.**

Choosing a result will take you to the listing page for the library in question. From there, you click on the link and make a Telnet connection, as I just described.

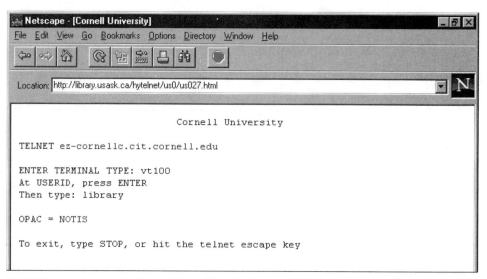

FIGURE 5.18: A university library listing will contain a Telnet link. When you select it, your browser will attempt to open a Telnet connection.

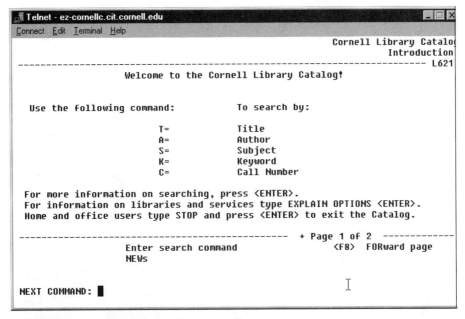

FIGURE 5.19: Searching the Cornell University library

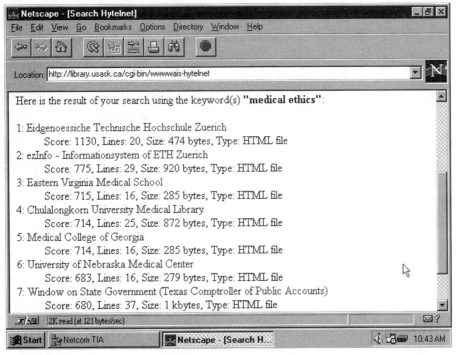

FIGURE 5.20: The results of a Hytelnet search

Chapter 6

PLUGGING IN TO MULTIMEDIA

FEATURING

- **Installing media viewers**
- **Setting up helper applications**
- **Installing browser plug-ins**
- **Exploring popular media formats**
- **Using specialized Web browsers**
- **Viewing multimedia files with AOL, CompuServe, Lynx, Microsoft Internet Explorer, Mosaic, NetCruiser, and Netscape**

Part of the fun of the Internet and the Web is that there are a lot of different media out there to explore. What do I mean by media? Well, the most basic medium is text. The next most common media are various forms of pictures. Beyond that, media available on the Internet include sounds, movie clips, animations, and even more elaborate formats combining the basic media in all sorts of different ways. We still haven't reached a point where your computer is going to be as flashy as a television, and I'm not sure we'll ever get to that point. For one thing, the more snazzy the medium, the bigger the files. For example, even the smallest picture file is bigger than most text documents you find on the Internet.

To actually see, hear, or otherwise experience these media, you need a computer equipped with the right hardware (such as a sound card, enough memory to make movies play smoothly, a big enough hard drive to store large-format files, and so on) and you need software installed on your computer, either as part of a Web browser or as a stand-alone program, that can interpret and display—or just "play"— the various media file formats. If you can put together all of the ingredients, then you can start to experience the Internet as the world's largest CD-ROM, with new content appearing online daily.

Every Web browser can at least download files. So if you can get a stand-alone program to interpret a multimedia file you've downloaded, then you can experience that medium even without a sophisticated Web browser. In this chapter, I'll show you the various ways to handle these media, depending on the flexibility of your browser.

Downloading and Installing Applications

In Chapter 5, I told you how to download a file using a Web browser. To experience just about any medium, you first have to download a large file. Depending on your browser, the file will be displayed inside the browser window; the browser will automatically start up a program that can display the file and the file will appear outside the browser; or, at minimum, the browser will store the file on your computer where you can open it yourself using the right player program.

The type of program that you launch separately to display a file is called a *viewer* or *player program.* If your browser can automatically start up an external program whenever it needs to display certain types of files, then the program is referred to as a *helper application* (since it helps the browser with this extra job). The type of program that becomes part of the browser and enables the browser to display a file within the browser window is called a *plug-in* (or, in some programs, an *add-in*). I'll cover all three variations in the sections coming up.

At Web sites that offer multimedia files, you will often find additional hypertext links to sites from which you can download the appropriate player software. Generally, just follow these links to the Web site housing the software, read the installation instructions, and download the correct program for your type of computer. Once the file is safely on your computer, place it in an empty, temporary directory (unless the instructions specify otherwise), double-click on it, and unless it starts installing itself after the first double-click, install it by double-clicking the Setup or Install program that gets unpacked from the primary downloaded file.

Different Ways to View Other Media

As I just alluded to, there are different ways to view various media files depending on the type of browser you have, the media format you're working with, and the additional software you install. Here's a quick run-down of the different approaches.

> **TIP**
>
> Don't be put off by the use of the word *viewer* to describe multimedia player applications. Because the first media (after text) to be widely distributed were picture (image) formats, the viewer terminology took hold and is now used even for media, such as sounds, that you can't actually see.

Viewers and Players

A viewer program is one that can be used to view or play a specific type of file. (Even the ones used to play, for example, sounds are still referred to as *viewers* in browser instructions, so viewers and players are two names for the same thing.) Even with a character-based browser like the Unix program Lynx, you can still download files. It's true that you'll then have to get the file from your Unix account to your desktop computer, but after that, you can "play" the file you downloaded if you have the appropriate software (such as Sound Recorder for Windows) installed on your PC. This approach will also work with browsers, such as AOL's, that are not equipped to launch external programs automatically.

The trick, then, is finding the appropriate viewer program to display the media files you download. As I mentioned earlier, this is usually a matter of following the suggestions from the Web site where you found the original file.

Helper Applications

Mosaic, Netscape Navigator, and other browsers based on that graphical model have the ability to launch external programs—called helper applications—when a non-standard file format is selected. Helper applications will let your browser open files in formats it could not otherwise handle, such as a Sun audio file. They do have to be "taught," though, where to look for the helper application. You can either do this in advance, by entering the Options or Preferences area of the browser and looking for the Helper Applications (or Helper Apps) section, as shown in Figure 6.1, or you can attempt to download a media file and then, when the browser tells you it doesn't recognize the file format, you can educate it about which viewer to use with that type of file. You do this simply by typing in the path and file name for the correct program, or by clicking on a Browse button and rummaging around on your hard disk for the program you need. After that, your browser will automatically launch the right helper application whenever you select that type of media file again.

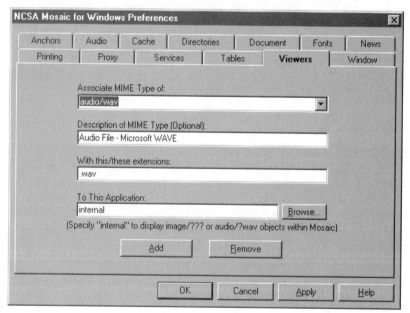

FIGURE 6.1: Here's how you tell Mosaic where it can find helper applications on your computer.

Plug-Ins

The most sophisticated way to work with multimedia files is to plug special add-on software directly into a browser. Such a program, usually called a plug-in, is an application that works in tandem with another program, enhancing its features as if you had taken a piece of hardware and added it to your computer to give it more features. Only Netscape Navigator has really exploited this approach fully. (It helps that Navigator has become the de facto standard in the Web browser field.) Its nearest competitor, Microsoft Internet Explorer, so far—at the time of this writing—can handle only one specific add-in, what Microsoft, which always uses its own terms, calls plug-ins. (This add-in is VRML 2.0, which I'll discuss later in this chapter.)

With plug-ins installed, a browser can then display an unusual format *in-line,* meaning inside the browser window, instead of launching an external program to display the file.

The Types of Media out There

The multimedia world on the Internet is still in a sort of "Wild West" phase, with many competing formats for the various types of media. In this section, I'll describe some of the media you'll encounter and enumerate the different file formats used to get those media onto your screen.

> **TIP**
>
> For more (or more up-to-date) information on multimedia file formats available on the Net, check out `http://ac.dal.ca/dong/contents.html`.

Pictures

The first graphical Web browser, Mosaic, could only display one picture format when it first appeared—CompuServe's *GIF* (*Graphic Interchange Format*), which is a compressed file format. The other major picture format is called *JPEG* (named for the *Joint Photographics Experts Group* that designed the format). At first, Mosaic could only display JPEG files in a helper application. When Netscape came along, it sported in-line JPEGs, which most browsers can now also handle.

Some GIFs are *interlaced,* which makes them appear to load faster on your screen. GIFs can also have transparent backgrounds; this accounts for the illusion of images with irregular (non-rectangular) edges. The images actually do have square edges, but their transparent background makes their content appear to float on the page (see Figure 6.2).

FIGURE 6.2: We made this word balloon (on the cover of Enterzone episode 4) appear to have rounded edges by making its real corners transparent.

JPEGs can be compressed to much smaller file sizes than equivalent GIFs, but the more they are "squished" the worse the quality of the image becomes. Figure 6.3 shows the *splash screen* (the first page that briefly appears) before my real home page. I cropped out a small image of my face from a scanned photograph and then compressed it as a JPEG as much as possible. This resulted in the low-quality effect of big patchy squares each with their own averaged-out colors. Then I displayed the picture in the full window size of the Web browser to exaggerate the sloppy quality of the image. Nice, huh?

Sounds and Music

There are many different sound file formats available on the Net. The most common of these include Microsoft's *.WAV* (wave) format, perhaps the most widespread; the Macintosh *AIFF* format; and the Unix (originally NeXT) *.au* format. Many Web sites will offer sounds in more than one format, in order to make it easier for each user to download a file format native to their type of computer.

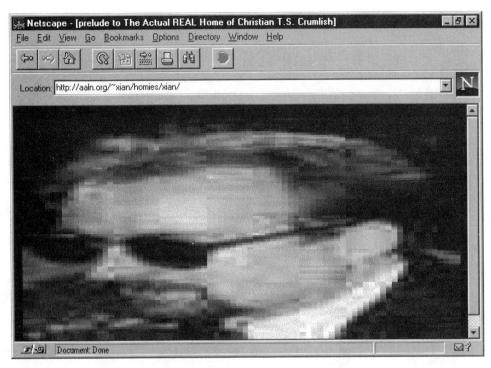

FIGURE 6.3: I'm much better looking in real life.

Other sound formats out there include *MIDI* (*Musical Instrument Digital Interface*); the Amiga SND format; the *.VOC* format for the SoundBlaster sound card; and MP2 or MPA, which are *MPEG* sound formats. (MPEG is a movie format, but movies, of course, often also include sounds, so the MPEG standard specifies a sound format as well.)

After awhile, you'll start to recognize what programs you'll need to view or play files by the (usually) three-letter extension following a file name. This will tell you whether it is a movie, a sound file, or a picture, and what method of compression—if any—was used on it. Some of the more common file compression suffixes are zip, hqz, .Z, .gz, sit, sea, exe, and tar. For more on compression, see Chapter 10.

NOTE Microsoft Internet Explorer can now handle *in-line sounds*, which mean sounds will automatically start playing as soon as you arrive at a page (if you have the right sounds software installed, of course), whether you like it or not!

A new approach to sound files (and, eventually, for movie files as well) is *streaming*. Streaming is when files are sent a little at a time and start playing almost immediately. This model differs from those in which an entire file is sent and starts playing only after it has been completely downloaded. The most popular streaming format these days is called *Real Audio* (.RA). The tools needed to create and listen to such sounds are made by a company called Progressive Networks. This format allows sounds to be broadcast something like the way they are in radio. In fact, the National Public Radio Web site uses the Real Audio format to broadcast some of their reports over the Internet (see Figure 6.4).

FIGURE 6.4: NPR's Web site offers current broadcasts in Real Audio format.

Microsoft has also developed a competing sound-streaming format, called *TrueSound*.

Movies and Animations

As with sounds and pictures, there are various competing movie and animation formats available on the Net. Technically, the difference between a movie and an animation is that movies use video or film images (variations on photographic technology), while animations use drawn illustrations. With computer art tools being what they are, this distinction will probably fade eventually. A lot of computer art these days starts off as photography and is then manipulated into something entirely different.

Probably the most widespread movie format is the *MPEG* (*Motion Pictures Experts Group*) format, a compressed format. Another popular format is QuickTime, which started off on the Macintosh platform but can now be displayed on most computers. QuickTime files usually have a .qt or .mov extension.

A third common movie format, native to the Windows platform, is *.avi.*

3D Environments

The future of the Net may be glimpsed in the still-evolving 3D formats with which real or imaginary spaces are depicted in perspective and the user has the ability to move (walk or fly) around, viewing the space from multiple angles.

The most common format for 3D worlds on the Web is called *VRML*, which stands for *Virtual Reality Modeling Language.* While VRML is an evolving standard, there are multiple competing implementations of it out there, including a version of QuickTime called, naturally enough, QuickTime VR. VRML files usually have a .wrl extension.

One of the future goals of VRML developers is to create worlds in which many users can meet and interact, as if in person. The present state of VRML development, however, involves users downloading copies of 3D environments and then moving around in them all by themselves.

Figure 6.5 shows a VRML art gallery at Construct.net, designed by Michael Gough and curated by Annette Loudon, a Web artist.

> **WARNING**
>
> To see the gallery space shown in Figure 6.5, your browser may have to uncompress files compressed with Gzip. See Chapter 10 for more on compressed file formats.

There are also some special browsers out there, such as one called WebFX, designed specifically for viewing and moving through 3D spaces. (For more on this, see *A Few Words about Specialized Browsers* later in this chapter.)

> **TIP**
>
> To find info on VRML browsers, builders, tools, documentation, and sample VRML worlds, check out `http://www.sdsc.edu/vrml`.

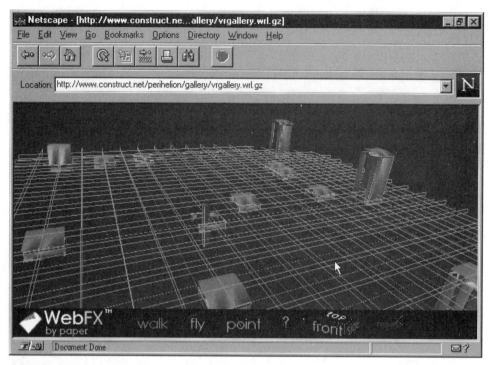

FIGURE 6.5: Construct's sample VRML art gallery

Document/Mixed-Media Formats

Aside from the familiar HTML format and plain text (.txt) files, which browsers can easily display, there are some document file formats intended to give designers and publishers more control over the precise look of a document. HTML is quite flexible but HTML documents look different in every browser because they have to use whatever fonts are built into the user's computer, and they even change their shape and layout depending on the size and shape of the browser window. For artists, publishers, and designers trained in the world of print publishing, most of these compromises are unacceptable.

The most popular document format is Adobe's PDF (Portable Document Format). The external helper application for viewing PDF files is called Adobe Acrobat. The Netscape plug-in that performs the same function is called Adobe Amber. Visit `http://www.adobe.com` for more information on the PDF format.

Another document format that requires special viewers is Postscript, which can be used for both text and images. Postscript files usually have a .ps extension.

Interactive Programs and Multimedia Presentations

The next wave of special media formats for the Web will involve interactive programs or demonstrations, running either in separate applications or in the browser window. Macromedia makes a product called Director that enables artists to assemble movies, animations, pictures, sounds, and interactive elements (such as clickable buttons and other user-influenced choices) into a single, self-running application. The Director plug-in is known as Shockwave.

The other up-and-coming application-development format for the Web is Sun's *Java* programming language, a variant of C++. With a special Java-savvy browser such as HotJava, Netscape Navigator 2, or earlier versions of Netscape with a Java plug-in, users can interact with fully operational programs inside of the browser window.

A Few Words about Specialized Browsers

One way to experience some of the latest multimedia offerings on the Web, even without customizing your browser, is to obtain a specialized browser designed to display one or more of the multimedia formats. In the long run, as general-purpose browsers become more flexible, this may no longer be a useful option, but for now, if you have the type of access that allows you to install and run your own browser, you can download such programs as Sun's HotJava browser (`http://java.sun.com`) or the WebFX VRML browser (`http://www.paperinc.com`). There are actually quite a few stand-alone VRML browsers, such as Fountain(`http://www.caligari.com/ftp/pub/fountain/fountain.exe`), WebSpace (`ftp://ftp.sd.tgs.com/pub/template/WebSpace/`), and VR Scout (`ftp://ftp.chaco.com/pub/vrscout/`) to name a few.

Staying Informed about the Latest Advances

There are new viewers and new file formats coming out on the Net all the time. It's literally impossible for the information I have at my disposal today and that I'm putting into this chapter to be fully up-to-date by the time you're reading it! As with any Internet software, you will have to take some responsibility for staying up-to-date with the latest developments. Your best bet is to visit your browser's home page (such as Netscape's page at `http://home.netscape.com`) from time to time and read the announcements to see if any new capabilities or plug-ins have been announced.

Multimedia for Specific Browsers

As in earlier chapters of this book, I'll finish up by running through many of the most popular Web browsers to tell you what alternatives you have (setting up helper applications or adding plug-ins) to increase the capabilities at your disposal and what media are viewable with them.

AOL's Web Browser

The AOL browser is built into the AOL software and is not really extensible. You can't even tell it how to launch helper applications, so your best bet for exotic media types is to simply download them with the browser and then view them with external programs (which you'll also have to download and launch by hand).

AOL's browser can display the most common of all media types (besides text), the GIF and JPEG picture file formats.

CompuServe Mosaic

CompuServe's version of Mosaic has the same helper-application capabilities as NCSA Mosaic and other up-to-date versions. Like Mosaic, it can display GIFs and JPEGs in-line.

See the Mosaic entry for more details.

Lynx (Don't Laugh!)

Naturally, a text-only browser like Lynx can't do much in the way of displaying multimedia files, but it *can* download any type of file to the Unix shell. The rest is up to you. See Chapter 10 for how to get files from a Unix account to your desktop computer.

Microsoft Internet Explorer

To set up a helper application for Internet Explorer, select View ➤ Options and choose the File Types tab in the Options dialog box (see Figure 6.6).

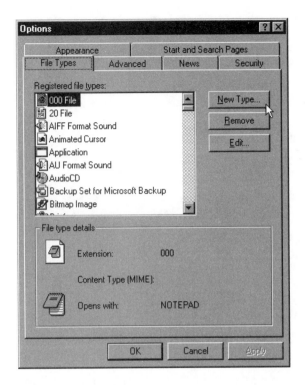

FIGURE 6.6:
Internet Explorer's Options dialog box with the File Types tab selected

Click on the New Type button. Type a description of the file format, press Tab, and type the file's extension. Then click on the New button. In the New Action dialog box that appears, type **open with**, press Tab, and then either type the path and file name of the helper application or click on the Browse button and hunt around on your hard disk for the correct program. When you've found it, click on OK, on Close, and then on Close again.

There is (at the time of this writing) only one add-in (plug-in) for Internet Explorer the VRML 2.0 add-in. It only works with the Windows 95 version of the browser. You can download the add-in from the Microsoft Web site (**http://www.microsoft.com**) and install it by double-clicking the .exe file when it finishes downloading to your computer.

Internet Explorer can display GIFs and JPEGs in-line. It can also play any of the standard Microsoft file formats (such as the .AVI movie format, the .WAV sound format, and so on). It also comes with the capability to play Real Audio sound files.

Mosaic

To set up a helper application for Mosaic, select Options ➤ Preferences and click on the Viewers tag (see Figure 6.7).

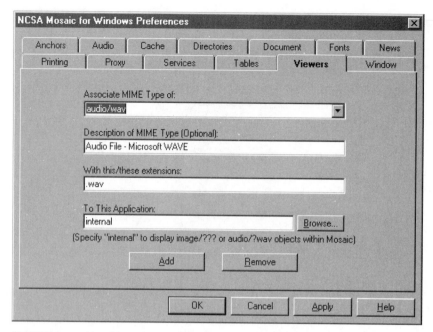

FIGURE 6.7: Mosaic's Preferences dialog box with the Viewers tab selected

Select a file type in the Associate MIME Type Of drop-down list box and type a path and file name for the helper application that can display that file type in the To This Application box near the bottom of the dialog box (or click on the Browse button to hunt around on your hard disk for the program you want). Then click on OK.

At this writing, there are no plug-ins for Mosaic. Mosaic can display GIFs and JPEGs in-line.

NetCruiser

The NetCruiser browser is built into the NetCruiser software and cannot connect to external programs. You can't even tell it how to launch helper applications, so to view any media beyond pictures, you'll have to download the files you want to display along with the necessary external viewer programs and then check out the files outside of the NetCruiser program.

NetCruiser can display the GIF and JPEG picture file formats.

Netscape Navigator

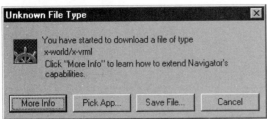

To tell Navigator about a helper application, either start downloading the file and then, when Navigator balks and the Unknown File Type dialog box pops up, tell it what program to use to view the file by clicking on the Pick App button and following the instructions that appear. Or, to plan ahead, select Options ➤ General Preferences and click on the Helpers tab in the Preferences dialog box that appears (see Figure 6.8).

Select a file type in the large list box at the top of the dialog box, click on the Launch the Application button in the Action area near the bottom of the dialog box, and then either type the path and file name of the helper application that can display the file type, or click on the Browse button to hunt around on your hard disk for the program you want. Then click on OK.

To set up a plug-in for Navigator, download the plug-in program and install it as instructed. Navigator will do the rest. The following table lists the plug-ins available for Navigator at the time of this writing (all available for download through the Netscape home page).

Name of Plug-In	File Format It Can View
Adobe Acrobat Amber Reader	PDF (Portable Document Format)
ASAP WebShow	Presentation files
Astound Web Player	Astound or Studio M multimedia documents
Corel Vector Graphics	CMX (vector graphics files)
Crescendo	MIDI sound files
Earth Time	Time and date for eight geographical locations
Envoy	Envoy (portable) documents
Figleaf Inline	CGM (vector graphics) files, among other picture formats
Formula One/NET	Spreadsheets (Excel-compatible)
Lightning Strike	Compressed image files
Live3D	VRML
OLE Control	Microsoft OLE objects
OpenScape	Microsoft OLE objects
PreVU	Streaming MPEG video

Continued on next page ➔

Name of Plug-In	File Format It Can View
RealAudio	Streaming compressed sound
Shockwave for Director	Director presentation files
Talker	Macintosh synthesized speech
ToolVox	Streaming speech audio
VDOLive	Compressed video
VR Scout	VRML
VRealm	VRML (and extensions)
WebFX	VRML
WIRL	VRML (and extensions)
Word Viewer	Microsoft Word documents

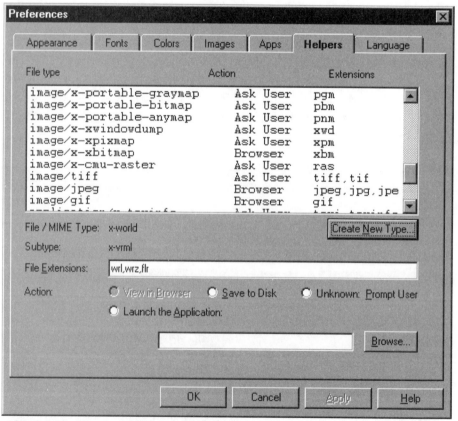

FIGURE 8.6: Navigator's Preferences dialog box with the Helpers tab selected

Navigator can display GIFs and JPEGs in-line, as well as *animated GIFs* (those are GIF files that contain multiple frames and instructions on how to show them). It has a built-in Java interpreter that you can instruct to use an almost unlimited number of helper applications. There are already many plug-ins for Navigator on the Net, as mentioned above, and undoubtedly many more on the way.

Chapter 7

GETTING ON MAILING LISTS

- **Finding interesting lists**
- **Subscribing to lists**
- **Getting off lists**
- **Putting in your two cents**

Another benefit of e-mail is that it gives you the opportunity to participate in *mailing lists.* Of course, I'm not talking about what you usually think of as a mailing list, such as the kind you get on after buying something from a catalog and that results in your getting two hundred catalogs the next year. No, electronic mailing lists enable people to send e-mail to large groups ("broadcasting the e-mail," it's sometimes called), and these lists usually function as discussion forums for people who are all interested in the same topics. The simplest kind of mailing list is an alias (or address book entry) that corresponds to a list of several e-mail addresses (see *Saving E-Mail Addresses* in Chapter 3 for a more in-depth explanation of aliases and address books), but the more interesting kind of mailing list (or *list* for short) allows anyone to send mail to a single address on the list and have it forwarded to everyone else on the list. These lists function as discussion groups on any subject you can imagine, with subscribers all over the globe.

Anyone with an Internet mailing address can participate in lists of this sort. And every subscriber can be a contributor as well. Sending a message to a mailing list is called *posting*.

Mailing Lists versus Usenet Newsgroups

Another way for people to share common interests by exchanging messages over the Internet is by participating in Usenet newsgroups.

Mailing lists have been around longer than Usenet and are more universal, as anyone with Internet access—even without Usenet—can participate in mailing lists. Lists generally have less traffic (fewer posts) than newsgroups, but there are some very large, very busy lists and some pretty dead newsgroups. Busy lists fill up your mailbox, whereas newsgroup posts are not sent to you directly. In Chapter 8, I explain how to "read" Usenet.

Sometimes mailing lists *become* newsgroups. Usually this means that there is a gateway between a list and a corresponding newsgroup, and all posts are shared between them. Most of these decisions are made by polling the readership. Some people feel that lists are more private, even when they are open to anyone, because they are harder to find—if you don't know where to look.

Once you've posted your message, one of two things will happen to it: An unmoderated list will be immediately resent to everyone on the list; a moderated list will go to the moderator (a volunteer) who determines if it's *on-topic* (directly related to the subject of the list), and then either sends it along to the entire list if it is or sends it back to you if it isn't. Most lists are unmoderated, however, and rely on peer pressure to keep posts in line.

NOTE   It should also be pointed out that mailing lists are free.

If you subscribe to a busy list or to several lists and then don't read and clear out your mail box for a while, it can fill up and even exceed your system's limitations. This could result in your losing mail. So if you *do* subscribe to some lists, be sure to check your mail regularly.

TIP Some lists are available as digests. This means that posts are grouped together and sent out less often. You might receive, say, ten posts in a single mailing. If you subscribe to a list and then find that the traffic is too much for you to handle—look into whether it is also available in a *digestified* form.

Finding Mailing Lists

So how do you find the lists you'd be interested in? There's no single way. To some extent, all information on the Net flows by word of mouth (or by e-mail, more likely). People will tell you about mailing lists. I've heard about some of the lists I subscribe to in Usenet newsgroups. There are also some large "lists of lists" out there that you can consult and peruse.

TIP These lists are long and will take up a lot of disk space. If you find what you're looking for, delete them. You can always get the updated versions in the future using the same method.

A General List of Lists

I know of two e-mail addresses you can send to so as to have lists of lists mailed back to you. The first one is so large that it is broken into twenty-one parts. (The second address is mentioned in the next section, *Specific Lists of Lists.*) Send mail to `mail-server@rtfm.mit.edu`. The Subject line can be anything—blank is fine. The message should contain just this line:

```
send usenet-by-group/news.answers/mail/
mailing/lists/part01
```

You will receive part01 as e-mail.

Then send the same message, but substitute **part02**, **part03**, and so on, all the way up to **part21**, to obtain the entire list.

If you'd rather peruse this same listing of mailing lists on the Web, point your browser at `http://www.neosoft.com/internet/paml` (that's an L at the end, not the numeral *one*). These lists are also posted regularly to the `news.announce.newusers` newsgroup. (See Chapter 8 for more on Usenet newsgroups.)

Specific Lists of Lists

You can seek out lists that relate to a specific topic by sending mail to `listserv@bitnic.educom.edu`. Leave the subject blank. Include the line **list global / topic** in your message and substitute whatever word you want for *topic*. (Also, don't include your signature if you've got one. The Listserv program will try to interpret it as a command.)

NOTE   You *can* send mail to this address and just include the line **list global** without specifying a topic, but then the message sent back to you will be incredibly long. You're much better off limiting the responses in some way.

Figure 7.1 shows the mail I got in response when I sent the message **list global / auto** to the Bitnic Listserv.

TIP   If you are interested in music, you might want to see the List of Musical Mailing Lists, which is updated regularly. Send mail to `lomml@arastar.com` and the current list will be sent to you, or look for it on the Web at `http://server.berkeley.edu/ayukawa/lomml.html`.

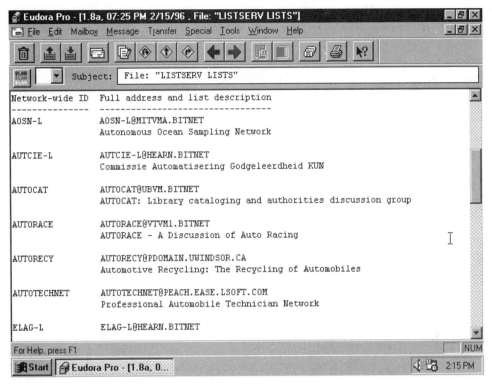

FIGURE 7.1: By using the topic word *auto* I got information about automobile mailing lists along with other lists related to words that start with auto (such as automatic).

Use the following table as a quick reference guide for getting general and specific lists of lists:

To Get Lists of Lists	Address	Message
General lists of lists	mail-server@rtfm.mit.edu	send usenet-by-group/news.answers/ mail/mailing/lists/part01 (then substitute **part02**, **part03**, and so on, all the way up to **part21** for future messages)
	http://www.neosoft.com/internet/paml	No message

Continued on next page →

To Get Lists of Lists	Address	Message
Specific lists of lists	news.announc .newusers	No message
	listserv@bitnic.educom.edu	Leave the subject line blank. Include the line **list global/ topic** in your message and substitute whatever word you want for *topic*
	listserv@bitnic.educom.edu	Leave the subject line blank. Just include the line list global in your message

Subscribing to Lists

The first and most important thing I can tell you is that to subscribe to a mailing list, you send a message to an address *different* from the mailing list address. People constantly make the mistake of sending their subscription requests directly to the lists in question. This results in everyone on the list having to read your mistaken post.

WARNING It's embarrassing to you and annoying to everyone else on a mailing list when you send your requests to the list itself instead of to the administrative address. Be careful.

The next thing you need to know is that there are two different kinds of lists. Once you're on the list, it won't make any difference to you. There are lists administered by real live people and there are automated lists. Lists that are run by programs are called *Listservs* (or, by their full name, *list servers*).

You'll need to know what sort of list you're subscribing to ahead of time. There are two types:

- If the address you've found for subscribing to a list is of the form *list-request@address* (with *list* being the name of the mailing list), then the list is handled by a person.

- If the address starts with `listserv@` or `majordomo@`, then the list is handled by a program (or *robot* or "'bot" for short).

People-Administered Lists

To subscribe to a people-administered list, send e-mail to the Request address for the list. This address should be of the form *`list-request@address`*.

Since this message will be read by a human being, you can write a normal sentence to the effect that you'd like to subscribe to the list. Include your e-mail address, just to be sure it comes through okay. The administrator will acknowledge your mail and send you the actual address of the list (for posting). She might also send you some additional information, such as where to find the list's FAQ or archive of posts.

So, for example, to join the they-might-be list to discuss the rock band They Might Be Giants, I sent to the address `they-might-be-request@super.org` a message that said something like

> Hi, I'd like to subscribe to the they-might-be list. My e-mail address is `xian@netcom.com`. Thanks!

Robot-Administered Lists

Subscribing to robot-administered lists is a little more involved. To subscribe to a robot-administered list:

1. Send mail to the contact address of the list, which should be of the form `listserv@`*`address`* (or `majordomo@`*`address`*).
2. Leave the subject line blank.
3. Include in your message only the line **subscribe *list Your Name***. Use the name of the list for *list*. Put your real first and last name on that line, not your e-mail address. You will receive a confirmation and a welcome message in response.

NOTE Only a computer program will read your message, not a human being, so don't gussy up the language to make it sound natural. Include only the key words listed here. To get help, send a message to the same address with just the word **help** in it.

So, for example, to join the Screen Writing Discussion List Top-Ten list, I sent to the address `listserv@tamvm1.tamu.edu` a one-line message that said, "subscribe SCRNWRIT Christian Crumlish."

Canceling Your Subscription

If you tire of a list, you can simply cancel your subscription to it. Again, it's different for people and robots.

People-Administered Lists

Send e-mail to the original *list*-request address, asking **Please unsubscribe me** or words to that effect.

Robot-Administered Lists

Send e-mail to the original listserv@ address, with no subject and only the line **signoff *list***, substituting the name of the list for *list*, of course.

Temporarily Unsubscribing

If you're going on vacation, you can temporarily cancel your subscription by sending to the listserv@ address the message **set *list* nomail**. When you return, send the message **set *list* mail** to start up your subscription again.

Posting to Lists

There are two ways to post to mailing lists. The first is to send mail to the list address. The other way is to reply to a message from the list, when the return address is set to the list itself. This varies from list to list, so watch out you don't do this by mistake when you mean to reply to someone directly.

> **TIP**   **Always look at the header of a message before replying to it. Normally, your reply will go to the return address, but sometimes there's a Reply-to line, and then your reply will go to that address.**

Remember that you always have the option of sending mail just to the person whose post you're replying to, though you may have to copy that person's address and then send mail to them directly.

WARNING In general, remember that many people will read your post. If you post, it is like speaking in public. You never know who is listening, or who is saving what you've written. Try to ensure that your posts are on-topic.

Participating in a List

Everybody was a newbie once, and while there's no such thing as a dumb question, there are such things as frequently asked questions. Most lists eventually get around to compiling a *FAQ*, a document of answers to frequently asked questions. Look for or ask for the relevant FAQ and read it before posting the first questions that come to mind. FAQs are usually fun and interesting to read—they are some of the best resources on the Net.

WARNING Some people just like to make trouble and post messages designed to arouse indignation, resentment, or anger. After a while, it's easy to tell when someone has posted *flame bait,* and you learn to just ignore it until it goes away. Unfortunately, there are always too many people too ready to jump in and debate even the most obviously insulting posts. Oh well. Fortunately, this seems to happen on mailing lists less often than it does on Usenet.

I highly recommend *lurking*— reading the list without posting to it for a while—to get caught up on the various threads of conversations that are going on. Once you've made reasonable efforts to get up to speed, plunge right in and start gabbing. Many people lurk most or all of the time. It's easy to forget how many people are out there when only a small number of them post regularly.

Lists are like communities and often have their pet peeves, their unassailable truths, their opposing parties, and so on. You might experience some campaigning if someone is taking a poll or a vote. Rules of e-mail etiquette become especially important in a one-to-many forum such as a mailing list. Bear in mind that sarcasm and other subtleties that are so easy to communicate when face-to-face do not translate well in cold, hard, ASCII text. Try to say exactly what you mean and read things over before posting them. Ask yourself if what you've written might be misinterpreted. And if the subject is heated or emotional, then remember: an advantage of e-mail is you don't have to send it immediately. Write your post and put it aside to think it over for a while before you send it.

Chapter 8

USENET NEWS— READ ALL ABOUT IT

FEATURING

- **Understanding Usenet newsgroups**
- **Preparing your newsreader**
- **Reading and replying to articles**
- **Posting and crossposting**
- **Filtering out bozos**
- **Reading news with AOL, CompuServe, Microsoft Internet Explorer, Mosaic, NetCruiser, Netscape News, NewsWatcher, News Xpress, and Tin.**

For many people, Usenet *is* the Net. *Usenet* is a network of other networks, BBSs, and computers, all of which have made bilateral agreements with other members of Usenet to share and exchange news. So what's *news*? Usenet is divided up into *newsgroups* (topic areas). Newsgroups consist of articles posted by readers and contributors. The word *news* is confusing in this context because Usenet news articles are posted by whoever wants to write them, not by a staff of reporters. The term *news* suggests instead the habit of reading or skimming a daily newspaper every morning or evening.

If you have Internet access, you probably have access to Usenet. This chapter discusses what Usenet is and how you can read news yourself.

What Is Usenet?

As soon as I log in to my Internet account, I immediately check my mail. After that, I compulsively run my newsreader and skim the newsgroups that I'm currently hooked on. In a sense, Usenet is where I "hang out" on the Net. I'm on some mailing lists as well, but Usenet is the mother lode of discussion groups.

Sometimes fast-breaking real-world events appear on Usenet before they appear on TV or in the newspaper, but generally, Usenet is not the information source "of record" in the way some newspapers are. Look for tabloid-style gossip in `talk.rumors` or among the `alt.fan` groups (such as the tasteless `alt.fan.oj.drive-faster` group created, oh, about a year or so ago).

People post about what they find interesting; however, if you post to a newsgroup looking for information, you might be told to "go to a library" to look it up for yourself. Every newsgroup sees its share of posts that begin something like "I'm writing a high-school paper on..." and end with "... please reply to me by private e-mail, since I don't read this group."

> **WARNING** It's been said that the fastest way to get information on Usenet is to post incorrect information because people will immediately post to correct you or flood your e-mail In box with the correct information. I don't recommend this. People out there skimming the newsgroups might see only your erroneous post and none of the corrections, but it gives you an idea of the culture of Usenet.

On the other hand, there are plenty of *wizards* out there who believe there's no such thing as a dumb question and who are willing to share their knowledge with anyone who asks.

Some Newsgroups Are Mailing Lists, Too

Some Usenet newsgroups, particularly those which evolved from mailing lists, maintain a gateway with a list, so that all posts to the newsgroup or the list are shared between both. Even if you don't have Usenet access, you should still be able to join lists that share posts with Usenet newsgroups. See Chapter 7 for more on lists, and later in this chapter I'll explain how to post to Usenet through e-mail.

One Way Not to Look Like a Newbie

Not that there's anything wrong with looking like a newbie, but here's one way not to give yourself away (besides not confusing Usenet and the Internet): Call a newsgroup a newsgroup. Don't call it a forum, a board , a bboard, a SIG, an echo, a file, a conference, a list (well, except for the ones that are also lists), an America Online folder, or a Prodigy folder.

On the other hand, who cares if you do, besides Usenet snobs?

Where Everybody Knows Your Signature

Usenet has been called the biggest bulletin board in the world. It can be more entertaining than television (hard to imagine?). I think of it as an enormous magazine rack, filled with magazines, each of which have infinitely long letters-to-the-editor pages and no articles.

WARNING   Usenet is also an anarchy—with rules. Nobody reigns from above, but the entire community is knit together through customs, traditions, and netiquette. More and more, this culture is coming under attack, most recently by greedy advertisers who deliberately misinterpret the acceptable use of the medium. If you are interested in Usenet, take some time to familiarize yourself with the existing culture, so that you can become a *net.citizen* (or *netizen*) and not one of the *net.barbarians* beating down the gates.

It's also been referred to as a huge writing project, and enthusiasts claim that we are now involved in a renaissance of the written word, as a direct result of e-mail and Usenet communication.

Fundamentally, Usenet is a way to share information. Many newsgroups that are technically not part of the Usenet hierarchy flow through the same *servers* (computers that store and share news) and are passed along as part of the *newsfeed* (electronic mail pouch) from computer to computer not unlike other long-distance carriers traveling on AT&T wires.

Your provider is not obliged to supply you with a full newsfeed. Many networks carry an incomplete feed, usually more for reasons of disk-storage limitations than corporate censorship, though some of the more controversial `alt` groups certainly experience a limited distribution because of their topics. Many system administrators refuse to carry *binaries*, which generally contain huge posts, each post part of a large *binary file* (a program, image, or other special-format file—as opposed to a text file), as much because of the enormous storage requirements as because of the pornographic nature of some of those files.

Most providers do carry all of the newsgroups in the Usenet hierarchy proper, as there are complicated plebiscite mechanisms in place to limit the proliferation of new newsgroups. In the `alt` hierarchy, pranksters create joke newsgroups every week, some of which are probably carried only by those providers that carry everything. Though these groups may wither on the vine from disuse, old `alt` groups never die.

What Is a Newsgroup?

So what exactly is a newsgroup? A newsgroup is an area for posting articles on a given topic. The topic names are arranged hierarchically, which means everything branches off from the main hierarchies like in a directory tree (This image is a familiar one to Windows' users who work in File Manager), so people can look for and find newsgroups of interest in a systematic way. This means, for example, that there's no newsgroup called `nintendo`, nor is there one called `rec.nintendo`, but there is one called `rec.games.nintendo`.

There are seven official Usenet hierarchies: `comp`, `misc`, `news`, `rec`, `sci`, `soc`, and `talk`, along with some "unofficial" ones (some of which are listed in the table below).

Newsgroup Hierarchy	Meaning
comp	Computers—from the extremely technical to help for beginners to geek wars between Mac enthusiasts and Amiga diehards
misc	Miscellaneous—anything that doesn't fit into the other hierarchies
news	News—information about Usenet itself, discussion of new newsgroups, advice for Usenet newbies

Continued on next page ➜

Newsgroup Hierarchy	Meaning
rec	Recreation—games, sports, music, entertainment, etc.
sci	Science—discussions of research, developments, techniques, policy
soc	Social—both in the sense of socializing and in the sense of talking about society
talk	Talk—some think this hierarchy should be called "argue"; these newsgroups house some of the eternally polarized debates, such as those on gun control and abortion
alt	Alternative—topics that don't fit into the mainstream newsgroups
bitnet	Bitnet listservs—for newsgroups gated to bitnet listservs
bionet	Biologists
biz	Business—advertising explicitly acceptable
gnu	Free Software Project
k12	Education—grade-school students, teachers, parents, etc.
local hierarchies	Geographical regions—examples include, ca for California, uk for United Kingdom, and de for Germany (Deutschland)

why.group.names.look.weird

Newsgroup names are in the form of two or more words or abbreviations, separated by periods. Figure 8.1 shows the start of the full list of newsgroups that you can subscribe to and a window with the group that my friend Nick subscribes to. The other window shows what new newsgroups have been created since Nick last logged in.

NOTE

So how do you pronounce these names? Remember, you pronounce a period "dot," so that `comp.sys.mac.games` is pronounced "comp-dot-sys-dot-mac-dot-games." While that's the traditional pronunciation, many people drop the "dots;" for instance, they would pronounce that newsgroup's name "comp-sys-mac-games." Regulars in a newsgroup often refer to the group by its initials—"c.s.m.g" or "csmg" or "CSMG," for example. Soc—one of the seven major newsgroup hierarchies—can be pronounced "soak" or "soash."

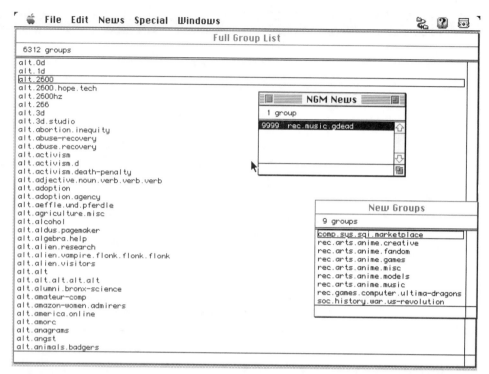

FIGURE 8.1: Nick subscribes to this group. (What's shown is a window in the Mac NewsWatcher program.) Notice how the newsgroups' names provide a way to organize the groups into hierarchies.

The words between the dots correspond to directories on the machines (usually Unix boxes) that store the Usenet postings. If more than one word is needed to describe something, the two words are joined by hyphens, not periods. There can be at most fifteen characters between two periods.

Newsgroup Names Are Not Always Obvious   Unfortunately, the hierarchical system does not always help you find the newsgroup you're looking for. For instance, the jazz newsgroup is called `rec.music.bluenote`—look for the perennial "rap is not music" flame war there. Likewise, you'd never know that the newsgroup `alt.fan.warlord` is devoted to reposting and spoofing monstrous signatures from other Usenet newsgroups, especially those with ASCII art such as enormous swords, crude Bart Simpsons, and maps of Australia with Perth pointed out on them. (Read that newsgroup to find out what "tab damage" is.) Sometimes you have to ask around a bit.

Especially in the `alt` hierarchy, sometimes two or more newsgroups will cover the same topics but have slightly different names. There's `alt.coffee`, `alt.food.coffee`, and `alt.drugs.caffeine`. (Purists hate to see a specific word like coffee as a first-level hierarchical distinction, but coffee lovers know that coffee is a basic element of life—comparable to music and sex.) A similar debate surrounded the formation of the newsgroups named `alt.philosophy.zen`, `alt.religion.zen`, and `alt.zen`.

What Kinds of Groups Are Out There?

This is just a brief sampling of the sorts of topics that are discussed on Usenet. There are over 11,000 newsgroups, and more are being created all the time.

There are newsgroups on art, entertainment, writing, just about every hobby you can imagine, games, sports, sex, politics, pets, science, school, computers, television shows, music, theater, cooking, want ads, religion, *net.personalities,* and so on.

Since most of the original Usenet readers were scientists, researchers, or computer programmers, the range of topics available on Usenet is still skewed toward techie interests, even among recreational topics. There are at least seven newsgroups devoted to some aspect of Star Trek, including one called `alt.sex.fetish.startrek`. The `misc.writing` newsgroup leans heavily towards science fiction and fantasy writing. And, of course, there are entire hierarchies devoted to computers and science.

If you can't find a newsgroup on the specific topic you're interested in, look for a more general newsgroup whose topic would include yours. Then post to that group about the subject you're interested in. Someone may point you toward a mailing list. Or you'll start a series of threads about your subject. If the interest is high enough, you can look into creating a splinter newsgroup for your particular interest. There is a long-standing procedure for broaching this topic on the Net. You start with a *request for discussion*—of course, there's an acronym for that too, *RFD*—and work up to a *call for votes* (*CFV*).

What Is an Article?

An article, also called a *post*, is a message sent to a newsgroup. Posts are very similar to e-mail messages, although the header information at the top is different. An article can be posted apropos of nothing or as a reply in regard to a previous post. A series of articles and replies is called a *thread*.

Eventually articles expire, meaning they are deleted from the directory in which they are stored. How long after they were posted varies from site to site. On my system, articles expire after two weeks. When you start reading a newsgroup for the first time, your newsreader program might tell you that it's "skipping unavailable articles" or something like that. This means that some of the posted articles have expired.

You can also cancel your own articles after you post them (though you can't cancel anyone else's). This won't prevent some people from seeing the canceled article in the meantime because some machines will already have propagated it beyond your network's server. Eventually, it will disappear from cyberspace, but the cancel message has to follow the thread of the original post.

Common Acronyms

Inevitably, as you start reading Usenet newsgroups, you'll notice certain acronyms showing up in posts. Most of these have come about as a way to save typing, although others were invented as jokes or to sow confusion. Some are used as disclaimers. You'll often see *IMHO* (in my humble opinion) attached to comments that are anything but. I'm waiting for *IMOO* (in my obsequious opinion) and *IMUO* (in my unctuous opinion) and a host of others, but I haven't seen them yet. Here's a brief and arbitrary listing of some common acronyms:

Acronym	What It Stands For
BTW	By the way
FAQ	Frequently asked questions
FOAF	Friend of a friend
FQA	Frequently questioned acronyms
FUQ	Frequently unanswered questions
FWIW	For what it's worth
IMO	In my opinion
IMHO	In my humble opinion
IMNSHO	In my not-so-humble opinion
LOL	Laughing out loud
MOTAS	Member of the appropriate sex
MOTOS	Member of the opposite sex
MOTSS	Member of the same sex
ROTFL	Rolling on the floor laughing
SO	Significant other
UL	Urban legend
WRT	With respect to
YMMV	Your mileage may vary

What Is a Newsreader?

A *newsreader* is a program you run to read Usenet news. With any newsreader you can:

- See which newsgroups are available
- Subscribe to newsgroups
- Read articles in a newsgroup
- Post articles to a newsgroup

There are many popular newsreader programs. Later in this chapter I'll explain basic newsreading principles and then explain the details of using a couple of the more popular newsreaders. I'll also show you how to use a Web browser as a newsreader.

> **TIP**
>
> Remember when you're reading Usenet that not everyone else is seeing the exact same things that you are seeing. Other readers may be getting their feed more slowly or their articles in a different order. They may be reading a newsreader with a different number of characters per line or with different keyboard shortcuts from yours.

Usenet as a Public Forum

While not completely public, Usenet is essentially a public forum, and you should consider anything you post to have been published. Your words may be noted or ignored by thousands or hundreds of thousands of readers. Anything you write will be available to strangers anywhere in the world. Some people say you should never post anything to the Net that you wouldn't want to see on the front page of a newspaper.

> **WARNING**
>
> For the same reason, you probably should not put your telephone number in your .signature file or in your posts in general. While strangers still might be able to figure out your phone number if you give your name and address or by fingering your account or looking you up in the membership directory of your online service, at least you will not seem to be inviting people to call.

Semi-Anonymity on the Net

Because you'll never see the vast majority of people whose posts you read on the Net, this creates a veil of semi-anonymity. Because of this, people fly off the handle more easily, misunderstandings proliferate, and people simply behave in ways that would be much more difficult, if not impossible, in a face-to-face encounter. Bear that in mind and try to ignore the occasional vicious, unprovoked attack.

> **NOTE** This *semi-anonymity* I speak of should not be confused with true *anonymity*, which can be used to disguise the origins of a post or e-mail message.

Unfortunately, this same semi-anonymity makes it possible for losers to harass females (or anyone with a female-sounding name) on the Net. For this reason, some women may prefer to use a genderless login or real name when posting.

How People Identify You on Usenet

There are three ways people can identify you on Usenet. The first is by your e-mail address, or at least the login part of it before the @ sign. The second is by your real name. This will appear in the author column of the article listing in a newsreader (although some put the e-mail address there). Third, people will see your .signature file, if you have one, attached to the end of your posts.

Being a Good Netizen

Try to get yourself up to speed before you start contributing to Usenet. Read the newsgroups you're interested in for a while to get caught up and avoid posting something that's been repeated so often it's become nearly a mantra in that group.

Also, read the newsgroup's FAQ before jumping in. One of the purposes of a frequently-asked-questions list is to save people the trouble of answering the same few questions over and over to the end of time. A newsgroup's FAQ will be posted to the newsgroup on a regular basis, anywhere from every two weeks to every two months. FAQs are built and maintained by volunteers, just like every other institutional aspect of Usenet.

Shooting Stars and net.spewers

Once you've been reading a newsgroup long enough, you will recognize a certain phenomenon of the eager new contributor. This should not be confused with the

September flood of new .edu postings from university students with their first Internet accounts. When a new contributor starts posting to a group, often they will spew hundreds of posts, following up every thread that's around and attempting to start new ones. (I'm not really criticizing, I did this exact thing myself.) Eventually, though, they will run out of the bottled-up ideas that have been waiting years for an audience and settle down to become regular or occasional contributors.

Reading a group without posting is called *lurking*, and there's no shame in it. It's easy to forget that many people are lurking out there and to think in terms of the few hundred or more people who post regularly, but most newsgroups have more lurkers than contributors.

There are also a set of answers newsgroups—`misc.answers`, `comp.answers`, `rec.answers`, etc.—which consist only of posted and reposted FAQs (and similar informational postings). Look there if you can't find the one you need. You can also FTP to `rtfm.mit.edu` and look in the /pub/usenet-by-group directory for FAQs. Chapter 11 explains FTP.

A newsgroup is a sort of community. The people in the group interact with each other in a recognizable way. Once you are familiar with the dynamics of a newsgroup, you will find it easier to contribute. Remember that, just as with mailing lists, sarcasm and other subtleties of spoken communication do not translate well into black-and-white text. Try to say exactly what you mean and read things over before posting them. Ask yourself if what you've written might be misinterpreted.

Getting Help

If there's something going on with Usenet, or your feed, or your newsreader, just ask people flat out. Sure, some people will tell you to *RTFM* (read the f***ing manual) or call you a *clueless newbie,* but we were all clueless newbies once and most manuals are tortuous to read. Just go ahead and ask. Some people are very kind.

So enough on the "what" of Usenet—on to the "how." You'll learn much more about the Net through the medium of Usenet itself than I could ever tell you.

The Quality of Usenet

When newsgroups get very popular or are filled with single-thread posts asking general or repetitive questions, they are said to have a low *signal-to-noise ratio*. To deal with this, some newsgroups are moderated. Usually, they will have the word *moderated* at the end of the newsgroup name (as in `soc.history.moderated`), but not always (as in `alt.folklore.suburban`, the moderated version of `alt.folklore.urban`. This means that all posts first go to a volunteer moderator, who decides if they are on-topic and then posts those articles to the newsgroup. However, some people prefer the messiness of open debate to the clarity of moderated discussion.

You will also notice that the quality of writing varies greatly from post to post. Some people are just better writers (or better fast writers) and some people are in too much of a hurry to worry about style or typos. Editing messages with Unix tools can be frustrating, and there is a certain amount of tolerance for typos and common errors, such as confusing *they're* and *their*, or spelling seperate *separate*. It's considered very bad form to correct someone's spelling or usage—it implies that you are not equipped to counter the substance of their post.

Imminent Death of the Net Predicted
—Film at 11

With participation in the Internet, and Usenet, growing at an exponential rate, there is never a shortage of Chicken Littles out there decrying the state of the Net now that the philistines have arrived and predicting the imminent demise of the medium. Such dire warnings have become so common, and reports of the Net's death have been so often exaggerated, that the expression "Imminent Death of the Net Predicted—Film at 11" has arisen to parody the jeremiads. Sometimes the "—Film at 11" tag is also appended to old news that's been breathlessly posted to the Net as if it's timely.

The type of writing done on Usenet is different from other kinds of writing. In some ways it is closer to spoken language—especially in its immediacy and informality. It is also constrained by typical line lengths and screen heights. An idea that can be expressed in one screenful is more likely to convince people than one that drags on for ten. If you spend time reading Usenet, you'll see that there are some experts out there who are quite adept at this new medium of communication.

How to Read Newsgroups

Before I get into the details of newsreading, let me mention that your newsreader program will probably seem complicated at first—the screen display won't totally make sense, you'll have to memorize a new set of commands, and so on. Try not to let this discourage you. You'll be over the threshold in no time, and once you've set things up, you'll do most of your newsreading by just pressing a few keys over and over.

Nevertheless, newsreading is more or less the same no matter what program you use to do it. As with e-mail, I'll first sketch out the generic newsreading process—the things you'll do no matter what newsreader you use. Then I'll explain the specifics about several of the most popular programs.

> **TIP**
> You can also search Usenet newsgroups with some Web search engines, such as DejaNews, as explained in Chapter 5. Another Web site from which you can search Usenet is called the NetNews Overview Index (`http://harvest.cs.colorado.edu/Harvest/brokers/Usenet/query.html`).

Net News by Mail—If You Don't Have Usenet Access

If your system does not provide you with Usenet access, you can still read newsgroups and even post articles via e-mail. In general, these methods don't support all newsgroups, though many will.

This alternative is easiest for newsgroups that are gated to mailing lists. With them, you subscribe to the list or digest and read and post as you would with any mailing list (see Chapter 7 for more on mailing lists). To receive a list of mailing lists that are gated to newsgroups, FTP to `rtfm.mit.edu`, go to the `/pub/usenet-by group/ news.announce.newgroups` directory and get the files `Mailing_Lists_Available_in_Usenet` and `Changes_to_Mailing_Lists_Available_in_Usenet` (FTP is explained in Chapter 10).

To read newsgroups via e-mail, send mail to `listserv@ccl.kuleuven.ac.be` with only **/nnhelp** in the body of your message (delete your signature too). You'll receive an informational file telling you how the listserv/usenet gateway works. Read this carefully before starting and then save it for future reference. Start off by replying to the listserv mail with just **/newsgroups** in the body of your mail. You'll be sent a list of groups. To subscribe to one, reply to the mail, deleting all extraneous text and keeping only the **/group lines** for newsgroups you want to read. Next you'll be sent mail including a list of available articles. Again reply, delete as much as you can, and keep the **/article lines** for articles you want to read.

Another way to read Net news by e-mail is to subscribe to a filtering service. To do so, first send mail to `netnews@db.stanford.edu` with any subject in the Subject: line (blank is fine) and only **help** in the body of the message. You'll be sent an introductory file. Essentially, you will send mail to the same address with any subject entered on the Subject: line (blank is okay), and include the lines

```
subscribe keyword1 keyword2 etc.
period n
end
```

Choose your keywords carefully to limit the mail you get. The number *n* is the number of days between mailings to you. You'll receive the first twenty lines of any Usenet articles that contain enough of your keywords to be a possible match. If you want an entire article, you can send another message with the line **get news.*group.name.article-number***. You'll find the group name and article number in the Subject: line of the article abstract.

If you have a Web browser (see Chapter 4), you can point it at `http://sift.stanford.edu` and subscribe to the news filtering service by filling out a form, a much simpler alternative.

Finally, if you want to post to a Usenet newsgroup via e-mail, send your article to one of the following addresses:

```
newsgroup-name@cs.utexas.edu
newsgroup-name@news.demon.co.uk
newsgroup.name.usenet@decwrl.dec.com
newsgroup.name@undergrad.math.uwaterloo.ca
newsgroup.name@nic.funet.fi
```

Use dots or hyphens as indicated above in the username portion of the address.

Newsreading Basics

Here are the basic things you'll do with any newsreader:

0. (That's right, step zero.) Prepare the newsreader and set up a reading list with which to start.
1. Start the newsreader.
2. Select a newsgroup to read.
3. Select articles to read.

4. Browse the articles:
   - Read articles.
   - Save articles.
   - Reply to articles via e-mail.
5. Post responses.
6. Start a new thread.
7. Quit the newsreader.

Also, you'll want to know how to get help when you need it, how to *crosspost* (post an article to more than one newsgroup at a time) and how to filter out bozos (although not all newsreaders can do this for you).

Preparing the Newsreader

Before your newsreader can pick up and sort out new articles for you, it has to know where to look. This means you have to do a little set up on your newsreader, which is somewhat analogous to the sort of information you put into a mail program so *it* knows where to look. There are two categories of information you have to supply: (1) the name of the news server you have access to *and* (2) your identity.

Obviously, you can't be expected to know the name of the news server off the top of your head. Your provider will have to supply it for you. In some cases, such as with online services, you don't have to do this, as all the appropriate information is automatically supplied. As for your identity, this is exactly the same information as with an e-mail program: you supply your "real name," your e-mail address, and the address of the mail server that handles your outgoing mail, so you can reply to newsgroup posts by mail when you want to reply directly to the poster. You can look this information up in the Preferences or Options dialog box of your mail program. (See Chapter 2 for more about setting up and using mail programs.)

Also, the first time you run your newsreader, it doesn't know what you want to read about: Fly fishing or macrobiotic cooking? Urban legends or international conspiracies? So you're stuck with a massive all-or-nothing problem. Some newsreaders start you off with a subscription to every single newsgroup, leaving it up to you to unsubscribe to the ones you don't want to read.

> **TIP**
>
> The process of subscribing or unsubscribing to newsgroups is instantaneous and completely reversible. Your list of newsgroups will most likely shrink and grow in some organic fashion. You'll realize that you never read certain groups and possibly unsubscribe to them. You'll hear about new ones and add them.

Others start you off without subscribing you to any newsgroups. You then browse through a list and add the newsgroups you're interested in. I think this is the better approach. If a newsreader starts you off with no groups, you'll be asked if you want to download an up-to-date list of groups. Say yes, but then go have lunch or something, because it will take a while. When the list is complete, you can usually search for and subscribe to groups by entering key words to select the groups you want.

In newsreaders that subscribe you to every group automatically, you're best off finding the .newsrc file (or whatever it's called in your program) and editing it, changing every colon (indicating a subscribed group) to an exclamation point (indicating an unsubscribed one).

Starting the Newsreader

Starting the newsreader is just a matter of clicking on an icon (for a Windows or Mac newsreader) or typing a short Unix command and pressing Enter. In most cases, when you start the program, it will let you know if any new newsgroups have been created since you last ran it. You can subscribe to any of the new groups at this point.

Selecting a Newsgroup

The newsreader will show you a list of the newsgroups you subscribe to and allow you to choose one to start reading. If you want to add a newsgroup to your available list, you can either search for it or add it if you know its exact name.

Selecting Articles

Once you've chosen a newsgroup to read, you'll be shown a list of the unread articles in the newsgroup, listed by subject line and usually author as well. (Some newsreaders may just show you the first unread article.) You can select, ignore, or delete articles.

Many newsreaders provide filtering capabilities, so you can screen out topics and authors or autoselect some you're especially interested in.

Browsing the Articles

Once you've selected some articles (or the first article), you can start reading. The first article you selected will appear on the screen. It will start with a bunch of header lines, similar to those in an e-mail message. The article itself starts after a blank line. Figure 8.2 shows the first screen of an article I selected in the `rec.humor.oracle` newsgroup.

If you get way behind in reading the articles in a newsgroup and don't want to wade through all the intervening posts, you can usually catch up by marking all current articles as read.

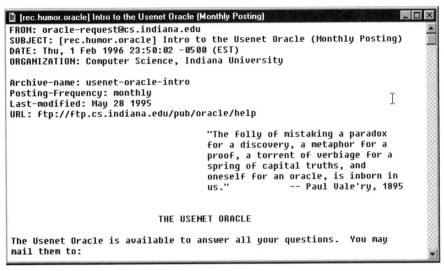

FIGURE 8.2: Reading an article with News Xpress

Reading Articles You can scroll through an article if it's longer than one screenful (or, in most programs, press the Spacebar to jump down one screen at a time).

What Does *Ob* Mean?

You may notice at the end of some posts, a cryptic line starting with *Ob*, such as ObDylan. The Ob stands for obligatory. The idea is that if you post something to a newsgroup, there must always be some content relevant to the topic of the group. When a post seems to lack that sort of content, the author will add an obligatory comment or quotation to satisfy the requirement. This is usually done partly tongue in cheek.

Saving Articles If an article looks interesting, you can mark it as *Unread* (most newsgroups delete articles after you read them—if your newsgroup doesn't, simply don't delete any article you want to read later). If you actually want to save it to a file to read later or to store, you can use the newsreader's Save command.

When I say that you're deleting articles, I mean that you are deleting them only from your list of unread articles. You are not actually deleting them from their source or even from the newsfeed that supplies your newsreader.

Replying to Articles There are two ways to reply to someone's post. One way is to post a follow-up article, including some or none of the previous post, and appending your comments. The other way is to send e-mail to the poster directly to discuss the post further. You have to decide when your follow-up is appropriate for the entire newsgroup (the thousands of invisible readers) or for the one person whose ideas caught your fancy.

WARNING **If somebody's post angers you, think twice before dashing off a reply, especially if you intend to post the reply to the entire group. It is easy to take people's writings in a spirit different from the intent of the writer. Most disagreements can be worked out more easily in private e-mail than in gladiatorial contests in front of the rest of the group. Angry, insulting posts are called *flames*.**

When you post a response to an article, your post becomes part of the thread of the original article. Usually, you keep the same subject line, although you can edit it if you like. As with replying by e-mail, you also have the choice of including the text of the preceding article or not.

If you include text from the article you're responding to, be sure to trim it down to the minimum amount of text necessary to give the context of your reply. It's just as bad form to quote an entire long message—just to add your own short reply—as it is to post a reply without any context at all, so the meaning is lost.

When replying, some newsreaders will give you a last chance to change your mind and not post. Some will even try to convince you not to, to save the resources of the Net.

TIP **If you're using a newsreader that doesn't handle word-wrapping for you, keep your lines down to 75 characters each (or 80 at the most). Many people, probably including you, can only get 80 characters on the screen at once, and any more will wrap to the next line and look bizarre. I recommend 75 instead of 80 so people can quote you without starting the bad-wrap problem.**

When you reply to the author of an article by e-mail, you also have the option, in most newsreaders, to quote the text of the post you're responding to. Your newsreader will then allow you to write and edit an e-mail message as usual, placing you into some sort of text editor. When you are done, exit the text editor if necessary and then send the mail.

> **NOTE**
>
> Not everyone's postings point back to their e-mail addresses properly. Sometimes, when you try to reply to a post via e-mail, the message "bounces." If so, it's probably not your fault.

Ignoring Flamers and Putting the R back in James R. Kirk

Arguments that rage on for a while or that become more and more incoherent or *ad hominem* are called *flame wars*. After you've been on the Net for a while you'll recognize flame wars in the making and learn how to avoid them. They might be entertaining at first, but they follow such regular patterns that they inevitably become boring.

Some people enjoy flaming and causing flame wars, so they post deliberately inflammatory articles designed to incite others. Such posts are called *flame bait*. Often the instigator will drop out of the conversation and watch how long the fire rages on its own. You'll also learn to recognize flame bait after awhile. By then, other newbies will be taking up the gauntlet every time it's thrown down.

A more subtle *net.pastime* than flame-baiting is called *trolling*. To troll is to deliberately post information so egregiously incorrect that most people will see that it's a joke. However, those with a strong desire to correct people and go on record with the right information will post follow-ups insisting that Bing Crosby and David Crosby are *not* actually father and son. (Everyone knows that David Crosby's father is Bill Cosby.)

Starting a New Thread

In any newsreader, there will be a separate command for posting a new article without any reference to previous posts. Use this command for starting a new thread, although it may grow no longer than your one post. (Even interesting posts do not always evoke follow-ups or e-mail replies.)

Quitting the Newsreader

When you are finished reading news (for now), it's time to quit the newsreader. (For information on your specific newsreader, see the section on *Reading News with Specific Newsreaders* later in the chapter.) If you've mucked things up and deleted articles you still want to read, you can usually quit without saving any changes made during the current session.

Getting Help and Avoiding Problems

Most newsreaders have some kind of help feature, even if it's only a list of available commands. If you're stuck, try looking for a Help menu or pressing **h** or **?**.

If you've deleted articles by mistake or done anything else to change the newsgroups you subscribe to or the articles you've read, and you want to scrap all your changes and go back to the way things were before you ran the newsreader, you can usually quit without saving your changes.

In a worst-case scenario, you can open up your .newsrc file in a text editor and edit it.

Some Advanced Stuff You Should Know

Here are some things you might not want to do right away but with which you should at least be familiar.

Crossposting

You can post articles to more than one newsgroup—if they are relevant to all of them. This is better than posting the same article more than once, because it will be stored only in one place even though it will be available to all the newsgroups it's posted to.

If you follow up someone else's article, be sure to check which newsgroups your reply is going to and edit the line (or the Follow-up line) if necessary. Look out for pranksters who've directed follow-ups to ***.test** newsgroups. Newsgroups such as **misc.test, alt.test**, and so on, exist so that you can test the propagation of articles that you post through your newsreader. If you post to them (on purpose or accidentally), automated Unix programs called *daemons* will send you e-mail verifying that your posts are getting through. Your mailbox can easily overflow as daemons from around the world send you electronic postcards.

NOTE   Articles can also have a Follow-up line that specifies different newsgroups from the ones it was originally posted to.

Killing and Autoselecting

Not all newsreaders allow you to kill or autoselect posts automatically, but the best ones do. The file of automatic commands that gets created when you do this is called a *killfile,* because most people use them to filter out unwanted posts, not to automatically select their favorite topics and authors. Killfiles are also sometimes called *bozo filters* since they allow you to filter out some of the bozos who fill newsgroups with their bleatings.

Reading News with Specific Newsreaders

The main distinction worth noting between newsreaders is whether they are *threaded* or *unthreaded*. Because they allow you to follow conversations from post to reply to follow-up, threaded newsreaders are better than unthreaded ones. Unthreaded newsreaders don't keep track of which posts are related to which. You have to figure this out from the context of the post or from the quoted text at the beginnings of some of them.

You can also read news through any of the online services, more or less the same way you read their local forums. Time for a couple of mild warnings: First, the ease with which an integrated "look and feel" allows you to jump into Usenet can be misleading. Old-timers are irritated when someone from an online service implies that Usenet is "part of AOL" or "just another folder on Prodigy, the world's largest online service™" or shows a blatant ignorance of Usenet or a seeming unwillingness to learn. In general, tread lightly and read your own posts to make sure they're coming out the way you intended.

The last distinction is between *offline* newsreaders and *online* newsreaders. Offline newsreaders download all the current articles in all the newsgroups you subscribe to and then log off. You can browse through the downloaded posts at your leisure without running up your phone bill or connect-time charges, compose posts and replies, and then log in again to send your replies. Still, offline newsreaders function more or less the same way online readers do, from your perspective.

If you plan to use a stand-alone newsreader with a network or dial-up connection and a PC or Macintosh, you'll have many options, some of which are free. In this section, I'll cover one for each of those two types of computers: NewsWatcher for the Macintosh and News Xpress for Windows. I'll tell you where to get those programs (they're free!) and I'll also name a couple of others and tell you where to get them so you can compare for yourself if you'd like.

AOL

AOL offers access to newsgroups in much the same way that it offers access to its own local bulletin boards. Since AOL is an all-in-one package, you don't have do any technical setup to get going reading news. You start by choosing newsgroups to read.

Selecting a Newsgroup to Read

To read newsgroups with AOL, first click on the Internet Connection button in the Main Menu window. Then click on the News Groups button.

To add newsgroups to your subscription list, click on the Add Newsgroups button in the Newsgroups dialog box (see Figure 8.3).

> **TIP**
>
> **The Add Newsgroups button gives you access to a selected number of newsgroups, excluding some of the racier ones, for example. You can also click on the Expert Add button to add any group if you know its exact name.**

This brings up the Add Newsgroups - Categories dialog box. Newsgroups are listed by plain English descriptions as well as by their top-level hierarchies. Double-click a category to see the subchoices associated with it. Repeat this process until you've zeroed in on a specific group. So, for example, to find your way to the `news.announce.newusers` newsgroup, you'd first choose the `news.*` choice, and then the `news.announce` choice, and finally the spelled-out Explanatory Postings for New Users choice.)

> **TIP**
>
> **If you'd prefer to see the Internet names of list newsgroups, click on the Internet Names button above the list.**

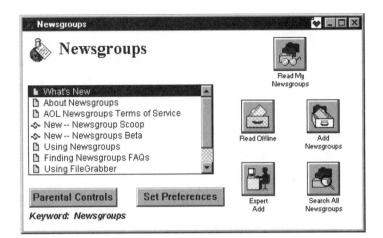

FIGURE 8.3:
AOL's
Newsgroups
dialog box

When you arrive at a group you want to read, click on the Add button to subscribe to it or click on the List Subjects button to immediately see its contents.

To go directly to your subscribed newsgroups instead of looking to add new ones, click on the Read My Newsgroups button in the Newsgroups dialog box.

To see the articles in a newsgroup you've subscribed to, click on the List Unread button in the bottom-left corner of the Read My Newsgroup dialog box.

Browsing the Articles

To read an article, double-click its subject or click on it and then click on the Read button (see Figure 8.4).

Then just scroll through the message area in the window that appears. To read the next article in a thread, click on the "Next–>" button.

To save an article so you can re-read it later, click on the Mark Unread button.

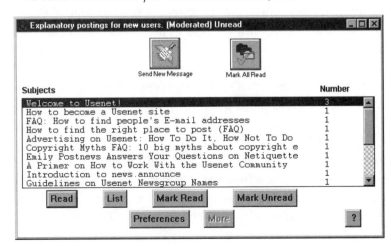

FIGURE 8.4:
Choose an article to read in a newsgroup's dialog box and then click on the Read button.

Replying to Articles

If you want to reply to an article, select the portion of it that you wish to quote in your reply and then click on the Reply to Group or E-Mail Author button. AOL will create a new message window for you with the selected portion of the original article already included. Write your reply and then click on the Send button.

Starting a New Thread

To post a new article to a newsgroup, click on the Send New Message button in the newsgroup or article window.

Closing a Newsgroup

When you're ready to quit reading news, just close all the windows you've opened related to newsgroups.

Getting Help

To get help, click on the ? button in the newsgroup or article window.

> **NOTE** AOL has no provision for crossposting or for filtering out unwanted authors or article threads.

CompuServe

CompuServe offers access to newsgroups built into its CIM (CompuServe Information Manager) interface. You don't have do any technical setup to get going reading news. You start by choosing newsgroups to read. (See the general information under *Reading News with Specific Newsreaders* earlier in this part of the chapter for some additional advice.)

It's also possible to read news with CompuServe using the version of Mosaic that comes with the package or using another external newsreader. See the entries for Mosaic, MS Internet Explorer, and Netscape News for more details.

Selecting a Newsgroup to Read

To read newsgroups with CompuServe, first click on the Internet button in the main window, or select Services ➢ Go, type **Internet**, and press Enter. Click on the Discussion Groups (Usenet) button in the Internet dialog box. Then choose USENET Newsreader (CIM) in the USENET Newsgroups dialog box and click on the Select button.

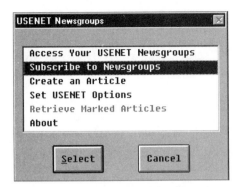

The toolbar will reduce itself to a few relevant buttons and it will take a few moments (more the first time) before CompuServe is ready to continue. A new USENET Newsgroups dialog box will appear. To add newsgroups to your subscription list, choose Subscribe to Newsgroups in the dialog box and click on the Select button.

This brings up the Subscribe to Newsgroups dialog box. Newsgroups are listed by plain English descriptions as well as their top-level hierarchies (see Figure 8.5).

You can also type a key word in the Keywords box to search for newsgroups containing that word.

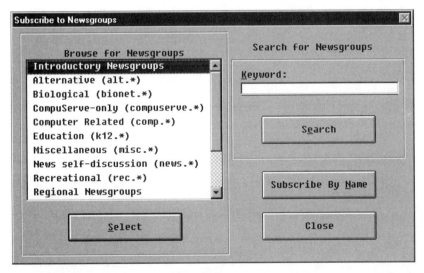

FIGURE 8.5: CompuServe's Subscribe to Newsgroups dialog box

Double-click on a category to see the newsgroups in it. Click on the check box next to the name of a group to select it, click on the Subscribe button, and then click on OK in the dialog box that appears. When you are done selecting groups in a category, click on the Cancel button. Repeat the process with other categories if you wish. Click on the Close button in the Subscribe to Newsgroups dialog box when you are done choosing categories.

TIP To subscribe to a group directly (if you know its exact name), click on the Subscribe by Name button, type the name, and press Enter.

To go directly to your subscribed newsgroups instead of first adding new ones, choose Access Your USENET Newsgroups in the USENET Newsgroups dialog box and then click on the Select button.

To see the articles in a newsgroup you've subscribed to, click on the Browse button in the bottom-left corner of the Access Newsgroup dialog box.

Browsing the Articles

To read an article, double-click on its subject or click on it and then on the Get button (see Figure 8.6).

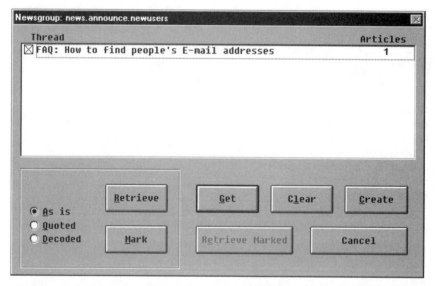

FIGURE 8.6: Choose an article to read in a Newsgroup dialog box and then click on the Get button.

TIP You can mark a number of articles and then get them all at once.

When you want to read an article, just scroll through the message area in the window that appears. To read the next article in a thread, click on the $>$ button under Article. To read the next thread, click on the $>$ button under Thread.

To save an article so you can re-read it later, click on the Hold button.

Replying to Articles

If you want to reply to an article, first select and copy (Ctrl+C) the portion of the article you wish to quote. Then click on the Reply button. CompuServe will create a new message window for you with the selected portion of the original article already included for context. Uncheck the Send via E-mail option if you don't want to send your reply directly to the original sender, and check the Post to Newsgroup(s) option to post your reply. By default, CompuServe will check off the current newsgroup's name in the Newsgroups' area, but you can select any of your subscribed newsgroups. If you select more than one, your article will be crossposted to all of the selected groups.

Write your reply, making it clear that you are quoting an earlier message, and then click on the Send button.

Starting a New Thread

To post a new article to a newsgroup, click on the Create button in the main Newsgroup dialog box. (If you've got an article window blocking the original Newsgroup dialog box, click on the Cancel button first.). Type a subject in the subject box. After typing your article, click on the Send button.

Closing a Newsgroup

When you're ready to quit reading news, click on the Leave button.

Getting Help

To get help, click on the ? button on the toolbar.

NOTE CompuServe has no provision for filtering out unwanted authors or article threads.

Microsoft Internet Explorer

Internet Explorer can function as an adequate newsreader for a network or dial-up account (or for the Microsoft Network, for that matter).

Preparing the Newsreader

Before you can use Internet Explorer as a newsreader, you have to find out what news server you have access to. (Ask your system administrator or service provider). Then, select View ➤ Options and click on the News tab in the Options dialog box (see Figure 8.7). Check the Use Internet Explorer to Read Internet Newsgroups option at the top of the dialog box. Press Tab and then type the address of your news server into the News Server Address box. In the Posting area, click in the Name box, type your name, press Tab, and then type your e-mail address. Then click on OK.

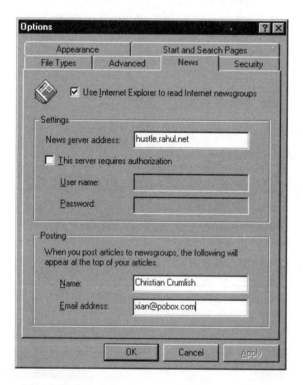

FIGURE 8.7:
The News tab of Internet Explorer's Options dialog box

Reading News

 To start reading news, either click on the Read Newsgroups button or select Go ➤ Read Newsgroups.

Internet Explorer will download the current, complete list of groups from your news server and display them in a window, with each group as a hypertext link.

Selecting a Newsgroup

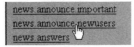

To select a newsgroup, just click on its name.

Internet Explorer will display a list of subject articles (including subject and author name).

You can go directly to a specific newsgroup by typing its address into the Address box, in the format **news:*news.group.name***, and pressing Enter.

Browsing the Articles

Just scroll through the list looking for articles you'd like to read. To read an article, click on its subject or author's name. Internet Explorer will display the article (see Figure 8.8).

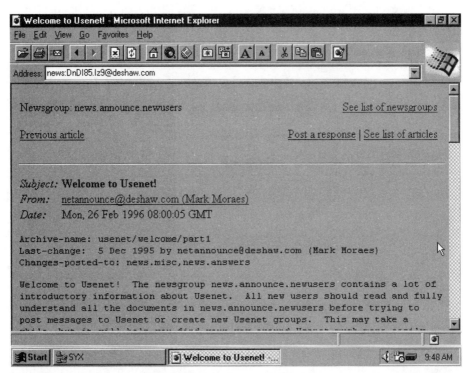

FIGURE 8.8: A newsgroup article displayed in Internet Explorer

WARNING There's no way to mark an article as Unread with Internet Explorer.

To go to the next article, click on the Next Article link. To return to the list of articles, click on the See List of Articles link. To return to the newsgroup list, click on the See List of Newsgroups link.

Replying to Articles

If you want to reply to an article by e-mail, click on the author's name in the From: header line. Internet Explorer will launch your mail program (or switch to it if it's already running) and open a new message window. Send mail as explained in Chapter 2. To quote from the article, copy text from the Internet Explorer window and paste it into your mail program's message window.

If, however, you want to post a reply to the newsgroup, click on the Post a Response link. Internet Explorer will open a new Post to Newsgroups window with the contents of the original article already quoted in the message area. To crosspost to more than one newsgroup, type additional newsgroup names, separated by commas, in the Newsgroups box at the top of the window. Type your message (remember to reduce the quoted material as much as possible but leave enough for appropriate context) and then click on the Post button.

Starting a New Thread

When you're ready to post a new message to the newsgroup, click on the Post a Message link from the List of Articles page. Internet Explorer will open a new Post to Newsgroups window with the name of the current newsgroup already entered and all the other boxes blank. Enter a subject in the Subject box and type your article in the message area. Then click on the Post button.

Quitting the Newsreader

To quit reading news with Internet Explorer, just quit the program or enter a Web address in the address box and press Enter.

WARNING Internet Explorer has no provision for killing or autoselecting articles, authors, or threads.

Mosaic

Mosaic offers basic newsreading capabilities. If you want to read news with a Web browser, though, you might find the Netscape interface preferable.

Preparing the Newsreader

Before you can use Mosaic as a newsreader, you have to find out what news server you have access to (your system administrator or service provider can tell you). Then, select Options ➢ Preferences and click on the News tab in the Preferences dialog box. Click in the NNTP Server box. After pressing Tab, type the address of your news server, as shown in Figure 8.9. If you haven't yet given Mosaic your e-mail address, click on the Services tab and enter your name, e-mail address, and SMTP (outgoing mail) server there. Then click in the Name box in the Posting area, enter your name, press Tab, and then enter your e-mail address.

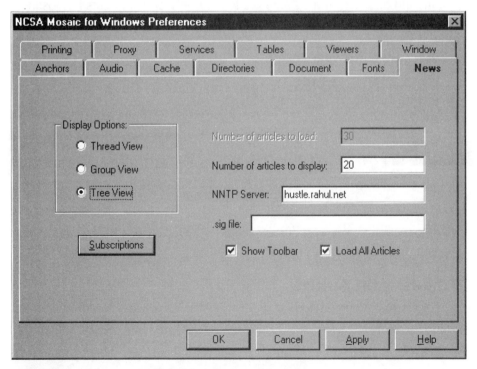

FIGURE 8.9: The News tab of Mosaic's Preferences dialog box

If you want to subscribe to a newsgroup, click on the Subscriptions button in the NCSA Mosaic for Windows Preferences dialog box. This brings up the News Subscriptions dialog box. To search for a specific group by name, start typing the name in the Search box. As soon as you've typed enough to specify the name, the list will scroll to the group you're looking for.

To subscribe to a group, click on its name in the Available box and then click on the Subscribe button. Repeat as often as necessary. Click on OK when you're done and then on OK again to close the Preferences dialog box and accept your selections.

Reading News

To start reading news, either click on the Read Newsgroups button or select File ➤ Newsgroups.

Mosaic will list your subscribed newsgroups, with each group as a hypertext link. It will also display an additional toolbar with shortcuts for moving forward and backward through articles and threads, and shortcuts for posting articles, replying by mail, and jumping from newsgroup to newsgroup.

Selecting a Newsgroup

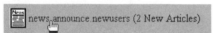

To select a newsgroup, just click on its name.

> **TIP**
>
> You can go directly to a specific newsgroup by typing its address into the Address box, in the format **news:*news.group.name*, and pressing Enter.**

Mosaic will display a list of subject articles, grouped together by topic, when appropriate (see Figure 8.10).

Browsing the Articles

Just scroll through the list looking for articles you'd like to read. To read an article, click on its subject, and Mosaic will display the article.

> **WARNING**
>
> There's no way to mark articles as Unread with Mosaic, but you can "catch up" (mark all the articles as read) by clicking on the Catch Up button when viewing the articles in a newsgroup.

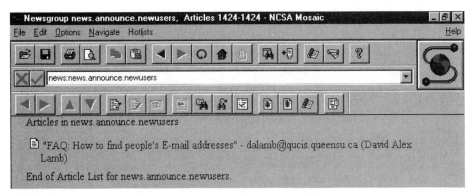

FIGURE 8.10: Mosaic groups articles by topic, when possible.

To go to the next article, click on the Next Article button. To return to the list of articles, click on the name of the newsgroup (in the header of the article). To return to the newsgroup list, click on the Read Newsgroups button. You can also use the normal Back button on the main toolbar to retrace your steps through a newsgroup.

Replying to Articles

When you want to reply to an article by e-mail, click on the author's name at the top of the article or click on the Reply button. Mosaic will open a new message window. Send mail as explained in Chapter 2. To quote from the article, click on the Include Text button and then on Yes. Write your reply and then click on the Send button.

If, instead, you want to post a reply to the newsgroup, click on the Follow Up button. Mosaic will open a new message window. To crosspost to more than one newsgroup, type additional newsgroup names, separated by commas, in the Newsgroups box near the top of the window. To quote from the original message, click on the Include Original Article button. Type your message (be sure to reduce the quoted material as much as possible but leave enough for appropriate context) and then click on the Post button.

Starting a New Thread

To post a new message to the newsgroup, click on the Post button. Mosaic will open a new window with the name of the current newsgroup already entered and all the other boxes blank. Type a subject in the Subject box and type your article in the message area. Then click on the Post button.

Quit Reading News

To quit reading news with Mosaic, just quit the program or enter a Web address in the address box and press Enter.

 **WARNING** Mosaic has no provision for killing or autoselecting articles, authors, or threads.

For help in Mosaic, select Help ➤ Help Contents.

NetCruiser

NetCruiser has a passable newsreader built into its all-in-one interface, so you don't have do any technical setup to get going reading news.

It's also possible to read news with NetCruiser and another external newsreader or Web browser. See the entries for Mosaic, MS Internet Explorer, and Netscape News for more details about Web browsers and the entries for NewsWatcher and News Xpress for details about newsreaders.

Starting the Newsreader Module

 To start reading news, click on the Read Netnews Newsgroups button on the toolbar.

Subscribing to Newsgroups

If you want to choose newsgroups to subscribe to, an alternative to clicking the Read Netnews button is to select Internet ➤ Choose USENET Newsgroups. This brings up the Select USENET Newsgroups dialog box (see Figure 8.11). Click on a button for one a category, or click on the All button if you don't want to try to guess what category the newsgroup you're looking for is filed in. Then choose a newsgroup from the box on the left side of the Newsgroup Mover area of the dialog box. Click on Subscribe to add the group to your list of subscribed groups (listed in the My Reading List box on the right). Repeat the process as often as necessary. Click on OK when you're done.

Selecting a Newsgroup to Read

The Select a Newsgroup dialog box will appear whether you click on the Read Netnews button or start by subscribing to newsgroups. Select a newsgroup to read and click on OK. When the Retrieve Article Headers dialog box appears, click on OK.

Browsing the Articles

To read an article, double-click on its subject in the top half of the Read USENET window (see Figure 8.12).

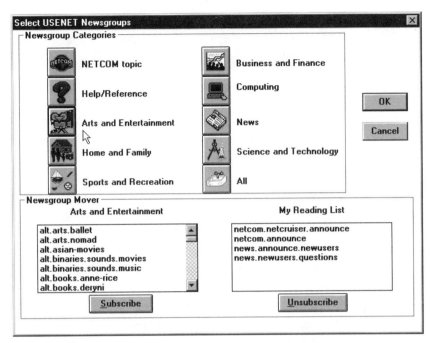

FIGURE 8.11: NetCruiser's Select USENET Newsgroups dialog box

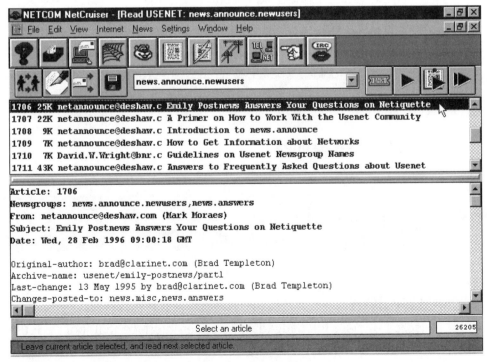

FIGURE 8.12: Double-click the article header to read the article.

TIP You can single-click on a number of articles to preselect them before you start reading.

Getting around in an article is simple; just scroll through the message area in the window that appears. To read the next selected article, click on the Read Next Selected Article button. To save an article so you can re-read it later, click on the Save button to save the article as a text file to your hard disk.

Replying to Articles

If you want to reply to the author of an article via e-mail, click on the Reply to Current Article button. Click on Yes to include the original article in the reply. NetCruiser will open a new Send Mail window. Send mail as explained in Chapter 2.

However, if you want to post a reply to the newsgroup, click on the Post a Follow Up to Current Article button. NetCruiser will open a Post to Usenet window. To cross-post to more than one newsgroup, type additional newsgroup names, separated by commas, in the Newsgroups box near the top of the window. Type your message (reduce the quoted material as much as possible but leave enough for appropriate context) and then click on the Send button.

Starting a New Thread

To post a new article to a newsgroup, click on the Post to Netnews Newsgroups button on the main toolbar. Type a newsgroup name (or names, separated by commas) in the Newsgroups box. Type a subject in the Subject box, and then type your article. When you're done, click on the Send button.

Quitting the Newsgroups

To stop reading news, close all the Netnews windows.

NOTE NetCruiser has no provision for filtering out unwanted authors or article threads.

Netscape News

Netscape offers a full-fledged newsreader interface that looks a lot like its mail interface.

Preparing the Newsreader

Before you can use Navigator as a newsreader, you have to find out what news server you have access to. Then, select Options ➤ Mail and News Preferences and click on the Servers tab in the Preferences dialog box. Click in the News (NNTP) Server box in the News area and type the address of your news server, as shown in Figure 8.13. (If you haven't yet given Netscape News your e-mail information, enter it in the Mail area at the top of dialog box.)

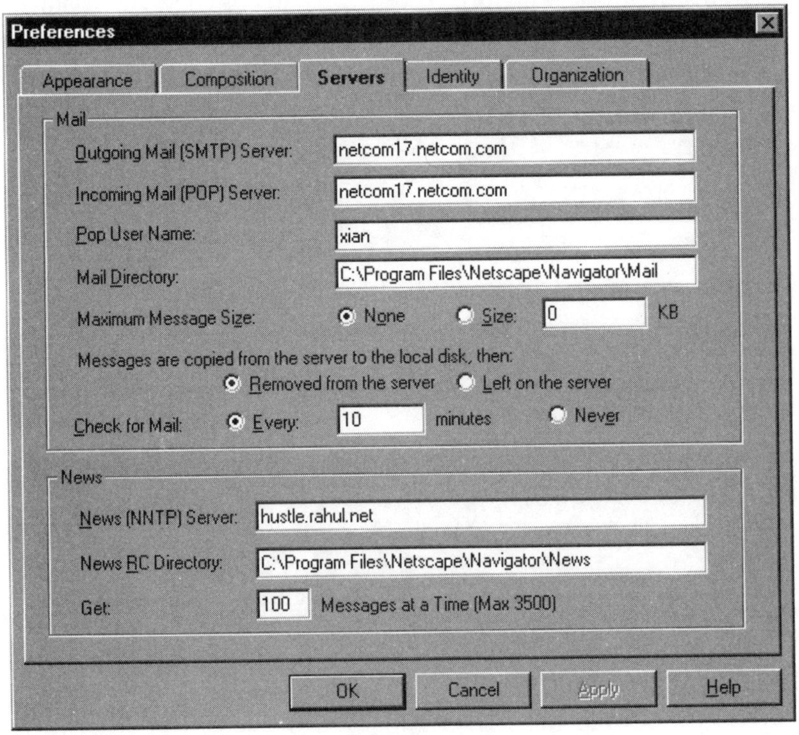

FIGURE 8.13: The Servers tab of Navigator's (Mail and News) Preferences dialog box

Reading News

To start reading news, select Windows ➤ Netscape News. This will open up a new window (the Web window will still be around, just behind the new one).

Netscape starts you off subscribed to the most essential news information newsgroups (such as news.announce.newusers). To subscribe to other newsgroups, select Options ➤ Show All Newsgroups and click on OK.

WARNING It will take a while for Netscape to download your entire newsgroup list.

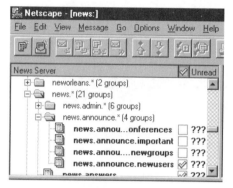

Netscape will display the newsgroups generally as folders representing the top level hierarchies. Click the plus sign to the left of a folder to see the next level of organization.

When you get down to the level of actual newsgroup names, click to place a checkmark in the box to the right of a newsgroup to subscribe to it.

When you're done, select Options ➢ Show Subscribed Newsgroups.

Selecting a Newsgroup

To select a newsgroup, just click on its name. Netscape will display a list of subjects, grouped together by thread when appropriate, in the upper-right pane of the News window (see Figure 8.14).

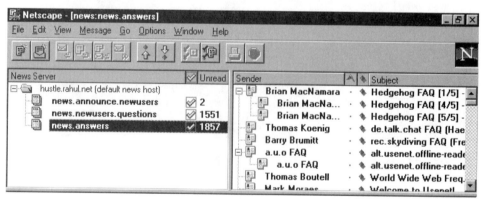

FIGURE 8.14: Netscape groups articles by topic, when possible.

Browsing the Articles

Just scroll through the list looking for articles you'd like to read. To read an article, click on its subject. Netscape will display the article in the large pane in the bottom half of the window (see Figure 8.15). To go to the next article, click on the Next Unread button. To mark an article as unread, select Message ➢ Mark as Unread.

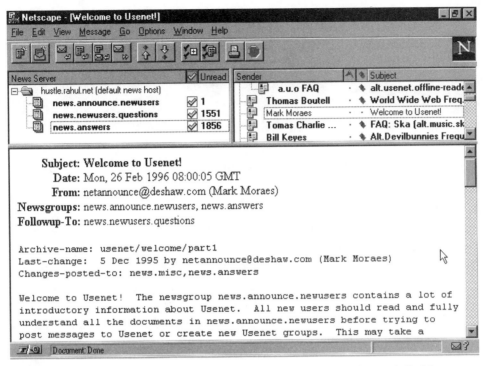

FIGURE 8.15: Netscape displays news articles in the large main pane in the bottom half of the News window.

Replying to Articles

If you want to reply to an article by e-mail, click on the Reply button. Netscape will open a new message window. Send mail as explained in Chapter 2.

However, if you want to post a reply to the newsgroup, click on the Post Reply button. Netscape will open a new message window. To crosspost to more than one newsgroup, type additional newsgroup names, separated by commas, in the Newsgroups box near the top of the window. Type your message (reduce the quoted material as much as possible but leave enough for appropriate context) and then click on the Send button, exactly as you would for a mail message.

Starting a New Thread

To post a new message to the newsgroup, click on the Post New button. Netscape will open a new message window with the name of the current newsgroup already entered and all the other boxes blank. Type a subject in the Subject box and type your article in the message area. Then click on the Send button.

Closing the Netscape Newsreader

To quit reading news with Netscape, just close the News window.

 **WARNING** | **Netscape has no provision for killing or autoselecting articles, authors, or threads.**

To get help, select Help ➤ Handbook.

NewsWatcher

NewsWatcher

NewsWatcher is the most popular Macintosh newsreader. You can download it (for free) from `ftp://ftp.acns.nwu.edu/pub/newswatcher/`. Another popular Macintosh newsreader is Nuntius (`ftp://ftp.cit.cornell.edu/pub/mac/comm/test/Nuntius-archive-mirror/`). It may be shipped to you as a compressed file; just click on the icon you receive to unpack it. When it is ready to run, it will look like the icon above.

Starting the Newsreader

Run NewsWatcher by double-clicking on its icon. When it first starts up, it will read the full list of newsgroups from whatever server you instructed it to connect to (under Preferences ➤ Startup). This may take a few moments.

Subscribing to Newsgroups

NewsWatcher will check for any new newsgroups that have been created since your last session and then will display a dialog box listing them. If this is your first session, it will simply display the full list of newsgroups on your server, in a window marked Untitled. This is what NewsWatcher calls a User Group List window. You start with no subscribed groups, so this window is empty.

To subscribe to a group, select it and then copy and paste it into your User Group List window, or select it and pull down to Subscribe under the Special menu.

TIP | **You don't have to subscribe to any groups the first time you run the program if you don't want to. You can always subscribe to groups later.**

To unsubscribe to a group, select it in your User Group List window and press the Delete key, or choose Special ➢ Unsubscribe.

After subscribing to your initial groups, close the Full Group List window. Now the only window on your screen is your untitled User Group List window. (To show the Full Group List again, just select Show Full Group List under the Windows menu.)

Use the File ➢ command to save your modified User Group List, with a name like "My News Groups." A NewsWatcher icon will appear with the name you have designated underneath.

> **TIP**
>
> **When you want to read the news, double-click your personalized news file instead of opening the NewsWatcher application. This opens to your saved user group list and automatically checks to see if any new articles have appeared.**

To look for other newsgroups, simply choose Windows ➢ Show Full Group List to call up the window with a list all of the newsgroups available.

Selecting a Newsgroup

To start reading a newsgroup, just double-click on it. This will open a new window with a list of the articles displayed (see Figure 8.16). You can arrange or resize the windows easily, as you can with all Macintosh applications.

Browsing the Articles

Articles are threaded (listed by topic), if possible. To jump from thread to thread, pull down to Next Thread under the News menu. To jump to the next newsgroup in your list, choose News ➢ Next Group. Double-clicking on an article opens it up in a new window (see Figure 8.17).

To mark an article as unread, select News ➢ Mark Unread (or press Ctrl+U). To mark the rest of the articles as read, drag down to the Mark Others Read command.

Replying to Articles

To reply to an article, click the Reply button. NewsWatcher will open a new message window. Click in the message area and type your reply. Cut as much of the quoted article as possible, retaining enough to preserve context. When you're done, choose whether you wish it to be sent as private e-mail, a post to the entire group, or a message to yourself by choosing one of the three icons at the top of the window. Then click the Send button.

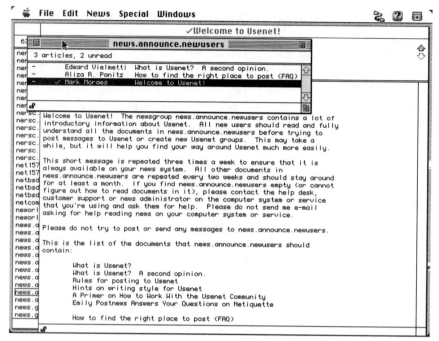

FIGURE 8.16: Articles in the newsgroup **news·announce·newusers**, with the last article open in the window behind.

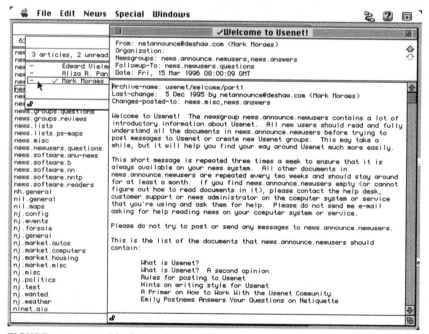

FIGURE 8.17: An article displayed in NewsWatcher. Notice the list of articles in the window on the left, behind the front window.

To crosspost to more than one newsgroup, type additional newsgroup names, separated by commas, on the Newsgroups line at the top of the window. Type your message (reduce the quoted material as much as possible but leave enough for appropriate context) and then click the Send button.

Starting a New Thread

To post a new message to the newsgroup, drag down to the New Message command under News. NewsWatcher will open a new window with the name of the current newsgroup already entered. Type a subject in the Subject box and type your article in the message area, then click the Send button.

Quitting NewsWatcher

To quit NewsWatcher, select File ➤ Quit

Getting Help

NewsWatcher has excellent on-line help available—try downloading their 151-page manual or other help files from: `ftp://ftp.acns.nwu.edu/pub/newswatcher/helpers/`.

News Xpress

News Xpress is an excellent—and free—Windows newsreader. You can download it from `ftp://ftp.hk.super.net/pub/windows/Winsock-Utilities/`. Look for a file name that starts with "nx" and ends with ".zip," such as nx10b4-p.zip, and download that file. The higher numbered files are the more recent.

> **TIP**
>
> **Other popular, free Windows newsreaders are Free Agent** (`http://http://www.forteinc.com/agent/`) **and WinVN** (`ftp://ftp.ksc.nasa.gov/pub/win3/winvn`).

Starting the Newsreader

Nx

Run News Xpress by double-clicking on its icon.

Subscribing to Newsgroups

News Xpress will check for any new newsgroups that have been created since your last session and then display a Newsgroups dialog box listing them. After clicking on the check box to the left of any groups you want to add to your subscription list, click on the Subscribe button. Then click on Close.

To subscribe to existing groups, select View ➤ All Groups (or press Ctrl+G) and wait for the entire group list to be displayed. Then select any group you want to subscribe to and select Group ➤ Subscribe (or press Ctrl+S).

Select View ➤ All Groups (or press Ctrl+G) again to show only a list of subscribed groups.

Selecting a Newsgroup

To start reading a newsgroup, just double-click on its name.

> **TIP**
>
> You can limit the newsgroups shown to those that match a key word or even just a few characters by typing the word (or characters) into the Filter box at the bottom of the window.

This will open up a new window with articles displayed. The old window will still be there, but behind the new one. Select options on the Window menu to bring a different window to the front or to arrange all the windows.

Browsing the Articles

Articles are threaded (listed by topic), if possible. Threads appear as folder icons. Double-click on a thread title to display all the articles in the thread. To read an article, double-click on its subject. The article will appear in a new window (see Figure 8.18).

To mark an article as unread, select Article ➤ Mark Unread (or press Ctrl+U). To mark all articles as read, click on the Catch Up button.

Replying to Articles

If you want to reply to an article by e-mail, click on the Reply button. News Xpress will open a new message window. Click in the message area and type your reply. Cut as much of the quoted article as possible, retaining enough to preserve context. When you're done, click on the Send button.

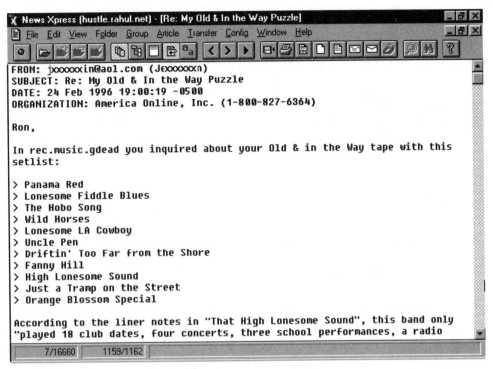

FIGURE 8.18: An article displayed in News Xpress

To post a reply to the newsgroup, click on the Follow Up button. News Xpress will open a new message window. To crosspost to more than one newsgroup, type additional newsgroup names, separated by commas, in the Newsgroups box at the top of the window. Type your message (reduce the quoted material as much as possible but leave enough for appropriate context) and then click on the Send button.

Starting a New Thread

When you want to post a new message to the newsgroup, click on the Post button. News Xpress will open a new message window with the name of the current newsgroup already entered and all the other boxes blank. Type a subject in the Subject box and type your article in the message area. Then click on the Send button.

Quitting the Newsreader

To quit News Xpress, select File ➢ Exit.

Getting Help

News Xpress's help features are minimal—what do you want for free? Select Help ➤ Topics to see what there is.

WARNING | **News Xpress has no provisions for killing or autoselecting authors, articles, or threads.**

Tin

One of the most popular threaded Unix newsreaders is called Tin. Tin is available on most Unix systems. (Other common Unix newsreaders include Trn, Nn, and Rn. If you plan to use any of these, see their manual pages online—for example, type **man trn** at the Unix prompt and press Enter to see the Trn manual.)

Preparing the Newsreader

I recommend first preparing the .newsrc file. What's the .newsrc file? It's the Unix name for a text file that keeps track of what newsgroups you are subscribed to and which articles you've read. If you run a newsreader and it doesn't find a file like this, it will immediately create one—and that's when some newsreaders subscribe you to every newsgroup. Here's how to create a starter .newsrc:

1. Type **vi .newsrc** and press Enter.
2. Type **i** to start inserting text.
3. Type **news.announce.newusers:** (including the colon) and press Enter.
4. Press Esc. Type **:wq** and press Enter.

You could also open Tin and then quit immediately (type **q**, repeatedly if necessary). Then edit the .newsrc file that was created. To edit it, type **vi .newsrc** and press Enter. Then type **:%s/:/!/** and press Enter to change all ":" (subscribed) to "!" (unsubscribed). Then manually change back the ones you actually do want to subscribe to.

Starting the Newsreader

To start Tin, you type **tin** and press Enter. Tin will first respond with something like

```
tin 1.2 PL1 [UNIX] (c) Copyright 1991-93 Iain Lea.
Reading news active file...
```

Then the Group Selection screen will appear, listing all the groups you're subscribed to and how many new articles each group has, as shown in Figure 8.19.

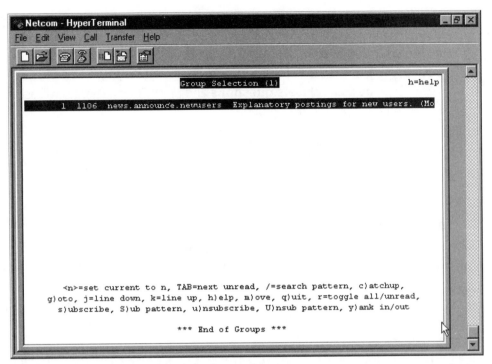

FIGURE 8.19: I've created a .newsrc file and am now running Tin. It shows me that there are 1106 unread news articles in **news.announce.newusers.**

TIP

If you want to read just one specific newsgroup, you can type **tin** *newsgroup.name* and press Enter.

Selecting a Newsgroup

If you don't want to read the first newsgroup on the list, press **j** to go down to the next line. If you do want to read the current newsgroup, press Enter. Press **k** to go up to the previous line. (Or try using ↑ and ↓.)

As you find that you read some newsgroups more than others, you can move those groups to the top of your list, so you see them first. To move a newsgroup, type **m**. Then, to put the newsgroup at the top of the list, type **1** and press Enter. To put it at the end of the list, type **$**. To place it somewhere in between, type the appropriate number.

To go to a specific newsgroup (and subscribe to it if you aren't already), type **g**. Tin will respond with `Goto newsgroup [ ]>`. Type the newsgroup name and press Enter. Try this:

1. Type **g** and press Enter.
2. Type **news.newusers.questions** and press Enter again. Tin will ask you where to put the newsgroup:

   ```
   Position news.newusers.questions in group list
   (1,2,..,$) [2]>.
   ```

3. Press Enter.

Selecting Articles

Don't worry if the number of articles listed is sometimes fewer than the number mentioned when you first ran Tin—it just means that some articles have expired since you last checked this newsgroup.

Once you've pressed Enter to start reading a newsgroup, you'll be shown a list of unread articles and you can choose which articles to read, which to save for later, and which to delete.

1. Highlight the `news.newusers.questions` line (press **j** or **k** if you're not there already).
2. Press Enter. Figure 8.20 shows the available threads in this newsgroup. Threads with a plus next to them contain unread articles. The number next to a thread represents the number of replies to the original article.
   - To choose an article you want to read, either type its number and press Enter or move the cursor to it (**j** for down, **k** for up). Then press *****.
   - To skip over an article for now, just ignore it.
   - To delete an article, move the cursor to it and press **K**.
   - To skip to the next screenful of articles, press the spacebar. To go back a screenful, press **b**.

> **TIP**
>
> You're choosing whole threads here, not single articles. To read only specific articles in a thread, press l to list the articles in the current thread so that you can read the ones you're interested in. Press q to go back to the originally selected thread when you've finished reading. At any point, you can read a thread by pressing Enter while it is highlighted.

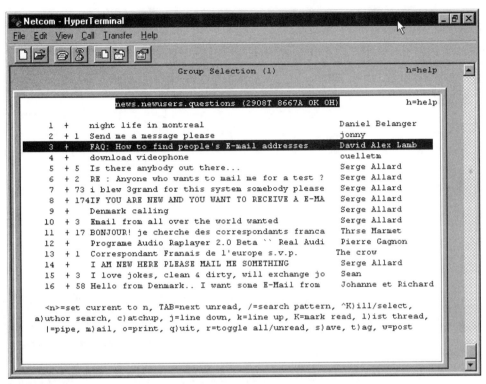

FIGURE 8.20: Here's the first screenful of unread articles (actually threads) in news. newusers.questions. I'm selecting "FAQ: How to find people's E-mail addresses" by pressing **3** and then Enter.

If you start reading a newsgroup and there are far too many articles, press **c** to catch-up (mark as read) all the current articles. Tin will ask you to press **y** if you're sure. Then the newsgroup will appear empty until someone posts something new.

Browsing the Articles

To start reading a thread, press Enter. If the article is longer than one screenful, press the spacebar to see the next page. The bottom of the screen will tell you how much of the article you've seen so far, expressed as a percentage.

When you get to the end of an article, press the spacebar to go to the next unread article or type **q** to go back to the original thread selection.

> **TIP** If you want more room on the screen for the articles you're reading, press **H**. This removes the menu of options at the bottom of the screen. Press **H** again at any time to bring it back.

To mark an article as unread, so you can read it later, press **z**. Tin will respond with something like "Article marked as unread." To save an article as a file, first type **s** and then **a**, enter a file name, and then press Enter twice. See Chapter 9 for more on files and directories.

Replying to Articles

If you want to send an e-mail reply to someone whose post you're reading, press **r**. Tin will drop you into a text editor. Write your message and exit the editor (by pressing Ctrl+X). Then press **s** to send the mail or **q** to cancel it.

> **TIP** To mail an article to someone, press **m**, press **a**, type an e-mail address and press Enter. Type **s** or **e** to edit the message first.

Before posting a reply to an article, mark it as unread first and read through the thread. You never know when someone else has already posted what you were planning to post. Then, if you do actually reply, check the Newsgroups: and Follow-up To: lines in the original post so you know where your post is going. Edit these lines in your reply if necessary.

To post a follow-up, press **f**. Tin will put you in a text editor and include the text of the original article with an attribution. Trim down the quoted text as much as you can without losing the context. Write and edit your article. When you're finished, exit the editor. To post the article, press **p**. To cancel the article, press **q**. To go back and edit it again, press **e**. To check the spelling, press **i**.

Starting a New Thread

To start a new thread, press **w** while reading any post (or while selecting threads). Tin will ask you for a subject. Type one and press Enter. Remember this is the first thing people will see and some people will decide whether or not to read your post based on it. Then edit your article in the text editor Tin sends you to and exit the editor by pressing Ctrl+X. Then you have several choices:

- To go back and edit the article again, press **e**.
- To check the spelling, press **i**.

- To cancel the article, press **q**.

When you're ready to post the article, press **p**. Your newsreader will prompt you for the "Distribution." The default is world. Your choices range from local (just your domain) to geographical abbreviations such as usa, na (North America), ny, ca, and uk depending on your location.

Before letting you post, Tin asks

```
Are you absolutely sure that you want to do this?
[ny] n
```

Type **y** if you're sure.

Crossposting

To post to more than one newsgroup, either edit the Newsgroups line among the headers of your post by putting a comma between each pair of newsgroup names, or post by pressing **x** instead of **w** or **f**. If you press **x**, Tin will prompt you for the newsgroups you want to post to and then let you edit the post you're crossposting if you want. (But don't go crazy with crossposting—people get annoyed when they find irrelevant messages in their newsgroup.)

Quitting the Newsreader

To quit Tin, press **q**. If you are reading an article, the first **q** will just take you back to thread selection, so you'll have to press **q** again to go back to the newsgroup selection, and then you'll have to press **q** a third time to actually quit Tin.

Getting Help

To get help, or at least a list of commands, press **h**. You will see a list of options appropriate to the part of Tin you're in just now—choosing newsgroups, choosing articles, reading an article, or having reached the end of an article.

Killing and Autoselecting

If there's a subject you don't want to read about or a person out there who annoys you, you can selectively kill topics or authors to screen them out before you ever see the posts.

To kill a subject or author, and select an article on that subject or by that author, press Ctrl-K. This will bring up the Kill / Auto-Select Article Menu (see Figure 8.21).

On this screen, use the spacebar to switch among options and Enter to select the current option.

TIP **Press e to edit the killfile directly.**

If you want to kill the subject or author, press Enter. To have this author or subject selected automatically in the future, press the spacebar and then Enter. Then press Enter again to get down to the Kill Subject line. If it's the subject you want to kill, press Enter; if not, press the spacebar and then Enter. Either way this takes you down to the Author line. If you want to kill articles by this author, press the spacebar and then Enter; if not, press Enter. Finally, if you want to kill articles in the current newsgroup only, press Enter. If you want to kill such articles in all newsgroups, press the spacebar and then Enter.

Then press **s** to save the killfile entry (or **q** to cancel).

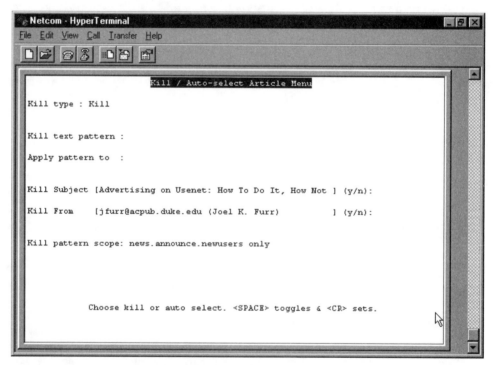

FIGURE 8.21: The Kill/Auto-Select Article Menu; Tin makes it very easy to kill or auto-select subjects and authors.

Chapter 9

CHATTING ON THE IRC

FEATURING

- **Understanding IRC**
- **Chatting with Irc**
- **Chatting with Ircle**
- **Chatting with mIRC**
- **Chatting with NetCruiser**
- **Chatting with Netscape Chat**

So far we've covered e-mail, mailing lists, and newsgroups, but there's one other way to communicate with people over the Internet. If you're in the mood for immediate communication, rather than tag games in e-mail or mass-market publication on Usenet, then you can look for people with similar interests and *chat* with them in *real time*.

WARNING This is also where the mass media go hunting for stories of "computer sex." That's because the immediacy and near-anonymity of this medium lead many an adolescent (or perpetually adolescent) male to *cruise* chat channels hoping to talk dirty. Watch out if you have a female sounding login or "real name."

Chatting is a form of immediate communication. With a chat program, you join conversations, and then whatever you type appears on the screen of everyone else who's participating in or listening in on the conversation (you can also direct messages to specific people). It's not unlike talking over the telephone with teletype machines. However, with too many people involved, conversations can degenerate into what *net.folk* call *noise* (when so much chatter is going on that the topic gets buried in the blizzard of messages). With the right amount of people, a sort of conversation or debate can take place.

The most popular and widely available chat form available is called *IRC*. IRC stands for *Internet Relay Chat*, and it's a set of protocols that allow multiple users to communicate quickly and easily over the Net.

The formal terms elucidating the difference between chat and e-mail are *synchronous* and *asynchronous*. Chat is synchronous (happening for all participants at the same time), and e-mail is asynchronous (taking place variously at different times). Telephones are synchronous, answering machines are asynchronous, beepers are synchronous, and voice mail is asynchronous. U.S. Mail is totally asynchronous.

TIP I prefer e-mail to chat because I like considering my replies in writing and responding when the time is best for me.

"Talking" from Screen to Screen

Talk is an even more intrusive form of communication possible across a lot of the Net, but it's generally only available on Unix shell accounts unless you have a special talk client program. Using the talk command (**talk *username@address***), you send words directly to someone's screen. Actually, first they'll get a "talk request" from a server (called a daemon). They'll have to type **talk *your-address*** to open the line of communication. I recommend that you use this only for emergencies and announcements.

How IRC Programs Work in General

IRC works because a series of IRC servers band together in a network to share *channels* of communication. This is the same metaphor as if you were communicating with someone or a group on a single radio frequency. If you connect to one server in such a network, you have access to all the channels and all the users connected to any of the servers on that network.

There are two major networks of IRC servers: EFNet, the traditional network; and the Undernet, a smaller, more community-oriented alternative network. (There seems to be a third, independent network called DALnet as well.) Most basic information provided in IRC client programs covers EFNet. For more on the Undernet, see `http://www.undernet.org:8080/cs93jtl/Undernet.html` or the Undernet IRC FAQ, `http://www.undernet.org:8080/cs93jtl/underfaq/`.

The first time you run an IRC client, you might have to select a server to connect to (or it might automatically select one for you). After that, you'll connect whenever you start the program. The next step is to list what channels (conversation "rooms") are available out there and choose one to join (or decide that none look interesting enough and start your own.)

> **NOTE** Some conversations are kept open by what are called *bots* or *'bots*. These are robotic participants in the conversation. Some of them are not bad conversationalists, compared with a lot of real people.

Then you join a channel. You'll be able to see who else is on the same channel, and you'll see what everyone types (except for their private communications).

> **TIP** Some conversations are *invitation only*. This means someone in the conversation has to give you a password or invite you to join.

You can type messages to the channel or send private messages (*whisper*) to individuals. When you're done, you quit the channel and then the program.

For more information about IRC, see the following documents on the Web:

- IRC FAQ (`http://www.kei.com/irc.html`)
- IRC Related Documents (`http://ftp.acsu.buffalo.edu/irc/WWW/ircdocs.html`)
- IRC Servers List (`http://www.funet.fi/pub/unix/irc/docs/server.lst`)

Other Real-Time Amusements

There are also games out there that you can play against other people on the Net in real time—everything from simple board games to MUDs (Multiple User Domain/Dungeon) which are huge role-playing text games with a large number of participants—supposedly they're very addictive. These games usually involve telnetting to some other system. Ask around on Usenet in the REC.GAMES hierarchy for specific host sites and ongoing games. (See Chapter 10 for more on Telnet and Chapter 8 for more on Usenet.)

There are also two new multimedia communications technologies that are somewhat similar to IRC—*Internet Phone* and *CU-SeeMe*. Internet Phone enables anyone with a microphone, speaker, and sound card in their computer to talk to other people on the Internet. CU-SeeMe enables anyone with a video camera and enough memory to play video images in their computer to see other people on the Internet.

For more information about Internet Phone, see the Internet Phone User Directory (`http://www.pulver.com/iphone/`). For more information about CU-SeeMe, see the CU-SeeMe Welcome Page (`http://cu-seeme.cornell.edu/`).

Chatting with Specific IRC Programs

I can't explain every chat program out there, but I want to cover some of the most popular ones. We'll discuss Irc, Ircle, mIRC, NetCruiser, and Netscape Chat. Irc is a Unix program, and Ircle is a Macintosh program. mIRC is a Windows program. NetCruiser is available for Windows and a Macintosh version is in the works, but so far Netscape Chat is only available for Windows.

> **TIP**
> AOL, CompuServe, and other online services have their own IRC equivalent, usually referred to as *chat rooms*. The concept is the same, but these conversations are not open to anyone on the Internet—only to members of the specific online service.

> **TIP**
> If your provider does not offer an IRC or a chat program, you can Telnet to a host that does. Chapter 10 explains Telnet.

Chatting with Irc

To run Irc, type **irc** at the Unix prompt and press Enter. If this command is not recognized, try typing **chat** at the prompt and pressing Enter. The program called Chat is older than Irc and has been replaced on most systems, but if it's all you've got, give it a try.

> **TIP**
> People will also be able to see your "real name" (or whatever you've set it to with chfn) with the /who command. If you don't want them to see your real name, you have to type **setenv ircname** and *"the real name you want between quotation marks"* at the Unix prompt and press Enter. (You can also put this command in any of your startup files, such as .login, .profile, or .cshrc.)

The program will start and tell you if your login conflicts with any other one currently on the system. If so, you'll have to change your Irc *nick* (short for nickname). You may want to change it anyway. To do so type **/nick *newnickname*** at the Irc prompt. (All Irc commands start with "/".)

See What's Going On

Use the /list command to see what conversations are going on. Conversation names all start with "#". You can specify a minimum and maximum number of participants for the groups the /list command should list. For example, try **/list -min 3 -max 4** and press Enter.

Join a Conversation

To join a conversation, type **/join *#conversation***. Type **/who *#conversation*** to get a list of who else is "on."

Your End of the Conversation

To talk to the whole group, just type whatever you wish to say and press Enter (see Figure 9.1).

If you want to send a message to just one person, type **/*their-nick your message***. When you're ready to leave the conversation, type **/join 0**. To quit Irc, type **/quit**.

At any point, you can get help by typing **/help** and pressing Enter. People will usually help you out if you just ask questions.

Chatting with Ircle

To obtain Ircle, point your Web browser at the office Ircle home page (`http://alf8.speech.cs.cmu.edu/ircle/`) and download the latest version.

To run Ircle, double-click on its icon. The program will open. To start a chat session, open File ➤ Open Connection, which will connect you to whatever server is selected. To change the server—or your name, nickname, or password—select Preferences under the File Menu.

After Ircle connects to the IRC server, the program will tell you if your login conflicts with any other one currently on the system. If so, you'll have to change your Ircle nickname, in File ➤ Preferences ➤ StartUp. You may want to change it anyway to be anonymous.

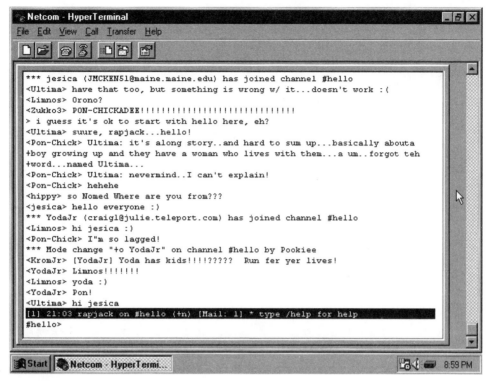

FIGURE 9.1: Talking on IRC in Unix

See What's Going On

To see what conversations are going on out there, pull down to List under the Command menu. Conversation names all start with "#". You can specify a minimum and maximum number of participants for the groups the /list command should list. For example, try **/list -min 3 -max 4** and press Enter.

Join a Conversation

To join a conversation, pull down to Join under the Command menu, then type in the name of the channel you wish to join, preceded by a **#** .

To get a list of who else is "on," pull down to Who under the Command menu, or open the small window marked User list, under the Windows menu. The name of the conversation will appear in the icon bar at the top of the Userlist window, with the names of the participants in the box below.

Your End of the Conversation

To talk to the whole group, just type what you wish to say, as if it were a command, in the window marked Input line, and press Enter (see Figure 9.2).

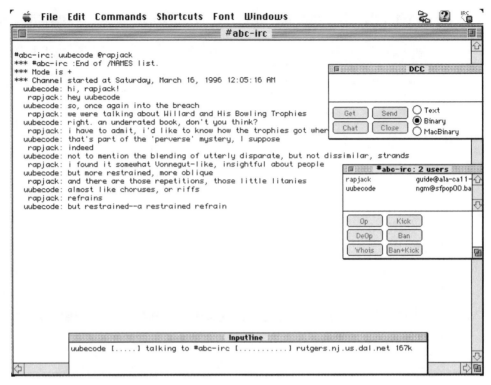

FIGURE 9.2: Talking on IRC in Ircle

Say you want to send a message to one person, type **/their-nick your message**.

To leave the conversation, just close the window, or select File ➢ Close connection if you want to leave the server. To quit Ircle, select File ➢ Quit.

Ircle has an extensive array of help documents at their Web site. There is also an entire web page devoted to help: go to `http://www.aloha.net/sputnik/irclehelp.html`.

Also, people you are chatting with will usually help you out if you just ask questions.

Chatting with mIRC

To obtain mIRC, point your Web browser at `ftp://cs-ftp.bu.edu/irc/clients/pc/windows` and click on the mIRC file to download it.

To run mIRC, double-click on its icon. The program will start.

Click on the Connect button to connect to a server.

mIRC will tell you if your login conflicts with any other one currently on the system. If so, you'll have to change your mIRC nick. mIRC will prompt you with the beginning of the command (/nick followed by a space). Just type the new nickname you want and press Enter. To change your nick at another time, right-click anywhere, select Other from the menu that pops up, and then click on Nickname. Type your new nick in the dialog box that appears and press Enter.

See What's Going On

To see what conversations are going on out there, right-click anywhere, choose Other from the menu that pops up, and then choose List Channel from the submenu that appears. Conversation names all start with "#". Just as in the other chat programs, you can specify a minimum and maximum number of participants by typing the /list command directly (for example, type **/list -min 3 -max 4** and press Enter). mIRC will list the available channels in a new window.

Join a Conversation

To join a conversation, double-click on the name of the channel you want to join. A new window will open for that channel.

If you want to get a list of who else is "on," right-click on the channel name in the list window and select List Users.

Your End of the Conversation

If you want to talk to the whole group, just type what you want to say and press Enter (see Figure 9.3).

To send a message to one person, double-click on that person's nick in the right pane of the channel window. From then on, everything you type will go to only that person.

When you are ready to leave the conversation, just close the channel window. To quit mIRC, select File ➢ Exit.

At any point, you can get help by selecting Help ➢ Contents.

Chatting with NetCruiser

 To connect to IRC with NetCruiser, click on the IRC icon. Then click on the Connect button on the dialog box that appears. The IRC Control Panel window will appear. It will tell you if your login conflicts with any other one currently on the system. If so, you'll have to change your IRC nick. To do so, type **/nick newnickname** in the area at the bottom of the IRC window.

See What's Going On

Type **/list** and press Enter to see what conversations (channels) are going on. As in other chat programs, channel names all start with "#". NetCruiser will display the

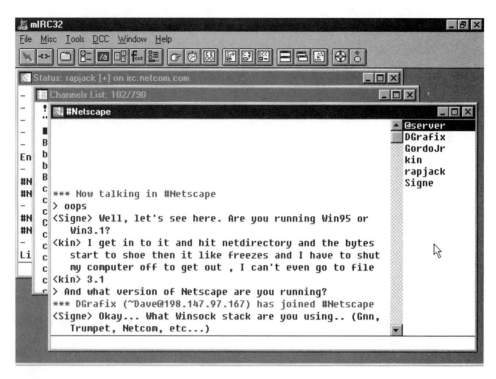

FIGURE 9.3: Talking on IRC in mIRC

channels in their own window. You can specify a minimum and maximum number of participants for the groups the /list command should list. For example, try **/list -min 3 -max 4** and press Enter.

Join a Conversation

 To join a conversation, either click the Join a Channel button, type the channel name, and press Enter; double-click on the channel name in the IRC LIST window; or just type **/join #channel** and press Enter.

Type **/who #channel** to get a list of who else is "on."

Your End of the Conversation

To talk to the whole group, just type your message and press Enter (see Figure 9.4).

To send a message to one person, click the Start a Private Conversation button, type their nick, and press Enter; or type **/their-nick your message**.

When you're ready to leave the conversation, close the channel window and click on Yes when asked if you're sure. To quit Irc, close the IRC Control Panel window and click on Yes.

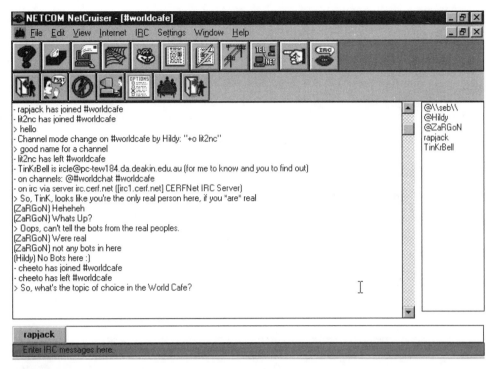

FIGURE 9.4: Talking on IRC with NetCruiser

At any point, you can get help by typing **/help** and pressing Enter. People will usually help you out if you just ask questions.

Chatting with Netscape Chat

Netscape Chat is a plug-in for Navigator that's so far available only for Windows 95. It enables you to chat on IRC and to link up your browser with other people on your channel so you can all visit Web pages together and discuss them.

To obtain Netscape Chat, go to the Netscape home page (**http://home.netscape.com/**), click on the Netscape Now link, and then fill out the form on that page, specifying Netscape Chat as the product you want to download. Then click on one of the listed download sites.

nschat

You have to run Navigator (see Chapter 4, *Browsing the Web*) before you can start Netscape Chat. Then double-click on the nschat (or Netscape Chat) icon.

The program will start. Click on the Connect button to connect to a server.

See What's Going On

To see what conversations are going on out there, click on the List button.

Join a Conversation

To join a conversation, double-click on its name. The nicks of other people already on the channel will appear in a pane down the left side of the window.

Your End of the Conversation

To talk to the whole group, just type your message in the area at the bottom of the window and press Enter (see Figure 9.5). To send a URL for everyone to visit, type the Web address in the URL box at the bottom of the window.

To send a message to one person, click on their nick before typing the message.

When you're ready to leave a conversation, close the window (not the program window; the window whose Close button is just below the main one).

To quit NS Chat, select File ➢ Exit.

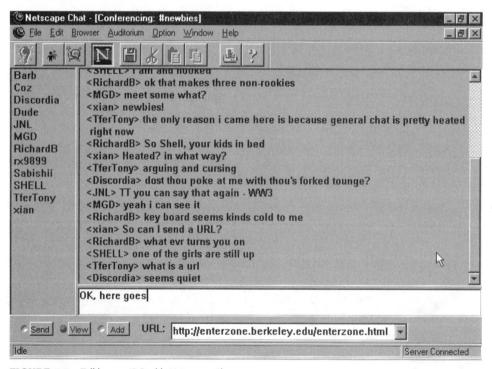

FIGURE 9.5: Talking on IRC with Netscape Chat

Chapter 10

FTP AND TELNET–THE TRANSPORTER BEAMS

- **Downloading files back to your computer**
- **Transferring files with xmodem and ymodem**
- **Finding FTP sites**
- **Doing FTP in general and with e-mail**
- **Transferring files from a Unix shell account**
- **Ftpping with a Web browser, Anarchie, Fetch, Ftp, ncftp, NetCruiser, and WS_FTP**
- **Finding a Telnet Program**
- **Telnetting from Your Web Browser**

Before the World Wide Web was invented, there were already ways to grab files from around the Net and connect to other computers out there. Now that we have the Web, we don't need to use those other methods too often, but there are some occasions when those protocols are still useful. (Such as when you need to send large files to an archive site.) In this chapter, I'll explain *FTP,* the *File Transfer Protocol,* and *Telnet,* a way of logging into remote computers. In Chapter 11, I'll discuss Gopher, a menu-oriented way of surfing the Net.

FTP—the File Transfer Protocol

You can send files attached to e-mail, but this is inefficient and wasteful of resources if the files are large. Instead, there's FTP (File Transfer Protocol), a method of retrieving files from (and sending files to) other computers on the Net.

Ideally, FTP will be built into the Windows and Mac operating systems some day (as it already is for Unix), so that managing files on the Internet will be as easy as managing files on your own computer. For now, though, you have to do FTP with either a special program designed for that purpose or with a Web browser.

You may also hear references to *anonymous FTP*. Most of the time you'll do FTP, you'll do it anonymously, at public *FTP sites*. This means you log in as **anonymous** and give your e-mail address as a password. If you use FTP to transfer files from a machine that you are authorized to access, then you won't do it anonymously. You'll log in as yourself and give your password.

How to Find FTP Sites

Say you're reading a Usenet newsgroup for a while (see Chapter 8) and then you wonder if the old posts you never got to see are archived anywhere. You post your question and someone e-mails you to tell you that, indeed, the archive is available by anonymous FTP at `archive.big-u.edu`. You cut the address and save it in a text file and then check out the FTP site with your FTP program. So that's one way to find out about sites.

There's also an anonymous FTP FAQ and a huge, alphabetically-organized, set of FTP site lists (eleven in all) posted regularly to `comp.answers`, `news.newusers.questions`, and many other Usenet newsgroups.

To have any or all of these documents mailed to you, send an e-mail message (no subject) to `mail-server@rtfm.mit.edu`. Include in it one (or both) of the following lines:

- send usenet-by-group/news.answers/FTP-list/faq
- send usenet/news.answers/FTP-list/sitelist/part1 *through* send usenet/news.answers/FTP-list/sitelist/part11.

These same files are also available via (what else?) anonymous FTP from `rtfm.mit.edu`. Look in the `/pub/usenet-by-group/news.answers/FTP-list/sitelist` directory for the eleven site list files, and the `/pub/usenet/news.answers/FTP-list/faq` directory for the FAQ.

> **TIP**
>
> More often than not, you'll find your way to an FTP site through your Web browser. Since you'll just be clicking on links, you may not even realize that you're connecting to an FTP site when you do this.

Many of the largest, most popular FTP archives have *mirror sites*, which are other FTP sites that maintain the exact same files (updated regularly to reduce the load on the primary site). Use mirror sites whenever you can.

How to Do FTP in General

The typical FTP session starts with you running the FTP program and connecting to a FTP site. Depending on the program you have, you'll either enter your login information before connecting or you'll be prompted to do it after you connect. If you're using a Web browser to connect to an anonymous site, the browser will prompt you to login. Type **anonymous** and press Enter. Then type your e-mail address and press Enter. This will put you at an FTP prompt.

> **TIP**
>
> Popular sites such as RTFM at MIT are often busy. It's best to do your file transfers during off-peak hours, such as at night or on the weekends, to minimize the load on the FTP site.

WARNING When logging into an FTP site as anonymous, never enter your real password. This is a security breach, as your password will appear in a log file that many people can read. If you do this by mistake, immediately change your password.

Now view file lists and hunt through the directory structure for the files you want. You might have connected to a Unix machine or to another type of computer on the Net. Fortunately, you won't have to know all the different commands they require. You only need to know the commands for your FTP program. The program will then translate your requests into whatever format the host computer requires.

If you're not sure where to start looking at the FTP site, start off by looking for a pub directory. If there is one, open it and then work your way through the subdirectories.

If the files you want to transfer are not simple text files (if they're programs, for example), specify *binary* before doing the transfers. When you find the files you want, transfer them with the Get command (or the Multiple Get command, to transfer several at once). Then quit the FTP program. You're done.

Recognizing Compressed Files by Their Extensions

Many files available by FTP have been compressed. This way they take less time to transfer and take up less storage space.

Files that have been squished down in size by the Unix compress command end with .Z. Files that end in .gz have been compressed by the Gzip program.

If the files you've downloaded are ultimately destined for a DOS machine, then they might end in .zip, .arc, or .lhz, and you'll need the correct DOS decompression program to expand them. If you don't have the program you need, look around for it at the FTP site where you got the compressed file. Likewise, compressed Mac files have extensions such as .hqx, .bin, or .sea.

Files that end in .tar contain several files all lumped together with the Unix lumping program Tar.

Programs like WinZip and StuffIt can uncompress many different compression formats.

FTP by E-Mail If You Don't Have "Real" FTP

If you don't have "real" FTP, you can access one of mail servers on the Net that will make FTP transfers for you and then mail you the resulting files. (It's a little like asking a third party to check out a book from the library and send it through the mail to you.) This method of transferring files is more wasteful and less efficient than real FTP, but it will work in a pinch if you don't have FTP available.

TIP   You'll find a thorough discussion of e-mail in Chapters 2 and 3.

To use FTPmail, send a message to either `FTPmail@pa.dec.com` or `FTPmail@decwrl.dec.com`.

Leave the subject line blank. Each line of the message should contain a single command, most of which are the same as the equivalent FTP command. The following table elucidates the commands you need to know:

Command	What It Does
connect *sitename*	Tells the service to connect to the FTP site whose name you include.
chdir *directory*	Tells the service to change to this directory, just like the cd command in real FTP.
ls	Sends you a listing of the current directory. You can then send another FTPmail message to get files.
binary	Must precede a get command for a binary (nontext) file, just like the binary command in real FTP.
uuencode	Uuencodes binary files so they can be attached to your return e-mail message as regular text.
get *filename*	Retrieves the specified file.
quit	Must include this as the last command in the message.

Transferring Files from a Unix Shell Account

If you get your access by dialing up a connection to a Unix shell account, then you'll need to know how to download files back from your Internet account to your desktop computer, as well as how to upload files over the modem to your Internet account.

> **TIP**
>
> **If your computer is on a network connected to the Internet or you dial up with a SLIP or PPP account, then you don't need to take the extra step of downloading files from your Internet account to your desktop computer. You'll simply store your Internet files on your regular computer and manage your directories (or folders if it's a Mac) in the normal way. If so, skip ahead to the next section, *FTP with Your Web Browser.***

Downloading just means bringing a file from a remote computer (such as the UNIX machine you log into) back to your desktop machine over the modem hookup. Similarly, *uploading* means sending a file over the modem from your desktop machine to a remote computer. They are essentially the same process in opposite directions.

Potential Problems Uploading Text Files

Because PCs and Unix machines use different systems to indicate line endings (if you must know, PCs use two characters—carriage return and line feed—while Unix machines use only one, carriage return), your text files might transmit with nonsense characters at the end of each line. This should not happen unless you mistakenly send a text file as a binary file. If your text file shows up on your Unix machine with ^M at the end of each line, you should be able to convert the file with the dos2unix program. If it's not available, ask your system administrator.

Downloading Protocols

The oldest downloading protocol (and consequently the most widely supported) is called Kermit. Kermit is slow! The Xmodem, Ymodem, and Zmodem protocols are all similar, as each is based on the previous one—Ymodem on Xmodem, Zmodem on Ymodem. Both Y- and Zmodem can download multiple files at once. Zmodem is the fastest protocol, but not every program offers it.

You may need to work with more than one protocol, because different software accommodates different protocols. The computers at both ends of a transfer must be using the same protocols for the transfer to work.

I'll list the basic commands for each of these two protocols, using transfers between your Internet account and your desktop computer as examples.

Before we get into the details of the two protocols, let's get one confusing thing out of the way. Even when you're sending only a text file, you have to tell your communications program what kind of binary transfer you want to make because from the point of view of your desktop machine, the file *is* a binary file (that happens to contain just text). The text transfer commands in your communications program deal with sending and receiving plain text. For more on this, see *Straight Text Transfers*, later in this chapter.

File Transfers in General

Before transferring a file, you have to tell your communications (terminal) program which protocol you're using.

Downloading Files To send a file back to your desktop computer:
1. Type the send command (see the table below) and press Enter.
2. In your communications program, select the command for receiving a binary file.

Protocol Name	Text Files	Binary Files
Kermit	kermit -s filename	kermit -s filename -i
Xmodem	sx filename -a	sx filename
Ymodem	sb filename -a	sb filename
Zmodem	sz filename -a	sz filename

Your communications program will show you the progress of the transfer (as a number of bytes and not as a percentage, because it doesn't know how long the incoming file is). When it's done, press Enter.

NOTE With Ymodem, you can send multiple files all at once by listing them all on the command line or using wildcards.

Uploading Files To send a file *from* your desktop computer, first make sure the file you want to send is not in use by any of the programs on your desktop computer. Then:

1. Type the receive command (see the table below) and press Enter.
2. In your communications program, select the command for sending a binary file.

Protocol Name	Text Files	Binary Files
Kermit	kermit -r	kermit -r -i
Xmodem	rx -a	rx
Ymodem	rb -a	rb
Zmodem	rz -a	rz

You'll then be shown a dialog box in which you can select the file you want to send.

Your communications program will show you the progress of the transfer (as a running percentage or visual graphic). When it's done, press Enter. The file on your Internet account will have the same name as the original.

Straight Text Transfers Your communications program should also provide you with commands for sending and receiving text over your modem. If you think about it, you'll realize that you are already sending and receiving text. When you type into the terminal window, the communications program is sending the characters you type over the modem to the computer at the other end of the connection. And when a Unix program produces output, it appears on your screen because it is passing over the modem to your PC.

The text transfer commands differ only in that they allow you to send text directly from a text file (instead of from what you type at the keyboard), and they allow you to store the text appearing on the screen in a file.

Besides typing text into the terminal window, there are two other ways to send text over your modem. You can type the text in some other program on your computer, select and copy the text, and then paste it into the terminal window. This should work most of the time, although you can overload the buffer or otherwise cause the modem to cough and stop sending text.

TIP

If you create a text file in a word processor, be sure to save it as a text file, and make sure there are hard returns at the end of each line. You may have to save it as a text document *with line breaks*.

The third way to send text is to send it from a text file. Again, create the file on your desktop computer, in a word processor or text editor. Save the text file and close it, so it's not in use by the program you created it in.

> **NOTE** Remember, if you're putting the text into a file with Vi, to first type i to start inserting text, before sending the text file.

In your terminal window, run the text editor or other program you intend to dump the text into. When you are ready, select the command to send a text file. When prompted, type the name of the text file and press Enter. You'll see the text start spilling out across your screen until the entire file has been dumped. Then save the text file you've created.

> **NOTE** Although you *can* systematically cut text from your terminal window and then paste it into a text file, it can get tiresome if you're transferring a great deal of text this way. To save text output into a file on your desktop computer, first type whatever commands you need to create the output but *don't press Enter yet*. For example, to send the contents of a text file to a file on your PC, type **cat** *textfilename* but don't press Enter yet.

By the way, most communications programs have an Append option for their receive text file command. This option allows you to attach various pieces of text to a single file.

FTP with Your Web Browser

You've already seen (in Chapters 5 and 6) how to download files from FTP sites with a Web browser (it usually involves just clicking a link). If you want to go directly to an FTP site, you can type its address in the browser's address box, starting with ftp://, for example, `ftp://rtfm.mit.edu/pub/usenet-by-group`.

With most browsers, you can only connect anonymously, and you can only receive files, not upload them. However, with Netscape, you can connect with a login by preceding the FTP address with the login and an @ sign. For example, to log in to the FTP site for my magazine with Netscape, I connect to `ftp://xian@ezone.org`.

Now you can also send files to a site. To do so, first connect to the site. Then select File ➤ Upload File. Choose the file you want to send in the Open dialog box that appears and then click on OK.

TIP You can also simply drag a file into the browser window and click on Yes to upload it.

Specific FTP Programs

Before going on to discuss Telnet, I'll explain the details of a couple of specific FTP programs. If you use a Macintosh, you'll want to do FTP with either Anarchie or Fetch. Anarchie combines an Archie program with an FTP program, so you can use it to search for programs (it also has a lot of built-in sites already listed), but you can only download files with it. Fetch is an easy-to-use FTP client for the Mac. If you're stuck in a Unix shell, you'll want to use Ftp or its slightly improved cousin Ncftp. If you're using Windows, then WS_FTP is your best bet for FTP. (These days, though, I use Netscape Navigator most of the time.)

TIP Most online services, such as AOL and CompuServe, offer FTP, but they generally also maintain their own archives of the most popular files and programs from the Net, and you may find it faster and easier to download them directly from those archives.

Anarchie

Anarchie

Anarchie combines Archie and FTP. Why didn't someone think of this sooner? To start Anarchie, you double-click on the Anarchie icon. Anarchie first brings up a window called Bookmarks, with a thorough, built-in list of FTP sites.

TIP Great instructions for Anarchie can be found on http://www/
mcp.com/59307192573003/hayden/iskm/iskm3/
pt4/ch23.html#aa2.

To make an Archie query, press Command-T. This brings up the Archie dialog box (see Figure 10.1).

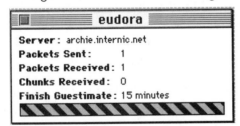

FIGURE 10.1:
The Archie dialog box. Type the file you're looking for and click on Find. I'm looking for Eudora.

The server in the Server box should be the nearest one to you. Choose the nearest one if it's not. Type the *filename* text into the Find box. Then click on the Find button (bottom right). Anarchie will display a window with the *filename* text in the title bar and a guesstimate of how much longer it's going to take.

When the search is done, Anarchie will display a window containing all the directories and files it's found with the *filename* search text, along with the host sites at which they're stored (see Figure 10.2).

To retrieve the file you want, just double-click on it.

Fetch

Fetch

On Macintoshes, the standard file-transfer program is called Fetch. You can obtain Fetch from `http://www.dartmouth.edu/pages/softdev/fetch.html`.

When you double-click on the Fetch icon, it brings up the Open Connection dialog box (see Figure 10.3).

If you don't want the default host, type a new one. Enter your password in the password window and enter a directory if you know the one you're headed for. (If you don't, just leave it blank.) Then click on OK.

Once you've connected to the host, you can navigate to the directory structure by clicking on the folder icons, just as with any Macintosh program. Click on the Binary

Name	Size	Date	Zone	Host	Path
eudora	-	7/1/94	3	dorm.rutgers.edu	/pub/Mac/eudora
eudora	-	8/15/93	3	dorm.rutgers.edu	/pub/msdos/eudora
eudora	-	2/25/92	3	hub.ucsb.edu	/pub/mail/eudora
eudora	-	12/4/91	3	pacific.mps.ohio-state.edu	/mac/comm/Mail/eudora
eudora	-	12/8/93	3	ftp.ucdavis.edu	/dos-public/windows/eudora
eudora	-	5/15/94	3	ee.utah.edu	/pop3/eudora
eudora	-	6/30/94	3	sutro.sfsu.edu	/training/eudora
eudora	-	11/21/93	3	ucsd.edu	/pub/mac/eudora
eudora	-	6/27/93	3	ftp.halcyon.com	/pub/eudora
eudora	-	7/8/92	3	ftp.cs.wisc.edu	/pub/misc/eudora
eudora-122.hqx	326k	4/4/93	3	ftp.wustl.edu	/systems/mac/info-mac/Old/comm/eudora-122.hqx
eudora-122.hqx	326k	10/15/92	3	ftp.cerf.net	/pub/software/mac/internet/eudora-122.hqx
eudora-131-accessories.hqx	768k	4/13/93	3	ftp.wustl.edu	/systems/mac/info-mac/Old/comm/eudora-131-accessories.hqx
eudora-131-accessories.hqx	768k	4/12/93	3	ftp.wustl.edu	/systems/mac/info-mac/comm/net/eudora-131-accessories.hqx
eudora-131.hqx	221k	4/4/93	3	ftp.wustl.edu	/systems/mac/info-mac/Old/comm/eudora-131.hqx
eudora-14-manual.hqx	938k	10/10/93	3	ftp.wustl.edu	/systems/mac/info-mac/comm/net/eudora-14-manual.hqx
eudora-14-manual.hqx	938k	10/10/93	3	ftp.wustl.edu	/systems/mac/info-mac/Old/comm/eudora-14-manual.hqx
eudora-14.hqx	336k	9/23/93	3	ftp.wustl.edu	/systems/mac/info-mac/Old/comm/net/eudora-14.hqx
eudora-offline-reader-unix.shar	23k	9/21/92	3	sumex-aim.stanford.edu	/info-mac/comm/tcp/mail/eudora-offline-reader-unix.shar
eudora-offline-reader-unix.shar	23k	9/21/92	3	mrcnext.cso.uiuc.edu	/pub/info-mac/comm/tcp/mail/eudora-offline-reader-unix.shar
eudora-offline-reader-unix.shar	23k	9/19/92	3	ftp.wustl.edu	/systems/mac/info-mac/comm/net/eudora-offline-reader-unix.shar
eudora-offline-reader-unix.shar	23k	9/19/92	3	ftp.wustl.edu	/systems/mac/info-mac/Old/comm/eudora-offline-reader-unix.shar
eudora-offline-reader-unix.shar	23k	9/19/92	3	ftp.wustl.edu	/systems/mac/info-mac/Old/comm/net/eudora-offline-reader-unix.shar
eudora-offline-reader.shar	23k	9/20/92	3	ftp.wustl.edu	/systems/mac/info-mac/Old/unix/eudora-offline-reader.shar
eudora1.2.2.i.sit.hqx	449k	12/4/91	3	pacific.mps.ohio-state.edu	/mac/comm/Mail/eudora/eudora1.2.2.i.sit.hqx
eudora1.31accessories.sit.hqx	768k	4/15/93	3	ftp.wustl.edu	/systems/mac/umich.edu/util/comm/eudora1.31accessories.sit.hqx
eudora1.31accessories.sit.hqx	768k	7/17/93	3	nigel.msen.com	/pub/systems/mac/mactcp/eudora1.31accessories.sit.hqx
eudora1.4.opt.hqx	371k	10/6/93	3	gumby.dsd.trw.com	/pub/macintosh/mail/eudora1.4.opt.hqx
eudora1.4.opt.hqx	371k	9/25/93	3	ftp.wustl.edu	/systems/mac/umich.edu/util/comm/eudora1.4.opt.hqx
eudora1.4docs.opt.hqx	938k	10/9/93	3	ftp.wustl.edu	/systems/mac/umich.edu/util/comm/eudora1.4docs.opt.hqx
eudoraunixreader.shar	23k	10/3/92	3	ftp.wustl.edu	/systems/mac/umich.edu/util/comm/eudoraunixreader.shar
Eudora_1.2	3k	9/3/91	3	ftp.wustl.edu	/systems/mac/rascal/comp.sys.mac.announce/+_annoucements_FTPable-fil
Eudora_1.2	3k	9/3/91	3	ftp.wustl.edu	/systems/mac/rascal/CSMA/+_annoucements_FTPable-files/Eudora_1.2
Eudora_1.2.2	3k	10/31/91	3	ftp.wustl.edu	/systems/mac/rascal/CSMA/+_annoucements_FTPable-files/Eudora_1.2.2
Eudora_1.2.2	3k	10/31/91	3	ftp.wustl.edu	/systems/mac/rascal/comp.sys.mac.announce/+_annoucements_FTPable-fil
Eudora_1.2.2_announce	3k	10/17/91	3	ftp.wustl.edu	/systems/mac/rascal/communications/Eudora_1.2.2_announce
Eudora_1.2b57_announce	1k	7/7/91	3	ftp.wustl.edu	/systems/mac/rascal/communications/Eudora_1.2b57_announce
Eudora_1.3b46_info	2k	8/6/92	3	ftp.wustl.edu	/systems/mac/rascal/communications/Eudora_1.3b46_info
README.TXT.pceudora.bin	2k	2/9/93	3	bcm.tmc.edu	/public/README.TXT.pceudora.bin
README.TXT.pceudora.bin	2k	6/25/93	3	ftp.msc.cornell.edu	/pub/dos/src/tmp/README.TXT.pceudora.bin

FIGURE 10.2: This window contains all the files and directories with *Eudora* in their names, along with the FTP sites they're stored at.

radio button to specify a binary file, or leave Automatic clicked to let the program figure it out. Highlight the file or files you want and click on the Get File button to get them (see Figure 10.4).

To send files, you can just drag and drop them onto the Fetch window.

When you are done, select File ➢ Quit.

FIGURE 10.3: The Open Connection dialog box in Fetch.

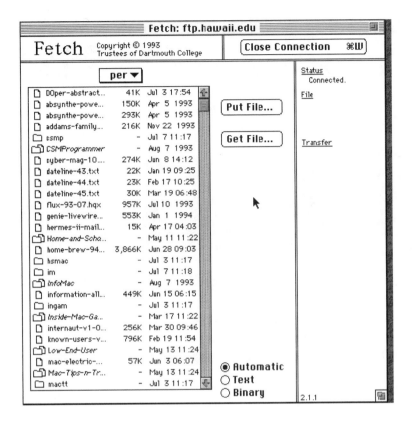

FIGURE 10.4:
The Macintosh interface makes fetching files simple.

Ftp and Ncftp

The basic Unix FTP program is called (what else?) Ftp. There's also a slightly more automated version of it called Ncftp that you might have available on your system. I will explain both.

Transferring Files with Ftp Every Unix shell has the Ftp program. If you've gotten the hang of working with directories and files in Unix, then Ftp should be a snap. To run the Ftp program:

1. Type **ftp *sitename*** at the Unix prompt and press Enter. You can also just type **ftp** and press Enter, and then at the ftp> prompt, type **open *sitename*** and press Enter.

2. Type **anonymous** and press Enter (or just press Enter if you mean to log in under your own name—you'll need a password to do that).

TIP If you mistype **anonymous**, type **u** and press Enter and then correct your spelling.

3. Type your full e-mail address and press Enter (or type your password if you're logging in under your real name). It won't show up as you type.

NOTE If your login fails (you'll know—the program will tell you), you'll still end up at an ftp> prompt, which can be confusing. Just try again by typing **user anonymous** and pressing Enter. Then continue with step 3.

Figure 10.5 shows me FTPing to **ftp.eff.org**, the Electronic Frontier Foundation site.

4. Read whatever information floods across your screen, if any. You should now be at a prompt that looks like this: **ftp>**.

5. Now type **ls** to list files and **cd** to change directories.

```
{netcom10:2} ftp ftp.eff.org
Connected to ftp.eff.org.
220 ftp.eff.org FTP server (Version wu-2.4(2) Thu Apr 28 17:19:59 EDT 1994) read
Name (ftp.eff.org:xian): anonymous
331 Guest login ok, send your complete e-mail address as password.
Password:
```

FIGURE 10.5: I've FTP-ed to **ftp.eff.org**, logged in as anonymous, and typed my e-mail address for a password.

TIP If you plan to transfer several files and you don't want to be prompted about each one, type **prompt** at the ftp> prompt and press Enter *before* getting the files.

6. To transfer a file, type **get *filename*** and press Enter. To transfer multiple files, type **mget *filename1 filename2*** etc. or use wildcards to get every file that matches a pattern. If you use **mget,** you'll have to type **y** for each file transferred.

   • If you are planning to transfer binary files, type **binary** at the ftp> prompt and press Enter. Otherwise, the program assumes that you are transferring text files. If you've transferred some binary files and *then* want to transfer some text files, type **ascii** at the ftp> prompt and press Enter.

- If you're transferring a big file, you can press Ctrl+Z to stop the job, and then type **bg** and press Enter to finish the transfer in the background so you can continue working.

7. Repeat steps 5 and 6 as often as you like.

> **TIP**
>
> If you're doing an FTP file transfer from a dial-up Unix shell account, and you're transferring a large file, there's the possibility that your modem will hang up if it doesn't pass along any characters for too long an interval. If this problem happens to you, type **hash** and press Enter before entering the Get command. Ftp will put a # symbol on the screen for every kilobyte transferred, which will in turn keep your modem awake.

8. When you are done, type **quit** at the ftp> prompt and press Enter. This should return you to the Unix prompt.

Ncftp—A Better Unix FTP Some Unix systems have a beefier version of Ftp available called Ncftp. To run Ncftp (if you've got it), type **ncftp *ftp-sitename*** at the Unix prompt and press Enter. The main advantages of Ncftp are:

- Ncftp assumes you want to use anonymous FTP and saves you typing that word (start it with **ncftp -u *ftp-sitename*** to log in with your username).
- Ncftp automatically takes you to the last directory you went to at the site.

NetCruiser

NetCruiser has a built-in FTP module. To use it, click on the FTP button. The FTP: Connect To dialog box appears. Type a host name and press Enter. This action brings up the FTP To dialog box, which assumes you want to log in via anonymous FTP. If not, uncheck Use Anonymous FTP and then enter a username and password. Then click on OK.

Once you've connected to the host, NetCruiser will show you the contents of the remote host in a new FTP To window. The top pane shows directories and the bottom one shows files. Highlight the file or files you want and click on the Download a File from the Remote Computer button to get them (see Figure 10.6).

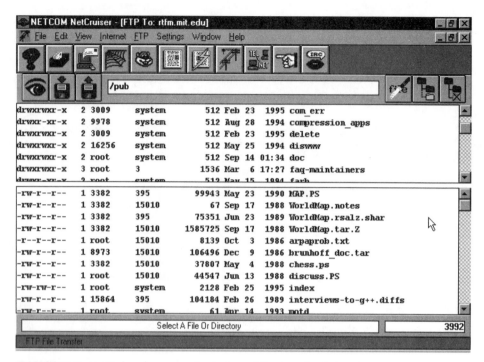

FIGURE 10.6: NetCruiser shows you directories and files in a simple layout.

To send files, click on the Upload button and select the file you want to send. When you are done, just close the FTP To window.

WS_FTP

A good FTP client for Windows is WS_FTP (`ftp://129.29.64.246/pub/msdos/`). To start it, double-click on the WS_FTP icon.

The Session Profile dialog box pops-up. If you don't want the default host, type a new one. Enter your login name and password and in the Remote Host box, enter a directory if you know the one you're headed for. Then click on OK.

Once you've connected to the host, WS_FTP will show you the contents of your own computer in the left two panes and the contents of the remote host in the right two (see Figure 10.7). The top panes show directories and the bottom ones show files. Click on the Binary radio button to specify a binary file. Highlight the file or files you want and click on the "<—" button between the Local System and Remote System areas to get them.

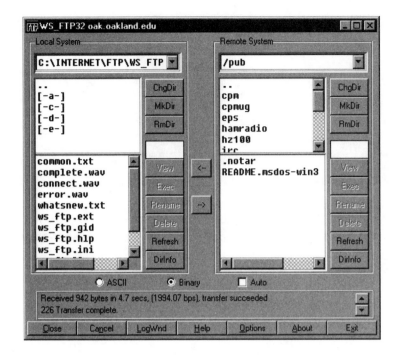

FIGURE 10.7:
WS_FTP gives you an easy way to get around a remote computer and retrieve files from it.

To send files, you can just drag and drop them onto the WS_FTP window. When you are done, select File ➤ Exit.

Telnet—A Computer in Your Window

One aspect of the interconnectedness of the Net is that you can log into other machines on the Internet directly from your own computer. With Telnet, you can log into any (Unix-style) computer or network for which you have a password, as well as thousands of public sites where passwords are not required.

Many university libraries now make their catalogs available by Telnet, as do countless other repositories of useful information. Of course, as with so many other Internet resources, you need to know where to go to take advantage of these public sites. Unfortunately, there's no overriding index or guide to available Telnet sites. One remote login program, Hytelnet, does include an up-to-date index of university libraries, so that's a start. (See Chapter 5 for more on Hytelnet.) In general, though, you have to ask around and collect remote login sites just as you have to with FTP sites.

> **TIP**
>
> If you have a Unix account, you can even telnet to your own service provider and log in to your own account, even if you're already logged in there! This is actually more useful when you are borrowing someone else's access and want to log into your own account to, say, check your e-mail.

You can also run the Telnet program by just typing **telnet** and pressing enter at the Unix prompt. This will put you at a telnet> prompt. Then type **open *host-sitename*** and press Enter.

Telnetting is easy. You run your Telnet program and open a connection to an Internet site as I just described. Then you have to log in. Logging in with Telnet is the same as logging into any computer system. You type your username and press Enter. Then you type a password and press Enter.

> **TIP**
>
> For public sites, you might have to log in under some special name, and either you won't be asked for a password or you'll be able to just press Enter when asked.

Figure 10.8 shows me Telnetting from my Unix shell account to California State University's Advanced Technology Information Network to get information about California agriculture. The Telnet site is `caticsuf.cati.csufresno.edu`, and the username that I log in with is **public**.

```
{netcom2:4} telnet caticsuf.cati.csufresno.edu
Trying...
Connected to caticsuf.cati.csufresno.edu.
Escape character is '^]'.


SunOS UNIX (caticsuf)

login: public
```

FIGURE 10.8:
Logging into the Advanced Technology Information Network via Telnet

The site doesn't ask for a password. Instead, a screen full of welcoming information appears.

From this point on, you're on your own. Depending on where you've telnetted to, you'll be either at a Unix prompt or, more likely, at the main menu of some information program. There are myriad such programs and each one works differently, but don't worry. They'll all prompt you, and they're designed for lay people. Generally, you can press Enter to accept defaults until you're given a menu of information. Then you have to make some choices.

Logging out from a Telnet session is either a matter of typing **bye** or **exit** or **logout** at a prompt, or pressing **q** (for *quit*) or choosing the appropriate menu choice from within an information program. Telnet will sign you off with "Connection closed by foreign host."

Finding a Telnet Program

Both Windows 95 and Windows 3.11 for Workgroups come with a perfectly fine Telnet client program called, as you might expect, Telnet (Telnet.exe, in full). Unix also has a Telnet program built in. To run it, just type **telnet *sitename*** at the Unix prompt and press Enter. For the Macintosh, you can download an excellent Telnet client program called NCSA Telnet (`http://www.ncsa.uiuc.edu/SDG/Software/Brochure/MacDownSoft.html#MacTelnet`).

Telnetting from Your Web Browser

Links to Telnet sites can be embedded into Web pages. When you select such a link, your browser will attempt to launch your Telnet program to connect to such a site. It will fail, though, if you've never told your browser where your Telnet program is. Solving this problem involves going to the Options or Preferences dialog box, choosing the Apps (or Applications, or Supporting Applications—not to be confused with Helper Applications) tab or Apps area of the dialog box, and then entering the path and file name of your Telnet program in the Telnet box. In Netscape Navigator for Windows, for instance, you have to do the fairly surreal action of choosing Options ➣ General Preferences, choosing the Apps tab, clicking in the Telnet box, typing **telnet**, and then clicking on OK.

> **TIP**
> If you're not sure of the exact path or file name of your Telnet program, you can click on the Browse button to hunt around on your hard disk for it.

Chapter

11

GOPHER AND GOPHERSPACE

FEATURING

- **Understanding Gopher**
- **Browsing Gopherspace**
- **Running specific Gopher programs**
- **Gophering with (Unix) Gopher, NetCruiser, TurboGopher, your Web browser, and WSGopher**

Gopher is a sophisticated Internet client-server system that allows seamless integration of different data types and protocols without regard to the type of computer the client (you, more or less) is running on. If you run Gopher from a character-based Unix account, you see things as lists consisting of text entries. If you run a Gopher client on another platform, the menus and items will look appropriate to that type of computer.

What Is Gopher?

Technically, Gopher sits (or rides) on top of FTP and performs Telnet logins, Archie searches, and other Internet services without requiring you to know (or type) the specific addresses and commands. Gopher does this by presenting everything to you in the form of menus. As long as you can highlight an item on a menu and select it, Gopher does the rest.

That's the beauty of Gopher: everything is presented to you in the form of menus (or lists). The items on the menus can be directories, documents, searchable databases, other menus, and more. It doesn't matter if the source material is stored on a Unix machine, or in VMS, DOS, Macintosh, Windows NT, or anything. With Gopher, it's all the same to you. Another advantage is that the menu entries can be plain English names, even when they point to a file, so you really know what you're getting or looking at.

You can start at any Gopher server (site) and get to almost any other one by choosing the Other Gopher Servers choice from the main menu. This feature brings the whole of *Gopherspace* within your reach, no matter where you start.

You can also follow any tangent that catches your fancy and leave bookmarks in any part of Gopherspace you might want to return to. When you find your way to a document, you can read it on screen or even download it directly to your desktop machine (if you dial up your account on a different computer).

NOTE Chapter 5 explains how to search for items that are locked in Gopherspace and not visible to popular Web search engines using Veronica and Jughead.

At one time, the Internet Gopher was one of the most useful and seamless tools on the Net. Then the Web came along and Web browsers could do everything Gopher browsers could and more. Web browsers can even connect to Gopher sites, so there's precious little reason to have a separate Gopher program now. Many dedicated gopher programs come with extensive bookmarks that make it easier to find specific information in gopherspace, though, so you may want your own gopher program. Even if you just plan to use your Web browser when entering gopherspace, you'll still want to read up on that later in this chapter.

NOTE Gopher is so-called either because it can "go fer" stuff and bring it to you or because the mascot of the University of Minnesota (where Gopher was created) is a gopher; it is not named after the Love Boat character played by (now former U.S. Representative) Fred Grandy.

Exploring Gopherspace

Here's the general procedure for running any Gopher client. First, start the program. You can specify a server when you start the program, but you don't have to. If you don't, the first menu you see will be for the default Gopher server that your client starts you off with.

From this point on, it's all a matter of selecting from menus. No matter which server you start from, you can always choose to go to other Gopher servers and keep searching from there.

When you find your way to documents, you can read them, one screenful at a time, search through them for key words, bring them back to your Internet account via FTP, have them mailed to your Internet address, or download them directly to your desktop computer.

TIP You can also ask questions about and discuss Gopher in the Usenet newsgroup `comp.infosystems.gopher`. See Chapter 8 for more on Usenet newsgroups.

To use your Web browser to explore Gopherspace, you can either start by following a link that points to a Gopher program, or you can enter the address of a Gopher server directly into the address box (in the form `gopher://gopher.netcom.com`, for example).

If you really do want to use a Gopher client and not just your Web browser, you can download one or use the built-in Gopher program available on just about every Unix system. There's an excellent Gopher program for the Macintosh called TurboGopher (`ftp://ftp.lanl.gov/pub/mac/gopher`). For Windows, you can download WSGopher (`ftp://dewey.tis.inel.gov/pub/wsgopher`).

I'll explain each of these approaches in more detail later in this chapter.

> **TIP**
>
> Don't worry if you get a *busy signal*—a message that you can't be connected right now because there are too many people using the server. Just try again a little later. As with other Internet resources, use Gopher in the evenings and on weekends whenever possible.

Browsing Gopherspace with Gopher

The original Unix Gopher program is called, naturally enough, Gopher. If it's installed on your system, you can run it by typing **gopher** at the Unix prompt and pressing Enter. To start the Gopher client with a different server from its default, type **gopher *server-sitename*** and press Enter. This is called *pointing* your Gopher client at the server.

Figure 11.1 shows the first-level menu that appears when I run my Gopher client and point it at the University of Minnesota Gopher.

Getting around the Menus

Browsing Gopherspace is then just a matter of selecting menu choices and following them where they go. You can always type the number of a menu item and press Enter. Depending on your communications program, you may be able to use your arrow keys to get around the menus ($\downarrow$ to go down an item, $\uparrow$ to go up one, $\rightarrow$ to select an item and follow it where it goes, $\leftarrow$ to go back to the previous menu). At any point you can return to the main menu by typing **m**. You can also connect to a new Gopher server by typing **o** and then entering the host name.

Otherwise, type **j** to go down an item and **k** to go up one item. Press Enter to select an item and follow it where it goes, and type **u** to go back to the previous menu.

> **TIP**
>
> The ability to always find your way back through previous menus (with u) is as useful as the proverbial trail of bread crumbs.

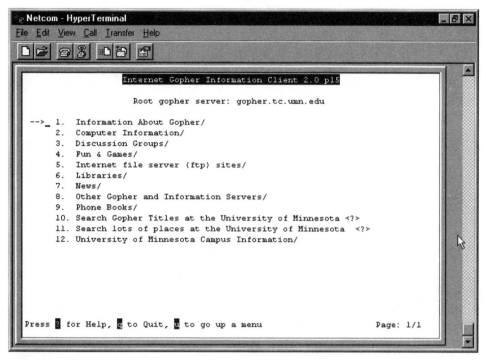

FIGURE 11.1: The main menu from the University of Minnesota's Gopher server. I pointed my Gopher client at the U of M Gopher by typing **gopher gopher.tc.umn.edu** and pressing Enter.

If a menu is longer than one screen, press the spacebar to go to the next screen (or press **>**, **+**, or PageDown). To go back to the previous screenful, press **b** (or **<**, **-**, or PageUp).

You can identify items in the gopher menus by the last character on the line:

- Items that end in a forward slash (/) lead to new menus.
- Items that end in a period (.) or no punctuation lead to text documents.
- Items that end in <?> or <CSO> lead to searchable indexes.
- Items that end in <tel> activate Telnet connections.

Reading Documents

Eventually, your selections will lead you to a document. (You'll have selected an item that ends in a period or no punctuation.) The document will first appear on the screen. If you're not interested in reading it right away, type **q**.

Documents are piped through the Unix paging program called More. To see the next page, press the spacebar. To go back one page, type **b**.

NOTE Actually, Gopher documents might be piped through any paging program, not necessarily the one called More, but the general rule remains the same: press the spacebar to advance another screenful.

To search a document in Gopher, type **/** and then type the text you'd like to search for and press Enter. To repeat a search with the same search text, just press **n**.

When you get to the end of a document, or quit reading it, you'll be given these options:

```
Press <RETURN> to continue, <m> to mail, <D> to
download, <s> to save, or <p> to print:
```

WARNING Don't choose the print option if you're connected to your Unix account by a modem. Gopher won't send the document to your printer—it will attempt to print it at your host computer, and it will probably fail.

Press Enter to return to the previous menu. Type **m** to mail the document to yourself. You'll be prompted for the address:

```
+------------------------------------------------------------------------+
|                                                                        |
| Mail current document to:  [                                        ]   |
|                                       [Cancel ^G] [Accept - Enter]     |
|                                                                        |
+------------------------------------------------------------------------+
```

Type **D** to download the document (be sure to type an uppercase **D**). You'll then be given a choice of download protocols. (See chapter 10 for more on downloading files to your desktop computer.) Choose whichever one you like to use with your communications program (by number). Then, in your communications program, choose to receive a binary file or a text file, if you prefer.

Type **s** to save a copy of the file in your home directory. Gopher will prompt you for a file name. Press Enter, or type a different file name and press Enter.

Getting to Another Gopher Server

To get to a different Gopher server from the one you started with, look for a menu item such as Other Gopher and Information Servers/ (this is how it's worded on the U of M Gopher main menu). Not all servers have this type of option, so if you're in a cul-de-sac, run your Gopher client again but point it at a server such as **gopher.tc.umn.edu** to start with.

You'll be taken to a top-level menu from which you can select either a large alphabetical list of Gopher servers or a general geographical area to start with.

If you know the name of the server you want, you can select the alphabetical option. Otherwise, start zeroing in with the correct region. I've found my way to the Electronic Frontier Foundation's Gopher server in Austin (see Figure 11.2).

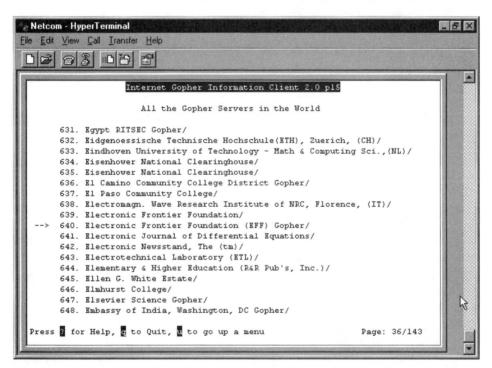

FIGURE 11.2: I searched for the word *electronic*, by typing **/electronic** and pressing Enter. It took me to item 640. I had to repeat the search a couple of times.

TIP

When a list is very long, such as a list of all the Gopher servers in the world, you can save time paging through it by searching for a keyword. To start a search, type a forward slash (/). This will bring up a box into which you can type the text to search for. Then press Enter.

Bookmarks in Gopherspace

If you find your way to or stumble upon an interesting Gopher site or stash of documents, you might want to create a bookmark there so that you can find your way back more easily.

To add a menu item to your bookmark list, type **a**. To add the current menu to your bookmark list, type **A** (uppercase). Gopher will prompt you for a name for the bookmark by suggesting the name of the item or menu:

```
+----------------------------------------------------------------------+
|                                                                      |
|  Name for this bookmark?   Ecological Wisdom                         |
|                                                                      |
|                                    [Cancel ^G] [Accept - Enter]      |
|                                                                      |
+----------------------------------------------------------------------+
```

Press Enter to accept the suggested name, or type a different name and press Enter. You can view your bookmark list at any time by typing **v**. (The bookmark list will appear as a Gopher menu, just like any other list, with the heading Bookmarks). To delete a bookmark from your bookmark list, type **d**.

To start your Gopher client with your bookmark list as the first menu, type **gopher -b** at the Unix prompt and press Enter.

Quitting Gopher

You can quit Gopher at any time by typing **q** or pressing Ctrl-C. Gopher will ask you if you're sure:

```
  Really quit (y/n) ? y.
```

Press Enter to quit. To quit without being prompted, type **Q**.

Getting Help for Gopher

You can get a quick reference of Gopher commands by typing **?** at any time. The help document can be saved, downloaded, or mailed just like any other document.

You can see the manual pages for Gopher by typing **man Gopher** at the Unix prompt and pressing Enter.

Browsing Gopherspace with NetCruiser

NetCruiser's Gopher module is really the same thing as it's Web browser. To start it, click on the Gopher icon

This starts you off at NetCruiser's site chooser, where you can accept the default Gopher site (**gopher·netcom·com**) or type in the name of another site. Clicking on OK takes you to Netcom Gopher's main menu. Items that lead to further menus appear as folders. Items that are documents appear with document icons (see Figure 11.3).

Getting around the Menus

Navigate Gopherspace by double-clicking on items you want to pursue. At any point, you can type in the site address of any Gopher server in the box at the top of the window.

Figure 11.4 shows a typical gopher menu in NetCruiser.

Reading Documents

Eventually, your selections will lead you to a document. If the information is longer than a screen, scroll down using the arrow at the bottom right corner of the window.

To search a document in NetCruiser, click on the Search button, and just type the text you'd like to search for and press Enter. To continue the same search elsewhere, click on Search and press Enter again.

You can save a document by clicking on the Save button.

If the document you have requested is not text—say, you've requested a Macintosh or PC application—when you click on it, TurboGopher will automatically download the

Bookmark Button

FIGURE 11.3: The NetCruiser Gopher's main menu

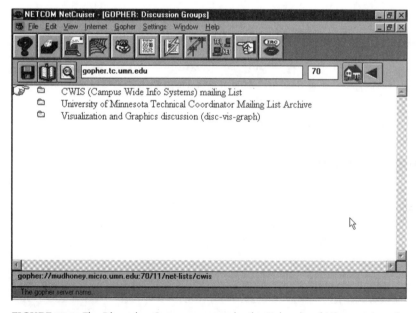

FIGURE 11.4: The Discussion Groups menu under the University of Minnesota's main gopher menu in NetCruiser

file to your hard drive. A standard Save As dialog box will pop-up, so you can name the file and store it where you wish. Most large files are compressed in Gopherspace, as they are elsewhere on the Net, so you may have to use one of the standard unzipping programs, such as WinZip or Pkunzip, to open up your new application.

Getting to Another Gopher Server

To get to a different Gopher server from the one you started with, double-click on the Other Internet Gopher Servers (via U.C. Santa Cruz) item.

You'll be taken to a top-level menu from which you can select either a large alphabetical list of Gopher servers or a general geographical area to start with.

> **TIP**
>
> **When a list is very long, such as a list of all the gopher servers in the world, you can save time paging through it by searching for a keyword.**

If you know the name of the server you want, you can select the alphabetical option. Otherwise, start zeroing in with the correct region.

Bookmarks in Gopherspace

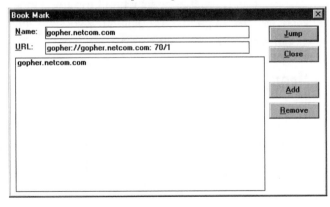

If you find your way to or stumble upon an interesting Gopher site or stash of documents, you might want to create a bookmark there so that you can find your way back more easily.

To add a site to your bookmark list, click on the Bookmark button.

NetCruiser will display the Book Mark dialog box. Click on the Add button. Then click on Close.

To jump to a bookmark, click on the Bookmark button, choose the bookmark you want to jump to, and click on the Jump button.

Quitting Gopher in NetCruiser

You can quit gopher at any time by simply closing the Gopher window.

Browsing Gopherspace with TurboGopher

TurboGopher is an excellent Gopher program for the Macintosh. Each menu is displayed in its own window. Documents are shown with a document icon, and menus are shown with a folder icon. For the Mac user, browsing Gopherspace feels just like opening files on your own hard drive: You click on folders, and they open into windows; you click on documents, and they open for you to read.

You can download TurboGopher from `ftp://boombox.micro.umn.edu`.

To start TurboGopher, double-click on its icon.

To connect to the default gopher server, pull down to Start Gopher under the File menu. If you want to connect to a different server, select File ➤ Another Gopher, type the address in the window, and press Enter.

Figure 11.5 shows the first-level menu that appears when I run my gopher client and point it at the University of Minnesota gopher. (I pointed my gopher client at the U of M gopher by typing gopher `gopher.tc.umn.edu` and pressing Enter.)

Getting around the Menus

Browsing Gopherspace is just a matter of pointing and clicking your way through folders, just like anywhere else in the Macintosh world. When you first connect to your server, a window will come up with a list of gopher choices, some folders, and a few documents. Clicking on any icon takes you to a subdirectory, or opens a document. If you wish to close a subdirectory or document and go back to the main menu, it's as easy as closing a window.

Figure 11.6 shows a typical Gopher menu in TurboGopher.

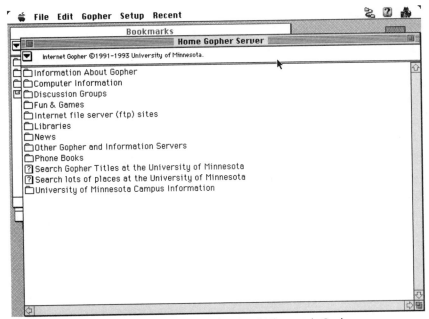

FIGURE 11.5: The main menu from the University of Minnesota's Gopher server in TurboGopher

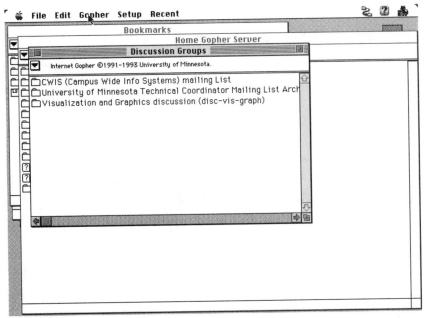

FIGURE 11.6: The Discussion Groups menu under the University of Minnesota's main gopher menu

Reading Documents

Eventually, your selections will lead you to a document. Read a document as you would in any other Macintosh application: if the information is longer than a screen, scroll down using the arrow at the bottom right corner of the window.

To search a document in TurboGopher, use the Edit ➤ Find command, type the text you'd like to search for and press Enter, as you do with any Macintosh Find dialog box. To continue the same search elsewhere, use the Edit ➤ Find Again command.

At the end of a document, you can print it or save it on your computer, using the File ➤ Save As Text command. If the document you have requested is not text—perhaps you've requested a Macintosh or PC application—when you click on it, TurboGopher will automatically download the file to your hard drive. A standard Save As dialog box will appear, so you can name the file and store it where you wish. Most large files are compressed in Gopherspace, as they are elsewhere on the Net, so you may have to use one of the standard unstuffing protocols, like StuffIt, to open up your new application.

Getting to Another Gopher Server

To get to a different Gopher server from the one you started with, select File ➤ Another Server.

Bookmarks in Gopherspace

If you find your way to or stumble upon an interesting Gopher site or stash of documents, you might want to create a bookmark there so that you can find your way back more easily.

To add a site to your bookmark list, drag down to Set Bookmark under the Gopher menu. TurboGopher will prompt you for a name for the bookmark (suggesting the name of the item or menu).

Save a bookmark for this document set as:

Discussion Groups

Cancel   OK

Press Enter to accept the suggested name or type a different name and press Enter. You can view your bookmark list at any time by choosing Gopher ➤ Show Bookmarks. (The bookmark list will appear as a gopher menu, just like any other list.) To edit the address or any other information about the bookmark, click on the bookmark you wish to edit in the Bookmarks window. When it is highlighted, you can choose Edit Bookmarks and change the information you wish, or choose Delete, if you wish to throw it away.

Quitting TurboGopher

You can quit TurboGopher at any time by selecting File ➤ Quit. Closing the window you're working in closes that connection but leaves the program open so you can choose another server and keep gophering.

Getting Help

You can get help within the program by selecting Gopher ➤ Help or Command+H. There are excellent help resources available at the University of Minnesota site as well, including a FAQ and several guides. Poke around the site to see what's available. That's one of the great aspects of gophering.

Browsing Gopherspace with your Web Browser

All Web browsers make perfectly adequate Gopher clients as well. One way to end up in Gopherspace from the Web is to click on a link that (whether you realize it or not) is linked to a Gopher address. This process is a little like tumbling down a rabbit hole. You'll lose the graphics and formatting of the Web behind and enter a limited (but still hyperlinked) world of folders and documents.

The other way to start browsing Gopherspace with a Web browser is to type a Gopher address into the address box, for example

```
gopher://gopher.netcom.com
```

Documents are shown with a document icon. Menus are shown with a folder icon. Figure 11.7 shows the Netcom Gopher server viewed in Netscape Navigator.

Getting around the Menus

Browsing Gopherspace is just a matter of pointing and clicking on links, just like anywhere else you visit using a Web browser. Clicking on any icon or link takes you to

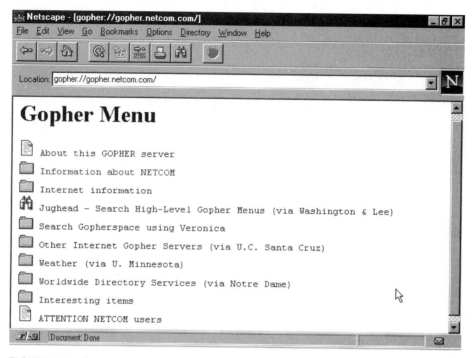

FIGURE 11.7: The main menu from the Netcom Gopher server in Netscape Navigator

a subdirectory or opens a document. If you wish to leave a subdirectory or document and go back to the main menu, you just use the Back button, as you would on the Web.

Reading Documents

Eventually, your selections will lead you to a document, which will appear unformatted and in a typewriter typeface (see Figure 11.8).

You read the document as you would any Web page, scrolling down if necessary.

Bookmarks in Gopherspace

If you find your way to or stumble upon an interesting Gopher site, you can make a bookmark to it as you would for any Web page or other resource in your browser.

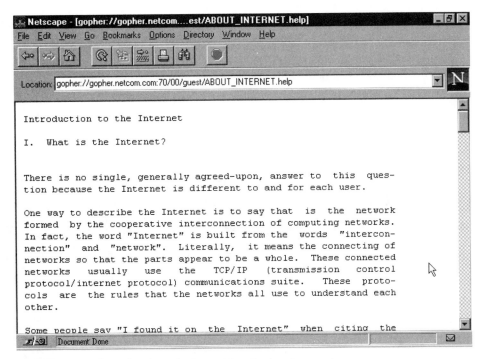

FIGURE 11.8: Information about the Internet in a Gopher document

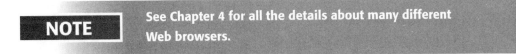

NOTE See Chapter 4 for all the details about many different Web browsers.

Browsing Gopherspace with WSGopher

WSGopher is a fine Gopher program for Windows. Each menu is displayed in its own window. Documents are shown with a document icon and menus with a folder icon. Browsing Gopherspace feels a little like opening files on your own PC: You click on folders, and they open into windows; you click on documents, and they open for you to read.

You can download WSGopher from an archive site (such as `ftp://boo-box.micro.umn.edu/pub/gopher/Windows/` or `ftp://sunsite.unc.edu/pub/micro/pc-stuff/ms-windows/winsock/apps/`). Look for ws-12.exe, a self-extracting archive file.

To start WSGopher, double-click on its icon.

WSGopher will automatically connect to its default Gopher server at the University of Illinois at Urbana-Champaign. Figure 11.9 shows the first-level menu that appears when I run WSGopher.

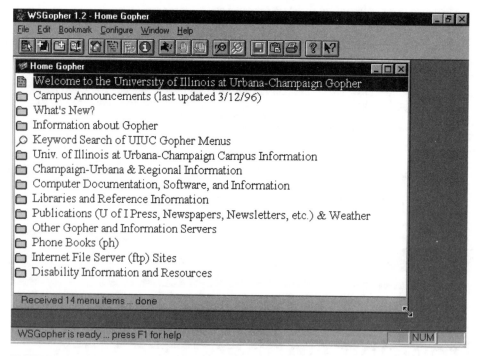

FIGURE 11.9: The main menu from the University of Illinois at Urbana-Champaign's Gopher server

Getting around the Menus

As with the other Gopher servers, browsing Gopherspace is just a matter of pointing and clicking your way through folders. When you first connect to your server, a window will pop-up containing a list of Gopher choices, some folders, and a few documents. Clicking on any icon takes you to a subdirectory, or opens a document. If you wish to close a subdirectory or document and return to the main menu, it's as easy as closing a window.

Figure 11.10 shows a typical gopher menu in WSGopher.

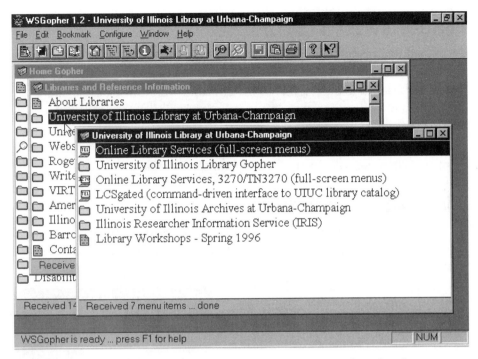

FIGURE 11.10: The contents of a folder in the Libraries and Reference Information directory

Reading Documents

Eventually, your selections will lead you to a document. Reading a document is the same as reading a document in any other Windows application.

To search a document in WSGopher, click on the Find button, and just type the text you'd like to search for and press Enter. To continue the same search elsewhere, press F3.

At the end of a document, you can save it on your computer, using the File ➤ Save Item command. If the document you have requested is not text—say it's a PC application—when you click on it, WSGopher will automatically download the file to your hard drive. The standard Save As dialog box pops-up, so that you can name the file and store it where you wish. Most large files are compressed in Gopherspace, as they are elsewhere on the Net, so you may have to use one of the standard unzipping programs, such as WinZip or Pkunzip, to open up your new file.

Getting to Another Gopher Server

To get to a different gopher server from the one you started with, double-click on Other Gopher and Information Servers.

You'll be taken to a top-level menu from which you can select either a large alphabetical list of Gopher servers or a general geographical area to start with (scroll down a little to get past the university's options).

If you know the name of the server you want, you can select the alphabetical option. Otherwise, start zeroing in using the correct region.

Bookmarks in Gopherspace

If you find your way to or stumble upon an interesting Gopher site or stash of documents, you might want to create a bookmark there so that you can find your way back more easily.

To add a site to your bookmark list, select Bookmark ➤ Add Bookmark. WSGopher will prompt you for a category to store the bookmark in. Select a category or type a name and click the Create button to create a new one, and then click on OK.

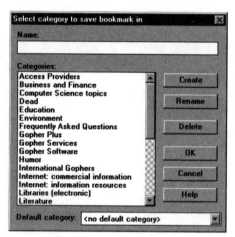

You can view your bookmark list at any time by choosing Bookmark ➤ Fetch. Select a category, then a bookmark, and click on OK to jump to the stored site.

Quitting WSGopher

You can quit gopher at any time by selecting File ➤ Exit.

Getting Help for Gopher

You can get help within the program by selecting Help ➤ Index. There are excellent help resources available at the University of Illinois at Urbana-Champaign gopher server, including a FAQ and several guides. Poke around the site to see what's available. That's one of the great aspects of gophering.

Chapter 12

MAKING A SIMPLE HOME PAGE

FEATURING

- **Finding and saving a home-page template**
- **Understanding a little HTML**
- **Editing an HTML document**
- **Inserting pictures and links into a page**
- **Previewing a home page**
- **Finding a home for your page**

This is the bonus chapter. You've now learned all you need to know to function on the Internet and explore the resources that are out there. The next step for you might be to put your own information up on the Net. You already know how to contribute to mailing lists and Usenet newsgroups—it's as simple as sending a message to the right address—but publishing your own home page can be a little trickier.

Why would you want your own home page? Well, it's a little like putting up a flag in cyberspace. One that says, "Here I am." A home page can be as simple as a yearbook entry with a few images, some facts about you and perhaps your family (and maybe your pets), and a list of your favorite Web sites (most likely taken from your bookmark file); or it can be as complicated as a full-service front end for a company or organization. Telling you all the ins and outs of making an elaborate Web site would take a whole book, but I can recommend an easy way to put together a simple home page and point you to a few other alternatives as well.

Creating a Home Page

A number of Web sites offer straightforward procedures that result in a fully assembled home page. Also, quite a few programs are available that do the same thing for you offline. I recommend the Home Page Construction kit at the GNN (Global Network Navigator) Web site.

To get there, point your browser at `http://gnn.com/netizens/construction.html` (see Figure 12.1).

FIGURE 12.1: Visit the Home Page Construction Kit to painlessly assemble a simple home page.

The GNN site offers stripped-down step-by-step instructions, as well as a useful HTML document template you can save to your browser and then edit, replacing the dummy information with your own personal text.

Another Approach: Making a Home Page with a "Wizard" Program

Windows users can download a tight little program called WEB Wizard (`http://www.halcyon.com/artamedia/webwizard/`). A Macintosh version is supposed to be available soon. The WEB Wizard program interviews you about your vital information: your name, what you do, and so on. It asks for the location of any art files you might want to include on your page and the Web addresses of any sites you might want to link to. Then it assembles your page for you.

Also, CompuServe offers a home-page wizard that members can download to set up home pages at the Our World (`http://ourworld.compuserve.com`) site. Visit that site to download their stand-alone program.

Visiting the GNN Site

Start by following the Creating a Home Page link (to `http://gnn.com/netizens/create.html`) for some background on how to make a home page in general. This page shows some examples of different types of home pages and demonstrates the HTML codes that make them work the way they do (see Figure 12.2).

NOTE

HTML stands for *Hypertext Markup Language*. It's the system of tags and codes that tell Web browsers how to display documents. Basic HTML is easy to learn, but it can also get quite complicated. Fortunately, there are a lot of new Web editors coming on the market that automate the process of inserting HTML into plain documents, so you never have to see how it looks or learn how to do it yourself.

Read through the rest of the page for a basic primer on HTML codes, hypertext links, and embedded images. When you've read this page, scroll back to the top and select the Back to Home Page Construction Kit link (or just use your browser's Back command) to return to the main page.

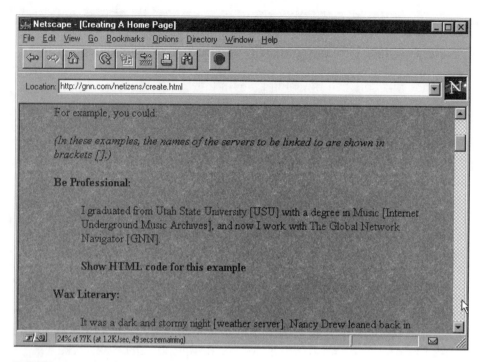

FIGURE 12.2: GNN's Creating a Home Page page

Going to the Template Page

Skip the next link, which discusses how to "publish" a home page, meaning how to find a place to store it on the Net and make it available to the public. That's important, but you have to create your home page first before you need to worry about where to store it. Instead, follow the link called Home Page Template (`http://gnn.com/netizens/template.html`). Read the instructions on that page and then follow the link that says GO to Home Page Template (`http://gnn.com/netizens/homepage.html`). This will take you to a dummy home page with lots of places to plug in information about yourself (see Figure 12.3).

Saving the Template

Next, save this file to your own computer. With most browsers, this means select-ing File ➤ Save As; be sure to specify HTML as the type of file. For example, in Netscape Navigator, the choice is called Source (*.htm, *.html). Make a note of where you're saving it.

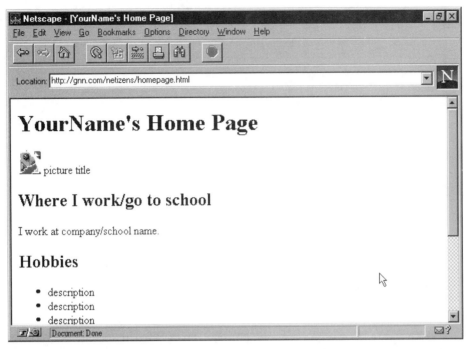

FIGURE 12.3: GNN's dummy home page includes most of the HTML tags you'll need to create a simple home page. You just have to fill in the actual information to be all set.

Looking at the HTML Document

Now you have to edit that HTML document, which you can do in any simple text editor. In Windows, I recommend using WordPad or Notepad. (WordPad has a few more features—such as Search and Replace—but you may be more familiar and comfortable with Notepad.) For the Macintosh, SimpleText will work just fine and BB Edit is ideal. In Unix, you're stuck with Vi (pronounced vee-eye and usually spelled all lowercase: vi).

The drill at this point is to open the HTML document and replace all the dummy text with your real information. You may be surprised at how simple and easy to read the HTML source file is (see Figure 12.4).

The document consists of regular text and HTML tags surrounded by < and > (typically less-than and greater-than signs but I think of them as *angle brackets*). Some of the brackets are required, so you shouldn't mess with those (such as <HTML> and <HEAD> and <BODY>). The following table briefly explains the tags you'll see, but you don't really need to understand them, so feel free to skip ahead.

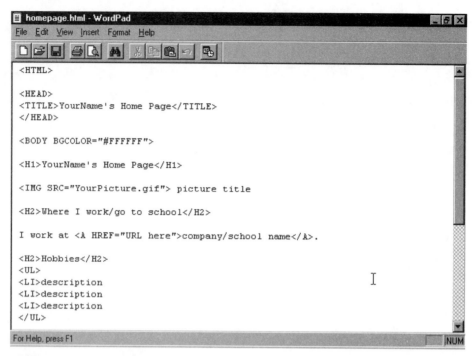

FIGURE 12.4: The HTML tags appear surrounded by < and >. The rest is regular text.

Tag	What It Means
H1 through H6	Headings. The number indicates the level of the heading, meaning its importance or priority
IMG	Image
SRC	Source
UL	Unordered list. Unordered means "with bullets," as opposed to ordered, which means "with numerals"
OL	Ordered list
LI	List item
A	Anchor. Indicates the beginning or end of a link
HREF	Hypertext reference
ADDRESS	Address
P	Paragraph break

Many tags appear in pairs, with an opening tag and a closing tag that starts with a slash, such as <H2> and </H2>. These particular tags mark the beginning and end, respectively, of a second-level heading. Now you know more HTML than 99 percent of the people on the planet.

Switch over to the browser window again and compare the "raw" HTML file to the file interpreted and displayed as a Web document. This result is what makes people say HTML is easy, since the browser does most of the work.

Editing the HTML Document

Okay, enough looking. Time to really edit your home page. Just start replacing the generic text with the real text. This is the easy part.

1. Replace **YourName** with your real name twice, once on the TITLE line (this controls what appears in the browser's title bar), and once on the H1 line.

2. Below the IMG tag and above the first H2 tag, type in anything you want to say about yourself, as much or as little as you want, but start with <P> (a paragraph break) so the picture title text beforehand doesn't run right into it.

3. Then select the dummy H2 text, **Where I work/go to school**, and replace it with the name of an employer.

4. In the sample text below the H2 heading, replace the text, **company/school name**, between the <A HREF=*blah, blah*> and </A> tags, with the name of the place where you work or go to school (or plot to overthrow the government, or whatever).

5. Then change the sentence however you want, but be careful not to mangle the <A ...> and </A> tags. Add more text as well. This is your chance to say a thing or two.

6. Do the equivalent thing with the <H2>**Hobbies**</H2> tag. This is your page, you can change the heading to anything you want.

7. Add more items to the list if you want (just start a new line with <LI> to do so).

8. Add introductory text after the H2 and before the UL starting tag if you feel like it.

9. If you'd like to have other, similar categories, copy the Hobbies section and paste it in again just below where it is now and just before the Personal Hot List section, as many times as you like.

10. If you want to break a section into smaller sections, start the first level of subsections with a <H3>Third-Level Heading </H3> and go from there.

Figure 12.5 shows what the top of my page looks like after Debussy Fields has gotten started with it.

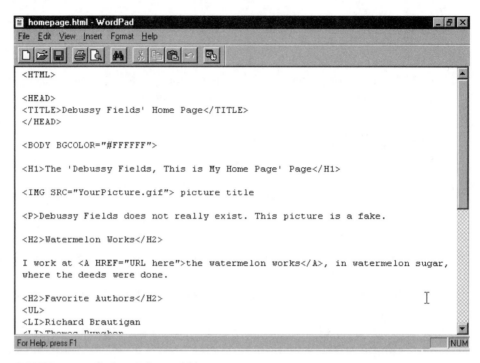

FIGURE 12.5: All about Debussy Fields

Next, scroll down to the bottom of the document. In the ADDRESS area, put your name and your e-mail address in parentheses, and then save the document.

Putting in an Image and the Links

Now you have to put the file names and locations of any Web pages you want to link to and any art or illustrations you want embedded in your page. First the image.

Putting in an Image

Go up to the <IMG SRC ... > tag just below the <H1> tag and replace **"YourPicture. gif"** with the actual file name of a picture you want to include on the page.

TIP
If you don't want to put a picture on your page, you can delete the line, or *comment it out*, by preceding it with <!— and following it with —> (in case you might get a picture together in the future).

The picture will have to be in a GIF or JPEG format, but other formats, such as PICTs, BMPs, and TIFs can be converted to either of those formats in a variety of image-manipulation programs (from the expensive, professional tool, PhotoShop, to the shareware tool, Lview Pro). You might find it easier to ask someone you know to do this for you.

> **NOTE** Copy your picture to the same directory (or folder) that the home page document is saved in.

Type a caption for the picture (replacing **picture title**). To make it bold, precede it with <B> and follow it with </B>.

Putting in Links

To insert your first link, go to the first A tag, the one in the first sentence after the first H2 heading. Replace the words **"URL here"** (but keep the quotation marks) with the full address of the home page of your company or school. (Hunt around on the Net for it if you don't have it handy.) You can erase the <A ...> and </A> tags if your affiliation does not have a home page.

Then go down to the Personal Hot List area. Change that heading if you want something different. Then replace the **description** text. Finally, you have to replace the **"URL here"** text with the actual addresses of your favorite links. You can go to those pages (easy, if you've made bookmarks) with your Web browser and then copy the links with perfect accuracy from the address box of your browser (Ctrl+C or Command+C will usually do this if you select the address first) and paste each of the addresses into the home page document you're working on. Figure 12.6 shows the document with hypertext links inserted. Then save the document.

Previewing the Home Page

Now switch back to your Web browser and select File ➢ Open File. Switch to the directory where you saved the home page originally (if necessary), and open the HTML document. Your browser will display your finished page (see Figures 12.7 and 12.8).

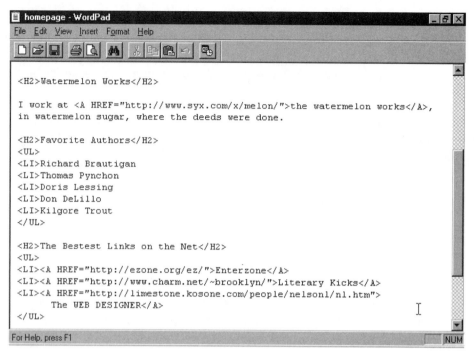

FIGURE 12.6: Debussy's employer and favorite sites have now been hyperlinked into the home page.

Learning More about HTML

In the future, you may want to expand the page, maybe link in some additional pages. In a similar way to how the IMG tag includes a SRC="*filename*" reference to connect a picture to a page, you can make *local links* to other documents stored in the same place as the home page by using the <A HREF="*local file*"> and </A> tags. If you want to learn more about HTML and Web-page creation, visit the Web Designer page (`http://www.kosone.com/people/nelson/nl.htm`), a central clearinghouse for Web-design related information. (That's a letter "l" by the way, not a numeral "one" in the filename of this page.)

FIGURE 12.7: The top of Debussy's home page as seen in Netscape Navigator 2.0 for Windows

FIGURE 12.8: The rest of Debussy's home page

Finding a Home for Your Page

The final question about your home page is where to put it. Many Internet service providers (and some of the online services as well) offer free space on their Web servers, up to some quota of disk space (often five megabytes), to all their customers. If your e-mail provider does not offer you access to a Web server, you'll have to find someone else to host your site. Look first at your company or any other affiliations you may have. There are also some free home-page hosting sites out there (though they may require that you include an ad for them on your page).

Some providers will ask you to send them your files via e-mail (see Chapter 3 for how to send files via e-mail). Others will prefer it if you use FTP to upload your files to them (see Chapter 10 for how to send files via FTP). They will assign you a URL for your home page, often in the format `http://www.their.name.com/~your-username`, but other variations are possible as well.

Once you get your page (and any associated art files or linked pages) out there on your provider's Web site, then anyone can drop by. E-mail your friends and ask them to visit. If you want to truly make your pages public, visit some (or all) of the directory and search sites mentioned in Chapter 5, and submit the URL for your page to each of them.

Now you're truly "on the Net."

Appendix A

GETTING CONNECTED AND GETTING STARTED

FEATURING

- **Understanding direct and modem connections**
- **Getting the equipment you'll need**
- **Getting a service provider**
- **Logging in and out**
- **Accessing help**

This appendix is here to help you out if you're looking for an Internet service provider, if you need to get the equipment together for a dial-up account, or if you've already got an Internet account or access to Internet e-mail but you'd like to shop around for better services.

Different Types of Connections

To start with, we need to go over the different types of Internet connections. First, there are *direct connections* and *modem connections*. A direct connection is a computer attached to a network that is itself connected to the Internet. Many university accounts work this way, as do some work-related Internet connections. Direct connections to Internet gateways allow the sending and receiving of Internet e-mail but not much more.

There are several types of modem connections:

- PPP or SLIP accounts
- Client-access accounts
- Host-machine accounts (including Free-nets)
- Online services
- BBSs (Bulletin Boards)

A PPP or SLIP account is a dial-up account that puts your desktop computer, when you're connected, directly on the Internet. The modem connection makes your computer part of a network attached to the Net. This type of access is by far the most popular and, once you get it set up, the easiest to use (aside from online services).

A client-access account makes a temporary connection to a server and downloads your e-mail, USENET news articles, and what-have-you and then logs off, allowing you to read and respond to your messages offline.

A host-machine account allows you to log on, using your desktop computer as a *dumb terminal*, (a keyboard-and-monitor device that sends information to a larger computer, e.g. a mainframe). In this case, the information would be sent to a host computer on the Internet. This account usually entails working in a Unix environment on the host machine, although there are many offline mailers and newsreaders available to help minimize your connect time and insulate you from the cryptic Unix commands. The host-machine account used to be the most common type of access, but it has been superseded by PPP and SLIP accounts.

An account with an online service may offer anything from partial to complete Internet access through the proprietary interface of the service. America Online, CompuServe, and the Microsoft Network, for example, offer complete Internet access.

Bulletin boards allow you to log on and then select options from menus. They can provide Unix command-line access to the Internet, but they do not necessarily do so.

So you can see that, depending on your type of access, you may be running programs in your desktop computer's native environment (SLIP, PPP, client-access, a host-machine account with offline readers), you may be working in a Unix environment (host-machine account), or you may be working in the interface provided by your online service or BBS.

This book covers the general procedures for using Internet services no matter what type of access you have, but it focuses on the most popular types of access: PPP/SLIP and online services.

Equipment You'll Need

If your computer is directly connected to the Net, then you don't need any special equipment. You run the client software installed on your computer for reading e-mail. If you don't have the client programs needed to use other Internet services, such as the World Wide Web, Usenet, FTP, and so on, you should be able to search for them on the Net.

| NOTE | See Chapter 5 for how to search the Net. |

Hardware

For every other type of connection, you'll need a modem. More and more often, PCs and Macs are sold with a modem preinstalled. If you were not so lucky, then you'll have to make a few decisions about what type of modem to buy.

You have to decide first of all if you want an *internal* modem or an *external* modem. An internal modem is a circuit board with a modem chip on it that you have to install into a vacant slot inside your computer (or pay or cajole someone else to install). An external modem is a flat box that plugs into a port on the outside of your computer.

| TIP | If at all possible, get a *Hayes-compatible* modem, since that's the most well established standard. This should not be difficult, as most modems on the market are at least somewhat Hayes compatible. |

Internal modems cost a little less than external modems and take up less space, but they're a real pain to mess with if a problem develops. Internal modems draw their power from the computer's power supply, while external modems require a separate power supply. Expect to pay from eighty to a couple hundred dollars for your modem.

The next thing you need to consider is the speed of your modem. This factor limits the speed of operations when you're connected. Like all things computerish, this year's standard model is next year's dud; this year's supercomputer is next year's idler. But from where I stand right now, I can suggest that you get at least a 14.4 kps modem (kps stands for kilobits per second). If you're forward thinking, invest in a 28.8 kps modem, as they'll be the standard before you know it. If you economize on something like a 9600 bps modem, your operations will be annoyingly slooooow.

> **NOTE**
> Actually, the speed of communication is a function of both the modems involved in the connection—the one attached to your computer and the one it dials up. Your connection will only proceed as fast as the slower of the two modems (if they differ in speed). Your 28.8 kps modem won't do you much good if you dial up a BBS with a 1200 bps Model T.

It goes without saying that once you install your modem, you must plug your phone into one of its jacks, and plug another cord into the other jack and into the wall jack.

> **TIP**
> You may want to consider getting a fax/modem as well. A fax/modem can send electronic information to fax machines and receive faxes as graphic images (though some can just receive and not send). They can be finicky, though, and you have to decide how much to burden your phone line with.

Software

If you'll be dialing up a connection with your modem, then you'll need to run some kind of communications software to communicate with the modem and to produce the terminal emulation so you can interact with the host computer. (If you'll be dialing up a PPP or SLIP connection, then you'll need the client software for the Internet programs you want to run and dial-up software (sometime referred to as a *dialer* or as a *dial-up stack*), but you won't need a communications program. Your provider should give you the software you need.

If you have Windows 95, make sure your provider realizes this and gives you the correct software and instructions. Ask if there are any conflicts with existing software you should worry about. You'll generally want to use the 32-bit version of most Internet software if you have a Windows 95 (or Windows NT) connection.

> **NOTE** Online services, such as America Online and CompuServe, will provide you with software designed for their services.

You might also want to get an offline mail reader or newsreader so that you can make your connection, collect your messages, and then read and reply to them while offline. You should be able to find such programs (such as Eudora Lite, a free mail program) on the Internet once you've connected. Client accounts offer this kind of service with their proprietary software.

No matter what kind of software you're running, you'll need to set it up the first time you run it. The software needs to know some crucial things about your modem and the type of connection it should make. The things you only have to tell it once include:

- Which COM port the modem is connected to.
- What type of *parity, data bits,* and *stop bits* to use. Your provider will tell you the information you need, so you don't need to know all the nitty-gritty details, e.g. what type of parity, data bits, and stop bits.
- What kind of terminal emulation to use for communication programs—most likely VT100.
- Some other Internet gibberish, which your provider should spell out for you in detail, since you'll never need to hear about it again once you've entered the information into the appropriate dialog boxes.

Going Online with a Macintosh

For Macintosh users, getting connected to the Internet will typically involve using a dial-up Internet protocol program such as MacPPP (or InterSLIP). You specify a server to connect to, your account number, and your password.

Some Internet service providers will give you a version of MacPPP—or a similar program—already configured with your account information and password. Then all you need to do is start the program and open whichever Internet application you wish to use.

> **WARNING** If your ISP charges you by the hour, be sure you log off or disconnect when you finish an Internet session. Quitting an Internet application will not terminate your connection.

Finding a Service Provider

Once you have all the equipment you need, you've got to find a service provider. The greatest consideration for most people is cost. One of the biggest cost factors can be the telephone charges for connect time.

If you can find a service with a dial-up number local to you, then you can reduce this charge to virtually nothing. If not, investigate several other options to see which will be cheapest for you. Look into services that provide 800 numbers or access via public data networks (such as CompuServe or AT&T). You'll have to compare total costs, including both phone charges and charges from the service. If you can't avoid phone charges, try to do as many of your activities offline as possible to minimize the charges.

> **WARNING** Although 800 numbers are free to call, your service will charge you extra to cover their cost, so choose carefully.

The next biggest charge issue is whether or not you are charged by the service based on how long you're connected (as opposed to paying a flat rate). The other cost issues are the monthly charge and a first-time connection charge, if any.

Located throughout the U.S., *Free-nets* are networks that charge nothing for an account or for connect time (although their public accounts may not always be available). You'll still need to pay phone charges unless the number you call is local.

> **TIP** If you're affiliated with a university, you can get a free university account.

Ironically, the best place to find up-to-date provider information is online. You could borrow someone else's access or connect to the Net through work and visit the sites I'll recommend in this appendix. You could also take one of the online services up on their offer of a free trial month, and then spend some of that time hunting for a more permanent provider.

The Chicken or the Egg

Here are two Web sites you can visit to get updated service-provider information once you're already online.

One commercial service on the Web is making an effort to assemble on a single Web page the various lists of providers out there, allowing users to look for providers by region. To see the current state of this effort, point your Web browser at `http://www.tagonline.com/Providers/` (see Figure A.1).

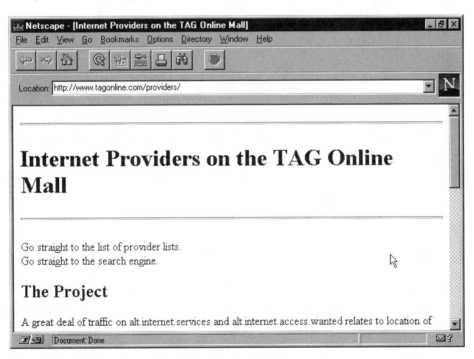

FIGURE A.1: TAG Systems' online listing of service providers

This is a searchable site you can browse based on area code (so you can get a provider that's only a local call away) and services offered.

Another site you can try is called The List at `http://www.thelist.com` (see Figure A.2). You can also search by area code, as well as in various other ways.

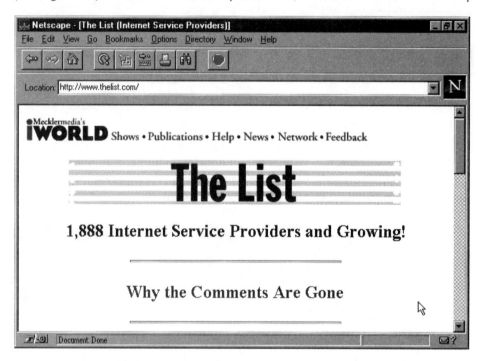

FIGURE A.2: MecklerWeb's "The List" site is another fairly comprehensive list of providers. (The List of Internet Service Providers [`www.thelist.com`] is owned and maintained by Mecklermedia Corporation. Copyright ©1996. Mecklermedia. All rights reserved. Image reprinted with permission.)

When you do choose a provider, hold off on distributing your e-mail address to everyone you know until you're sure you're happy with them. See if the connection works most of the time. (Nothing on the Net works all of the time!) Notice how often you get a busy signal when you're trying to connect. Decide how helpful they are when you have questions or something isn't working. Be a good consumer and shop around until you find a provider you're satisfied with. *Then* spread your e-mail address around. Good luck finding a service provider.

Getting Started

Whenever you want to connect to your provider, you'll run your dial-up or communications software, which will use your modem to phone your provider to make a connection.

Logging In

When you are connected, you will need to log in to your Internet account. First type your *login*, your Internet handle, and then type your password. (Your password will not appear on the screen.) Some software programs will remember your login information after you connect the first time and will, therefore, not require you to type it all in each time. (Having this ability means, though, your computer is not secure, in the sense that anyone who runs your dial-up software will automatically be connected to your account, whether they know your password or not.)

> **TIP**
>
> Your password should be at least eight characters long, contain both letters and numbers, and be meaningless (not your birthdate, your partner's name, your pet's name, your driver's license number, or anything like that).

You're on the Net!

Now you're ready to do whatever you got on the Internet to do. Read the rest of the book for specifics. When you are finished with an Internet session, you should log off to tell your provider's computer that you're done. (Eventually your modem would hang up for you if you walked away, but that's sloppy and wasteful of resources and could conceivably cost you more money too.)

You'll also want to hang up your modem (unless your software does this for you). Logging out is not hanging up. Even after you log out, your modem is still connected and charging time if that's how your phone system works. So after logging out, hang up. Then quit your software.

Dealing with Problems

Sometimes things will just freeze up on you, which could mean there's a problem with the command that you issued, a problem with an Internet server such as the mail server or the newsfeed, or a problem with your provider's network. First try to deal with it yourself. Then ask for help.

> **NOTE** There could also be a problem with your PC, your modem, or the phone lines. If any of these seems to be suffering or if they have conked out, try basic resuscitation procedures—reset the PC or modem, check the phone line, and try dialing again.

You may be surprised by problems you experience with your Internet connection. Some problems, such as busy signals, may be the fault of your service provider. But others are a reflection of the Internet itself, that big, loosely organized bundle of very different computers, spread all over an immense amount of territory. So, for example, if your IRC program bumps you off in the middle of a chat session, it might just be the vicissitudes of the Internet in this day and age, and not necessarily the fault of your provider.

Be patient and willing to tinker with things until they work properly for you. Sometimes this means simply quitting an application and starting over. Other times it may mean restarting your computer. As it is with netiquette, patience will go a long way toward smoothing your travel over the information superhighway.

Stop This Crazy Thing!

When things start going wrong or nothing is happening at all, you sometimes have to interrupt the process by pressing Esc so that your mail program gives up (for now) on trying to send your mail, by quitting the program (such as your mail, Web, or news program) and starting it again, by actually shutting down a piece of software that isn't responding, and so on.

Ultimately, if you can't get your software's or connection's attention, you can always just hang up your modem by quitting the dial-up software. This solution will (eventually) sever the connection to your provider, though it is always better to log out when you can.

Getting Help

Every program you run should have a help system, though admittedly some are more sketchy than others. In Windows or on the Mac, this usually means looking for a Help menu. In Unix, it usually means typing **h** or **?**.

Once you've looked at your software's documentation or help system and have made a good-faith effort to figure things out for yourself, the next step should be to get help from your service provider. Either phone them up (they should have given you a number for this purpose when you first signed on), or send them e-mail if your mail is working but something else isn't (send it to `info@their-address` if you don't have a more specific address). Some providers, such as Netcom, also offer technical support through their Web site.

> **NOTE** See Chapter 2 for how to send e-mail. See Chapter 4 for how to connect to the Web.

Another way to get help or answers to your questions is to contact *InterNIC*. InterNIC is a center funded by the National Science Foundation and founded to help Internet users and people interested in the Net. (*NIC* stands for Network Information Center.)

There are many ways to reach InterNIC with your questions. You can call their hotline at (800) 444-4345 or their regular number at (619) 455-4600. You can fax them at (619) 455-4640. Or you can send them e-mail at `info@is.internic.net`. In addition, they have a Web site (`http://www.internic.net`).

Finally, you can send them regular mail—what people on the net call snail mail—at the following address:

P.O. Box #85608

San Diego, CA 92186-9784

Appendix B

GLOSSARY OF INTERNET TERMS

If you've run into some jargon in this book that you don't understand, you should find an explanation here.

> **NOTE** If you want a more thorough compendium of Internet jargon, terminology, and culture at your fingertips, try my *Internet Dictionary*, also from Sybex.

$0.02
Appended to the end of a **Usenet post**, this means "my two cents."

:-)
The basic **smiley** symbol; this is often used to mean "just kidding," "don't flame me," or "I'm being sarcastic," but it can also mean "I'm happy."

^]
This garbage symbol may appear on your screen, or in text-transferred files, from time-to-time. It's an uninterpreted Esc character. Ignore it.

acceptable use
Internet service providers require that all their users agree to some guidelines of acceptable use of Internet and Usenet resources. Acceptable use guidelines vary from provider to provider.

account

A form of access to a computer or **network** for a specific **username** and password, usually with a home directory, an **e-mail inbox,** and a set of access privileges.

address

1. The name of a computer (also called a **host** or **site** on the **Internet,** in the form *host.subdomain.domain*; 2. An **e-mail** address in the form *username@ host.subdomain.domain*; 3. A **Web** address (**URL**) in the form *http://host.subdomain.domain/optionalpath/optional -filename.html.*

address book

In some **e-mail** programs, a list of abbreviations for e-mail addresses.

administrivia

Information regarding the administering of a **mailing list** or **moderated newsgroup** that is posted to the list or group.

AIFF

The Macintosh audio format on the **Internet.**

alias

An abbreviation for an **e-mail address,** sometimes called a *nickname.*

alt.

A quasi-**Usenet hierarchy** devoted to "alternative" topics. It is easier to create alt. groups than to create standard Usenet groups, and it's practically impossible to remove them.

alt.fan groups

Newsgroups devoted to a real-world or **Net** celebrity or villain.

America Online

The most popular **online service.**

Amiga

A line of desktop PCs, famous for their handling of graphics and the evangelical zeal of their users. Many Amiga users include an **ASCII**-graphic double checkmark in their **.sigs**.

Anarchie

An **Archie** program for the Mac.

anon.penet.fi

The most well-known anonymous remailer service.

anonymous FTP

The most common use of **FTP,** the **Internet file transfer protocol. FTP site**s that allow anonymous FTP don't require a password for access—you only have to log in as anonymous and enter your **e-mail** address as a password (for their records).

anonymous remailers

A service that provides anonymity to users on the **Net** by allowing them to send **mail** and **Usenet post**s through the remailer.

*.answers

Moderated newsgroups dedicated to the posting of **FAQ**s. The "*" in *.answers stands for anything. *.answers newsgroups include `news.answers`, `alt.answers`, `rec.answers`, `misc.answers`, and so on.

AOL

America Online.

application

A program (or piece of software) that isn't a **shell,** environment, or operating system.

archie

A **client-server** application that gives users access to databases that keep track of the contents of anonymous **FTP** archives (hence the name).

ARPAnet

The legendary predecessor to the **Internet.**

article

A **Usenet post.**

ASCII

American Standard Code for Information Interchange; ASCII is a standard character set that's been adopted by most computer systems around the world (usually extended for foreign alphabets and diacriticals).

ASCII file

A file containing only straight text. ASCII files are easier and quicker to transfer.

asynchronous

Not happening at the same time. **E-mail** is an asynchronous form of communication.

Attachment

Any **data file,** in any form, that your **e-mail** program will send along with your e-mail **message.**

.au

A **Unix** audio format

autoselect

In **Usenet killfile**s, to select automatically—the opposite of to kill. A killfile comprises instructions to search for certain key words and then either kills or autoselects the articles containing those words.

AutoSurf

A new **Mosaic** feature that will pull down and cache all of the pages at a site, letting you browse them at your leisure.

.avi

A movie format native to the Windows platform.

B1FF

A legendary persona from the early days of **BBS**s, B1FF liked to talk about *kool warez*—cool, pirated computer software.

back

1. In a **Web browser,** a command, often a shortcut button, for retracing your steps back to the previous page or **link;** 2. The command in a **Unix** paging program to go back one screen.

backbone

A large, fast **network** connection.

bandwidth

1. The amount of information that can pass through the wires in a certain amount of time; 2. Also, a more general term for what everyone is encouraged not to waste on the **Net.**

baud

Usually confused with **bps** (bits per second), baud is technically the number of times per second that your **modem** changes the signal it sends through the phone lines.

BBS

A **bulletin board system.** Many BBSs are connected to the **Internet.**

Bcc line

The portion of an **e-mail message** header where you list the recipients who will be sent *blind* copies of an email. This means that the primary (and Cc:) recipients will not see the names of people receiving blind copies.

Big Dummy's Guide to the Internet

The former name of **EFF**'s excellent, free **Internet** guide.

binaries

Newsgroups that generally contain huge **post**s each comprising part of a large **binary file,** usually a program, image, or other special-format file, as opposed to a **text file.**

binary file

As opposed to a **text file,** a file that contains more than simple text. It must be copied literally, bit for bit, or it will be corrupted. Also called an **image file.**

binary transfer

A **file transfer** in which every bit of the file is copied (as opposed to a **text transfer,** in which the text is transferred to whatever format the receiving machine prefers).

BinHex

A form of file **compression** native to the Macintosh.

bitnet

A huge **network,** distinct from the **Internet,** but fully connected to it, used largely for **e-mail** and **Listserv mailing list**s.

bitnet.

A **newsgroup hierarchy** in the **Usenet** mold, comprising newsgroups that correspond to **bitnet** mailing lists.

biz.

A **newsgroup hierarchy** in the **Usenet** mold that expressly permits advertising (biz stands for *business*).

bookmark

In a **Web** or **Gopher** browser, a record of a destination that allows you to immediately get back there at any time. (Also called Favorites or Favorite Places in some browsers, and Items on a **Hotlist** in others.)

'bot

A **robotic** entity on the **Net** that automatically performs some function that people usually do.

bounce

When **e-mail** fails to reach its destination and returns to you, it is said to have bounced.

bozo filter

A **killfile** that allows you to filter out the bozos whose **Usenet post**s you don't wish to see.

bps

Bits per second; a measurement of **modem** speed.

browse

To skim an information resource on the **Net,** such as **Usenet, Gopherspace,** or the **Web.**

browser

The program you use to read the **Web.**

BTW

By the way.

bulletin board

1. What some **online service**s call their **discussion group**s; 2. A **bulletin board system.**

bulletin board system

A set of computers and **modem**s running **bulletin board** software that allow users to dial in, send **mail,** participate in forums, and (sometimes) access the **Internet.**

cancel an article

On **Usenet,** to delete an article after you've posted it. It takes a while for the article to vanish everywhere, as the cancel message has to catch up with the propagating article.

cascade

A nonsensical series of one-line follow-up **post**s, each a play on the previous one and designed to create a huge triangle of >'s on the screen.

cc:Mail

A network-oriented **e-mail client** program.

Central Search Page

Most of the **Web browser**s have a shortcut to one or more **directory** or search pages built in to the program.

CFV

Call for Votes, a step in the creating of a **Usenet newsgroup** that comes after the RFD (Request for Discussion) step.

character-based browsers/readers

Internet programs, generally used in **Unix** systems, that can display only characters (and no graphics).

chat

Synchronous, line-by-line communication over a **network.**

client

An application that communicates with a **server** to get you information.

client-server application

An application whose process is distributed between a central **server** and any number of autonomous **client**s.

clueless newbie

A derogatory term for a beginner who POSTS IN ALL CAPS or betrays some ignorance of the **Net.** We were all clueless newbies once.

.com

An **Internet domain** that stands for *commercial.*

COM port

A communication port in your PC. Your **modem** plugs into one.

command line

The place in a character-based **shell,** such as a **Unix** or DOS shell, where you can enter commands directly (usually at the bottom of the screen).

commercial online service

A private, proprietary **network,** offering its own content and access to other network members, such as **CompuServe, America Online, Prodigy,** and **Microsoft Network.**

comp.

A **Usenet hierarchy** devoted to computers.

compress

1. (v) To squish a file; 2. (n) a **Unix** program that squishes files.

compression

The method of squishing a file or the amount of squishing.

CompuServe

A popular **online** service.

copyright

People debate how standing copyright law applies to articles posted to **Usenet** or to texts in general made available on the Internet. Some people attach copyright notices to their **post**s. *See also* **fair use.**

cracker

A **hacker** who breaks into computers.

Craig Shergold

See **Shergold, Craig.**

crosspost

To **post** a **Usenet** article to several **newsgroup**s at once. Crossposting takes up less disk space than posting it separately and repeatedly.

CU-SeeMe

A **protocol** that enables anyone with a video camera and enough memory to play video images in their computer to see other people on the **Internet.**

cyberspace

A term, popularized by author William Gibson, for the shared imaginary reality of computer **networks.** Some people use cyberspace as a synonym for the **Internet.** Others hold out for the more complete physical-seeming consensual reality of Gibson's novels.

daemon

In **Unix,** a program that runs all the time, in the background, waiting for things to do (possibly from Maxwell's Demon). When you post an article to a ***.test** newsgroup, daemon's all over the world send you e-mail confirming they received your post.

data bits

One of the things you have to set to use your **modem**. Usually set to 7 or 8, it depends on the modem you're calling.

decoding

Retranslating a file from some encoded format to its original format.

decrypt

To remove the **encryption** from a file or **e-mail message** and make it readable.

DejaNews

A service for searching **Usenet** (at `http://www.dejanews.com/forms/dnq.html`).

delurk

1. (v) To **post** to a **list** or **newsgroup** for the first time; 2. (n) A first post to a newsgroup or list after the writer has **lurked** for a while.

dial-up account

An Internet **account** on a **host** machine that you must dial up with your **modem** to use.

digest

A collection of **mailing list post**s, sent out as one message.

digestified

Turned into a digest. Not all **mailing list**s are available in a digestified form.

Direct-Access ISP

A **service provider** (usually just called an **ISP**) that offers direct **Internet** access, as opposed to an **online** service.

directory

A **Web site** where other Web sites are organized by topic and subtopic, something like a yellow pages phone book.

discussion groups

Any "place" on the **Net** where discussions are held, including **mailing list**s and **Usenet newsgroup**s.

domain

The three-letter code indicating whether the **address** is a business (**.com**), a non-profit (**.org**), a university (**.edu**), a branch of the government (**.gov**), a part of the military (**.mil**), and so on.

download

To transfer a file over a modem from a remote computer to your desktop computer.

.edu

An Internet domain, it stands for educational.

EFF

See **Electronic Frontier Foundation.**

EFF's Guide to the Internet

Formerly **Big Dummy's Guide to the Internet,** **EFF**'s excellent and free **Internet** guide, is available via the **Web** (`http://www.eff.org/papers/eegtti/eegttitop.html`).

EFNet

The traditional **IRC** network.

Electronic Frontier Foundation

Founded by Mitch Kapor and John Barlow, the **EFF** lobbies for the preservation of freedom on the cyberspace frontier.

elm

A popular **Unix** mail program.

.elmrc

A setup file for **elm.**

emacs

A **Unix** operating environment that doubles as a **text editor.**

e-mail

Electronic mail, but you knew that already, didn't you?

e-mail address

An **Internet** address that consists of a **username** (also called a **login,** a **log-on name,** a **userID,** an **account** name, and so on), followed by an "at" sign (@) and then an address of the form `host.subdomain.domain`.

emoticons

Those little **smiley** faces people use to indicate emotions.

encoding

Any method of converting a file into a format for attaching to **e-mail messages.**

encrypt

To scramble the contents of a file or **e-mail message** so that only those with the **key** can unscramble and read them.

encryption

A process of rendering a file or **e-mail message** unreadable to anyone lacking the right encryption **key.**

Eudora

An **e-mail** program.

fair use

The legal doctrine that allows limited quotation of other people's work if the use of their work does not undercut its market value.

FAQ

1. Frequently asked questions; 2. A file containing frequently asked questions and their answers, also sometimes called a FAQL (Frequently Asked Question List). To find FAQs, look in the ***.answers newsgroup**s or the **FTP** archive at `rtfm.mit.edu`.

Fetch

An **FTP** program for the Mac.

FidoNet

A **network** of **BBS**'s with **Internet e-mail** access.

file transfer

To copy a file from one computer to another.

film at 11

A common tag in **Usenet** follow-up posts mocking the timeliness of the news. Often follows **Imminent death of the Net predicted!**

finger

A **Unix** command that reports back on the status of a user or a **network.**

flame

1. An ill-considered, insulting e-mail or Usenet retort; 2. An insulting post.

flamebait

A **mailing-list** or **newsgroup post** designed to elicit **flame**s. Flamebait can be recognized by the fact that it goes beyond the premises of the list or newsgroup. Nobody objects to provocative or even argumentative posts, but posts to the `alt.fan.frank-zappa` newsgroup saying that "Zappa was a no-talent, potty-mouthed dweeb" betray a lack of legitimate interest in the subject at hand.

flamer

One who **flame**s or likes to flame others.

flame war

An out-of-control series of **flame**s and counterflames that fills up a list or newsgroup with noise. Traditionally, flame wars end when Nazis are mentioned.

FlashSession

An AOL process that enables its users to work **offline** and then send and receive **mail** and **newsgroup** articles and **download** files all at once, minimizing connect time.

FOAF

Friend of a friend.

follow a link

In graphical browsers, following a link entails positioning the mouse pointer over the link (the pointer will change to show you that you're over an active link) and then clicking once.

follow-up

A **post** that replies to and possibly quotes an earlier post.

follow-up line

In **Usenet** articles, if there is a follow-up line, follow-up articles will be posted to the **newsgroup**s listed there, and not necessarily to the original newsgroups. Always check the follow-up line before posting. Pranksters sometimes direct follow-ups to *.test groups, resulting in thousands of automated replies, stuffing the inbox of anyone hapless enough to follow up without editing the follow-up line.

FQA

Frequently questioned acronyms.

free-net

A free public **network** (also written as one word, *freenet*).

freeware

Free software available for downloading on the **Net.**

FTP

File Transfer Protocol, the standard **Internet** way to transfer files from one computer to another.

FTP site
A computer on the **Net** containing archives and set up for **FTP.**

FTPmail
A way to use **FTP** by **e-mail** if you don't have an FTP application.

full name
Your full name as it appears in **e-mail** messages and **Usenet post**s.

full-screen editor
A text editor that enables you to move the insertion point or cursor all over the screen, as opposed to a line-at-a-time editor that always keeps the insertion point at the bottom of the screen.

FUQ
Frequently unanswered questions.

FWIW
For what it's worth.

Indicates the author is grinning, similar to :-).

garbage characters
Nonsense characters that **modem**s sometimes spit out.

gate
Short for **gateway,** a computer that transfers files or **e-mail** from one **network** to another, or from a **newsgroup** to a list, and vice versa.

gated
Said of a **newsgroup** or **mailing list** that is connected to a mailing list or newsgroup, respectively.

gateway
1. A computer that connects one **network** to another, for the purpose of transferring files or **e-mail** when the two networks use different **protocols;** 2. A computer that transfers **post**s from a **newsgroup** to a **list,** and vice versa.

GIF
1. A **compress**ed graphics (image) file format (GIF stands for graphics interchange format) invented by **CompuServe;** 2. A file in the .gif format.

gnu.
A **hierarchy** in the **Usenet** mold devoted to the Free Software Foundation and to **emacs.**

gopher
A **client-server application** that performs **FTP** transfers, remote **login**s, **archie** searches, and so on, presenting everything to you in the form of menus. This saves you from having to know (or type in) the **address**es of the **Internet** resources being tapped. You run a **gopher client** program to get information from a **gopher server** running at a **gopher site.**

Gopherspace
A collective name for all the **gopher** servers on the **Net,** so called because all the servers can connect to each other, creating a unified "space" of gopher menus.

.gov
An internet domain that stands for government.

green-card lawyer
A derogatory term for people who **spam** the Net with unwanted advertisements and then go on TV to defend their actions.

<grin>
Equivalent to the :-) **emoticon.**

group
A **newsgroup.**

gunzip
The **Unix uncompression** program for **gzipped** files.

Gzip
A file **compression** program.

hack

To dig into some computer activity, going beneath the surface and reinventing things when necessary.

hacker

A computer adept. Among hackers, anyone who can bend a computer to his or her will is a hacker, whereas people who break into computer systems are called **crackers**. In the rest of the world, people generally refer to those who break into computers as hackers.

Hayes-Compatible

Modems that understand the Hayes AT instruction set are said to be Hayes compatible. (Hayes is a name-brand modem maker.) If you're buying a modem, make sure it's Hayes compatible. Most are these days, so that shouldn't be difficult.

hierarchy

1. In file storage, the arrangement of directories into a tree of parents and children; 2. In **Usenet,** the organization of **newsgroup**s into general areas, topics, and subtopics.

^H

In the standard **VT100** terminal emulation, Delete is used to erase characters, and Backspace either backs up over the previous character (without deleting it) or produces this character on the screen. It's a sign that a **clueless newbie** has tried to erase something and failed.

history

A record of your last so many actions. On the **Web,** a list of all the **page**s you've been to since you started your Web browsing program. The history list will actually show you only the pages you've visited in a straight line from your starting point. Any time you back up and then follow a different **link,** you will lose the original history path from that point onward.

$HOME

In **Unix,** a variable that means your **home directory.**

home directory

The directory you start off in when you log into your **Unix account.**

home page
1. The page you begin with when you start your **Web browser;** 2. The main page of a **Web site;** 3. A personal Web page.

host
A computer on the **Internet.**

HotJava
A **Web browser** made by Sun Microsystems.

hotlist
A **bookmark** list (especially in **Mosaic**).

HTML
Hypertext Markup Language; the **hypertext** language used in **Web page**s. It consists of regular text and tags that tell the **browser** what to do when a **link** is activated.

HTML source
The underlying source file that makes a **Web** document look the way it does in a **Web browser.**

HTTP
Hypertext Transfer Protocol; the Web **protocol** for linking one **Web page** with another.

hypermedia
Linked documents that consist of other media in addition to plain text, such as pictures, sounds, movies, and so on.

hypertext
Text that contains **link**s to other text documents.

hypertext link
A **link** from one text document to another.

Hytelnet
A **Telnet shell** that helps you find the Telnet **site** you want and then runs the Telnet session for you. It contains a huge list of university and public library catalogs.

image file
A **binary file.**

IMHO
In my humble opinion.

Imminent Death of the Net Predicted
A parody of the perennial warnings that traffic on the Net has gotten to be too much. Often followed by **film at 11.**

IMNSHO
In my not-so-humble opinion.

IMO
In my opinion.

inbox
A file containing your incoming **e-mail.**

info
Many **Internet** providers have an info **address** (`info@host.subdomain.domain`).

Internet
The worldwide **network** of networks. The Internet is a way for computers to communicate. It's not a place; it's a way to go through.

Internet address
See **Address.**

Internet Explorer
Microsoft's **Web browser.**

Internet Phone
A **protocol** that enables anyone with a microphone, speaker, and sound card in their computer to talk to other people on the **Internet.**

Internet Resources Meta-Index

A useful starting point on the **Web.**

Internet service provider (ISP)

A company that offers "just" access to the **Internet** and no local content (or only very limited local information and **discussion groups**).

InterNIC—

The Internet's Network Information Center, a repository of **Internet** information, a resource worth knowing about.

IP

Internet **Protocol.** the protocol that allows computers and **network**s on the Internet to communicate with each other.

IRC

Internet Relay Chat; A **protocol** and a **client-server** program that allows you to **chat** with people all over the **Internet,** in channels devoted to different topics.

Ircle

A Macintosh IRC program.

Java

A programming language from Sun that's a variant of C++. With a special Java-savvy browser such as **HotJava, Netscape Navigator** 2, or earlier versions of Netscape with a Java **plug-in,** users can interact with fully operational programs inside of the **browser** window.

JPEG

A **compress**ed file format for images with the extension .jpg.

Jughead

An index of high-level **gopher** menus.

k12.

A **hierarchy** in the **Usenet** mold, devoted to kindergarten through 12th grade education.

Kermit
A **protocol** for **download** and **upload file transfer**s.

key
In **encryption,** a code that allows you to **decrypt** encrypted text.

key word
A word used to search for a file, document, or **Web page.**

key encryption
A form of **encryption** that relies on **key**s.

Kibo
The **username** of James F. Parry. Some say he is the first deity of the **Internet.** Also known as "he who greps," Kibo reportedly notes every mention of his name on Usenet and replies to worthy posts. (Grepping means searching a file or an entire directory for a specific word; in this case, Kibo used to grep for his own name.) There is also an evil anti-Kibo named Xibo, whose legions are much fewer than the **troll**ing readers of `alt.religion.kibology`.

kibology
The religion (or is it a science?) of **Kibo.** Its main doctrine is that *You're Allowed.* Only Spot, Kibo's dog, is *Not Allowed.*

killfile
A file containing search instructions for automatically killing or **autoselect**ing **Usenet post**s. *See also* **bozo filter.**

Knowbot
An information service on the **Net** that, among other things, helps find **e-mail** addresses.

kps
Kilobits per second, a measurement of **modem** speed.

LAN
A **local-area network.** A computer network usually confined to a single office or building.

lharc

A file **compression** program for DOS.

library catalogs

Most university and public library catalogs are available via **Telnet** (and some via **Gopher**). **Hytelnet** has an excellent index of library catalogs.

Line-at-a-time

Said of programs that, as the name suggests, only allow users to see one line of type at a time.

link

On **Web page**s, a button or highlighted bit of text that, when selected, jumps the reader to another page.

list

A **mailing list.**

Listserv

A type of **mailing list** software that runs on **bitnet** computers.

local-area network

A small, local network, such as in an office **(LAN).**

log in

To start a session on your **Internet account.**

login

A **username,** the name you **log in** with.

log out

To end a session on your **Internet account.**

LOL

Laughing out loud.

lurk

To read a **mailing list** or **newsgroup** without **post**ing to it. You should lurk for a while before posting.

lurker

One who **lurk**s.

Lynx

An excellent, text-based, **Unix browser** for the **Web,** developed at the University of Kansas.

^M

In **text file**s transferred from DOS to **Unix** as **binary** files, this character will sometimes appear at the end of each line. Get rid of it with the dos2unix program.

mail

On the **Internet,** synonymous with **e-mail.**

mail box

A folder or area in a **mail** program where **messages** are stored.

mailing list

A list of people with a common interest, all of whom receive all the **mail** sent, or **post**ed, to the **list.**

.mailrc

A resource file for **mail** programs, other than **elm.**

mail reader

A program that allows you to read and reply to **e-mail,** and to send out new **mail** of your own.

mail reflector

A computer that sends copies of **mail** to a list of **address**es.

majordomo

A type of **mailing list** software.

MAKE.MONEY.FAST

A chain letter still making its rounds on the **Net.** It's a classic Ponzi/pyramid scheme. As someone replied last time I saw this garbage reposted, "Don't make your first act of fraud one that includes your name and address at the top!"

message

1. An **e-mail** letter; 2. A comment sent to a specific person on **IRC** and not to the entire channel.

MIDI

Musical Instrument Digital Interface.

MIME

Multipurpose Internet Mail Extensions, a **protocol** that allows **e-mail** to contain more than simple text. Used to send other kinds of data, including color pictures, sound files, and video clips.

.mil

An **Internet domain** that stands for military.

mIRC

A Windows **IRC** program.

mirror site

Another **FTP site** that maintains the exact same files (updated regularly), in order to reduce the load on the primary site.

misc.

A **Usenet hierarchy** devoted to whatever doesn't fit in the other hierarchies.

modem

A device that connects your computer to a phone jack and, through the phone lines, to another modem and computer. (It stands for *mo*dulator/*dem*odulator.)

moderated

Lists and **newsgroup**s whose **post**s must pass muster with a **moderator** before being sent to the subscribers.

moderator

The volunteer who decides which submissions to a **moderated list** or **newsgroup** will be **post**ed.

more

The most common **Unix** pager program.

Mosaic

A **Web browser,** developed by **NCSA,** for graphical user interfaces.

MOTAS

Member of the appropriate sex.

MOTOS

Member of the opposite sex.

MOTSS

Member of the same sex.

motto!

A **follow-up post** on **Usenet** proposing the previous post as a motto for the group.

MPEG

A **compressed** file format for movies with the extension .mpg.

MS Exchange

A Microsoft **e-mail** program.

MU*

Any one of a series of acronyms for multiuser role-playing game environments.

MUD

A multiuser **domain**/dimension/dungeon. A role-playing game environment that allows people all over the **Net** to play together in something like interactive text adventures.

MUSE

A multiuser simulation environment (for role-playing games).

my two cents

A tag appended to **Usenet** or **list post**s, indicating "this is just my opinion," or "I just wanted to get my two cents in."

Ncftp

A more sophisticated **Unix FTP** program than Ftp, the basic Unix FTP program.

NCSA

The National Center for Supercomputing Applications, founded by the **NSF** in 1985; inventor of **Mosaic.**

NCSA Mosaic

The original graphical **Web browser,** developed at the National Center for Supercomputer Applications and distributed for free.

NCSA What's New Page

The unofficial newspaper of the **Web** (found at `http://www.ncsa.uiuc.edu/SDG/Software/Mosaic/Docs/whats-new.html`).

Net, the

Often used as an abbreviation for the **Internet** or for **Usenet,** the Net is really a more general term for the lump sum of interconnected computers on the planet.

.net

An **Internet domain** that stands for **network.**

net.celebrity

A celebrity on the **Net.**

net.cop

Someone accused of trying to control others' **post**s in **mailing list**s or in **Usenet newsgroup**s.

NetCruiser
Netcom's all-in-one **Internet** access software.

Netfind
An **Internet** resource for finding **e-mail address**es.

net.god
An apparently powerful being on the **Net**.

nethead
A Dead Head (serious fan of the Grateful Dead) on the **Net**.

netiquette
The traditional rules of civilized behavior **online**.

netizen
A citizen of the **Net**.

net.personality
A somewhat well-known person on the **Net**.

.netrc
A file of **FTP** archive **site** names, **username**s, and passwords, used by Ftp and Ncftp to automate login to **FTP site**s.

Netscape Navigator
Hands-down the most popular **World Wide Web browser** program. It works very much the way **Mosaic** does but, with a number of additional features and improvements.

net.spewer
A new contributor to a group who spews hundreds of **post**s, following up every **thread** that's around and attempting to start new ones.

network
A linked-together set of computers and computer equipment.

newbie
A beginner, not as derogatory as **clueless newbie.**

newsfeed
The packet of news articles passed along from one computer to the next on **Usenet.**

newsgroup
A **Usenet discussion group.**

.newsrc
The list of **subscribed** and **unsubscribed newsgroup**s for a **Unix newsreader.**

newsreader
A program used to read **Usenet** articles.

NewsWatcher
A **newsreader** for the Macintosh.

News Xpress
A **newsreader** for Windows.

NFS
Not to be confused with **NSF,** NFS is the Network File System **protocol,** developed by Sun Microsystems, for transferring files over a **network.**

NIC
A **network** information center.

Nn
A **Unix newsreader.**

node
Any computer on the **Internet,** a **host.**

noise
Useless or unwanted information (as in **signal-to-noise ratio**).

NSF

The National Science Foundation; maintainers of the **NFSnet.**

NSFnet

A high-speed backbone, crucial but not essential, of the Internet; maintained by the NSF.

Ob

A prefix added to an obligatory addendum to a **Usenet** or **list post.**

offline

Not currently connected to the **Net.**

offline mail reader

A **mail** program that connects to the **Net, download**s your **e-mail,** and then disconnects, allowing you to read, reply to, and send mail without being charged for very much connect time.

offline news reader

A newsreader that connects to the **Net, download**s all unread articles in all subscribed **newsgroups,** and then disconnects, allowing you to read, reply to, and **post** articles without being charged for connect time.

online

Currently connected to the **Net.**

.org

An **Internet domain** that stands for (non-profit) organization.

page

A **hypertext** document available on the **World Wide Web.**

pager

A **Unix** program that presents text one screenful at a time.

parent directory

The parent for which the current directory is a **subdirectory.**

parity

One of the things you have to set to use your **modem.** It's usually set to None or Even, but it depends on the modem you're calling.

Pegasus Mail

A free **e-mail client** program.

PgP

A **shareware encryption** program (it stands for Pretty Good Privacy).

Pico

A **Unix text editor** based on the text editor built into the **Pine mail reader.**

Pine

A popular **Unix mail** program.

ping

A somewhat obsolete **Unix** command that checks on the status of another **network.**

pkunzip

The **uncompression** program for **pkzipped** files.

pkzip

A DOS file **compression** program.

.plan

A **text file** that is displayed when someone fingers (uses a program called Finger to see if you are **online**) your **e-mail address.**

platform

A type of computer or system.

players

Programs, also called **viewers,** used to display multimedia file formats.

plebiscite
Literally, popular vote. In a **newsgroup,** it means polling the readership.

plonk
A **follow-up post** that means, "I just put you in my killfile." (It's supposed to be the sound of the **bozo** falling into the **killfile.**)

plug-ins
Programs that can be plugged into a **Web browser** to add multimedia capabilities to it.

point at
To start a **client** program; such as a **Web browser,** by supplying it with an address, as in "Point your Web browser at `http://ezone.org/ez` to see the latest episode of *Enterzone*."

POP
1. Point of Presence; a local access number for a **service provider;** 2. Post-Office **Protocol,** a standard way to **download** and **upload e-mail.**

POP server
A type of **mail server** that "speaks" the Post-Office **Protocol.**

post
To send a **message** to a **mailing list** or an article to a **newsgroup.** The word *post* comes from the bulletin-board metaphor, in which scraps of paper are posted to the board, to be read by anyone who comes by.

Postmaster
The human being responsible for information requests for a **mail server** (`postmaster@address`).

PPP
Point-to-Point **Protocol;** a protocol for an **Internet** connection over a **modem.**

private key
In **key encryption,** the **key** that allows you to **encrypt** your outgoing messages.

.project

A **text file** that might be displayed when someone **fingers** your **e-mail address.** Not all fingers check for a .project file. You can describe the project you're working on in it.

propagation

The process of dissemination for **Usenet post**s, as they are passed from computer to computer. Propagation delays are responsible for the sometimes confusing situation that occurs when you read a **follow-up** to a post that hasn't yet appeared at your site.

protocol

Any agreed-upon method for two computers to communicate.

/pub

A **Unix** directory often found on **FTP host**s.

public data network

A public data **network** allows you to make a local call to connect to a national network.

public discussion area

See **discussion group.**

public key

In **key encryption,** the **key** that allows you to verify the **encrypted** signature of the person who has sent you **mail** or **decrypt** a **message** from that person, given out to anyone who asks.

query

A search request submitted to a database.

queue

A list of **messages** waiting to be sent.

QuickMail

An **e-mail client** program designed for **networks.**

QuickTime
A movie format originally on Macintoshes.

Real Audio
Progressive Networks' **streaming** audio format.

real name
Your full name as it appears on **e-mail message**s and **Usenet post**s.

real time
The time it takes real people to communicate, as on a telephone.

rec.
A **Usenet hierarchy** devoted to recreation.

remote login
Logging into another computer over a **network**. *See also* **Telnet**.

reply
An **e-mail message** or **Usenet post** responding to, and possibly quoting, the original.

repost
To **post** again. A subsequent post of the same information.

-request
Human-administered **mailing list**s have an address for sending administrative requests (such as subscriptions), with -request appended to the **username** for the list. So the administrative address for the imaginary list `epictetus@netcom.com` would be `epictetus-request@netcom.com`.

RFC
Request for Comments; one of a set of documents that contain **Internet protocol**s, standards, and information, and that together, more or less define the Internet in an open way. The standards contained in them are followed carefully by software developers (both commercial and **freeware**). The name Request for Comments can be confusing, since the contents are settled, but they arrived from free and open discussion on the **Net**.

RFD

Request for Discussion; a stage in the creation of a new **Usenet newsgroup,** preceding the **CFV.**

Rlogin

A **Unix** program that allows you to log on to another Unix machine without having to give your password.

Rn

A nonthreaded **newsreader** for **Unix.**

roboposter

A **'bot,** disguised as a person, that automatically **post**s and **repost**s huge numbers of articles to **Usenet.** Roboposters have rendered some **newsgroup**s without a **killfile** to filter out unwanted posters unreadable. A reputed roboposter, using the human name of Serdar Argic, single-handedly rendered **soc.history** (and a number of other newsgroups) unreadable. His howling through the wires (ranting holocaust revisionism about the Turks and the "x-Soviet" Armenians) came to an unexpected halt in the spring of 1994.

root

The directory with no parent. An **Internet address** at a **network** usually monitored by a **system administrator.**

ROTFL

Rolling on the floor laughing.

RTFM

Read the f***ing manual!

sci.

A **Usenet hierarchy** devoted to science.

Search Engine

A program, usually reachable through a **Web page,** used to search a Web **site,** the entire **Internet,** or some **domain** in between.

select articles

In **newsreader**s, to choose ahead of time (by their titles or authors) which articles you want to read.

semi-anonymity

Because you'll never see the vast majority of people whose **post**s you read on the **Net,** this creates a veil of semi-anonymity.

server

A **network** application providing information to **client** programs that connect to it. They are centralized repositories of information or specialized handlers of certain kinds of traffic.

service provider

A company that provides access to the **Internet.**

shareware

Software you're expected to pay for after evaluating it, if you decide to keep using it. It is available for a free trial and must be registered and paid for if you decide to use it.

shell

A computer operating environment.

shell account

An **Internet account** that gives you access to a **Unix shell.**

Shergold, Craig

If you get the chain mail telling you to send this poor kid (or someone with a very similar name, as in the popular misspelling, Shirgold) a get-well card, don't! He is the famous "dying boy" (no longer dying and no longer a little boy) who is said in endlessly circulating chain-mail **post**s and **e-mail** to be hoping to become the *Guiness Book of Records* champion for postcards received. It was true once—ten years ago. The hospital where he stayed still gets postcards.

.sig

A **signature** file.

signal-to-noise ratio

An engineering term adapted as a metaphor for the proportion of useful information to junk on a **list** or in a **newsgroup.**

signature

A few lines of text, usually including your name, sometimes your postal **(snail mail)** address, and perhaps your **e-mail address.** Many people also include quotations, jokes, gags, and so on. Signatures (also called sig blocks, **signature files, .signatures,** or **.sigs**) are a little like bumper stickers in this respect. Some **e-mail** programs do not support signature files.

.signature

A **signature file** (so spelled because of the convention used for **Unix** signature files).

signature file

A **text file** that is automatically attached to the end of your **e-mail message**s or **Usenet post**s, usually containing your name and other pertinent information about you.

site

An **Internet host** that allows some kind of remote access, such as a **Web** site, **FTP** site, **Gopher** site, and so on.

SLIP

Serial Line Internet Protocol; a **protocol** for an **Internet** connection over a **modem.**

SlipKnot

A program made by MicroMind that provides graphical access to the **Web** for people with character-based **Unix accounts.**

smileys

Sideways smiley faces, such as **:-), ;^)**, and **=%7o**, used to indicate emotions or facial expressions.

SMTP

Simple Mail Transport Protocol; this **protocol** is what enables **Internet e-mail** to flow so freely.

snail mail
Internet slang for surface mail.

SO
Significant other.

soc.
A **Usenet hierarchy** devoted to society (and usually sectarian groups in it).

spam
To **post** (or **robopost**) huge amounts of material to **Usenet,** or to post one article to huge numbers of inappropriate groups.

spew
To **post** excessively.

stand-alone program
For **online services,** a program that runs separately from the main access program, but one that can use the connection established by the main program.

stop bits
One of the things you have to set to use your **modem.** Usually set to 1 or 2, but it depends on the modem you're calling.

streaming
When files are sent a little at a time and start playing almost immediately.

subdirectory
A **directory** that is the child of another directory.

subdomain
A named portion of an **Internet domain,** usually a **network,** university, or company. In one of my **e-mail address**es, `xian@netcom.com`, *netcom* is the subdomain.

subscribe
To join a **mailing list** or start reading a **newsgroup.**

surf

To **browse**, following tangents. You can surf either **Usenet** or **Gopherspace**, but the **Web** is best for surfing.

synchronous

Happening at the same time. **Chat** is a synchronous form of communication.

sysadmin

A **system administrator.** Someone who runs or maintains a **network.**

sysop

A **system operator.**

system administrator

Someone who runs or maintains a **network.**

system operator

A type of **sysadmin** who runs a **BBS.**

talk

One-to-one **synchronous** chatting over the **Net.**

talk.

A **Usenet hierarchy** devoted to discussion, argument, and debate.

tar

1. (v) To lump a bunch of files together in an archive; 2. (n) The **Unix** program that does the said lumping.

TCP

Transmission Control Protocol; a **protocol** that transmits information over the **Internet,** one small piece at a time.

TCP/IP

The **Internet protocol** using **TCP.**

Telnet
A **protocol** for **remote login,** and the name of most programs that use that protocol.

*.test
Usenet newsgroups, such as misc.test, alt.test, etc., used for posting test **messages** to see if they propagate properly. If you **post** something to a *.test newsgroup, be prepared for a mailbox full of confirming replies to your post, sent back by **daemons** as your post propagates around the world.

text editor
A program for editing **text files;** less fully featured than a word processor.

text file
A file containing text only.

text transfer
A transfer of straight text over the **modem,** between the remote computer and a **text file.**

thread
A series of **post**s and follow-ups in a **newsgroup.**

threaded newsreader
A **newsreader** that organizes **post**s according to a **thread** and allows you to read your way up or down a thread.

time out
To fail, as a **network** process, because the **remote server** or computer has not responded in time.

Tin
A **threaded newsreader** for **Unix.**

Trn
A **threaded newsreader** for **Unix,** similar to **Rn.**

troll

To deliberately **post** egregiously false information to a **newsgroup,** in hopes of tricking dense know-it-alls into correcting you. Also, such a post itself. If you follow up a bizarre post to point out that Grover Cleveland Alexander was never president of the U.S., you may see an even more confusing reply to your post saying just "YHBT. YHL. HAND." This stands for "You have been trolled. You have lost. Have a nice day."

TrueSound

Microsoft's own **streaming** sound format.

TurboGopher

A **Gopher** program for the Mac.

UL

An **urban legend;** the **Internet** is a perfect communication medium for tracking down and verifying or debunking urban legends.

uncompress

To unsquish a **compress**ed file. A **Unix uncompression** program.

uncompression

The process of unsquishing a file.

Undernet

A smaller, more community-oriented alternative **IRC network** than **EFNet.**

Uniform Resource Locator (URL)

A **Web address.** It consists of a **protocol,** a hostname, a port (optional), a directory, and a file name.

Unix

An operating system common to workstations and on which most **Internet protocol**s were developed.

Unix shell account

An **Internet account** that provides access to a character-only **Unix command line.**

unmoderated
Said of a **newsgroup** or **list** whose articles are not vetted by a **moderator**.

unselect articles
To remove the selection tag from **Usenet articles** selected for reading.

unsubscribe
To remove yourself from a **mailing list** or to stop reading a **Usenet newsgroup**.

untar
To separate a **tar**red file into its component parts.

upload
To transfer a file over a **modem** from your desktop computer to a remote computer.

urban legends
Stories passed around and always attributed to a friend of a friend (a **FOAF**), frequently (but not always) based on a kernel of falsehood. The **Usenet newsgroup** `alt.folklore.urban` (and its less noisy cousin `alt.folklore.suburban`) is the home of **UL** debunkers.

URL
See **Uniform Resource Locator.**

Usenet
1. The collection of computers and **network**s that share news articles. Usenet is *not* the **Internet** (though they overlap to a great extent); 2. The **hierarchy** of **newsgroup**s.

username
Also called a **login** or userID. The name a user **log**s **in** with. Also the first part of your **e-mail address** (up to the @).

UUCP
Unix to Unix Copy. A **protocol** and a program for intermittent **network** connections and file and mail transfers.

uudecode

1. (v) To turn a uuencoded file back into its **binary** form; 2. (n) The **Unix** program that does this.

uuencode

1. To convert a **binary file** into a text form that can be sent as part of an **e-mail message**; 2. The **Unix** program that does this.

vacation

A **Unix** program that sets up a return message to be sent to anyone who sends you mail, telling them you're on vacation.

Veronica

An index of **Gopher** menus that you search. The results are presented to you as a Gopher menu.

Vi

A common **Unix text editor.**

viewers

See **players.**

virus

A program that deliberately does damage to the computer it's on.

.VOC

The audio format for the SoundBlaster sound card.

VRML

Virtual Reality Modeling Language; VRML files usually have a .wrl extension.

VT100

A terminal type, originated by DEC, that has become the standard terminal. If you dial up a **Unix shell,** then your communications program probably emulates a VT100.

w³

An abbreviation for the **Word Wide Web.**

WAN

A wide-area **network.** A computer network spanning a wide geographical area.

warlording

Reposting a **Usenet** article to `alt.fan.warlord` and mocking its **signature** for being overly large, ugly, or stupid.

.WAV

Wave format, from Microsoft; perhaps the most widespread sound format on the **Internet.**

Web

The **World Wide Web.**

Web address

A **URL.**

Web browser

A **Web client** program that allows you to view **hypertext page**s and follow **link**s.

Web page

A **hypertext** document on the **Web.**

Web server

A **Web** application that allows you to store **home page**s and make them available via the Hypertext Transfer Protocol. If you lack access to a Web server but have access to an **FTP site,** then you can store your home page there and make sure that **URL**s pointing to it use the ftp:// **protocol** instead of http://.

whisper

A private message to someone in an **IRC** session.

Whois

An **Internet** resource for identifying **e-mail address**es.

WhoWhere?

A **Web site** from which you can look for people.

WinZip

A **compression** program for Windows.

wizard

An expert, usually one willing to help **newbies.**

working directory

The current **directory.** The directory you're "in" right now.

World Wide Web

A collection of **hypertext** documents and associated files, **link**ed together, that spans the **Internet** (and hence, the globe).

worm

A program that duplicates itself, potentially worming its way through an entire **network.**

WRT

With respect to.

WSGopher

A **Gopher** program for Windows.

WS_FTP

1. An **FTP** program for WindowsWww; 2. A **Unix**-based **Web browser** developed at CERN, the European particle physics laboratory where the Web was invented. It is the original text-based Unix browser for the Web.

Xmodem

A **protocol** for **download** and **upload file transfer**s.

X window

A graphical user interface for **Unix.**

Yahoo

The most popular **Web directory.**

Ymodem

A **protocol** for **download** and **upload file transfer**s.

YMMV

Your mileage may vary.

zip file

A **compress**ed file.

Zmodem

A **protocol** for **download** and **upload file transfer**s.

Index

Note to the Reader: Main level entries are in **bold**. **Boldfaced** page numbers indicate primary discussions of a topic. *Italicized* page numbers indicate illustrations.

H

Q

R

S

V

W

X

Y

Z